MORE FRANCE
FOR THE $

GW00703244

by

ALAN AUSTIN

BERLITZ°

Series Editor: Barbara Ender
Design and Layout: Philippe Aquoise
Cartography: Hallwag AG, Bern
Back Cover Photograph: Leif Schiller

Publisher's Note

All the restaurants and hotels mentioned in this book were visited and evaluated by the author, Alan Austin; all opinions and ratings are strictly his own, not those of Berlitz Guides. The benefits offered with the coupons were agreed between the author and manager of the establishment. There is no time restriction, but in certain cases the validity of the coupon is subject to availability. Should any problem arise, present the reverse of the coupon or ask to speak to the manager. Berlitz Guides decline all responsibility for non-respect of the benefits described on the coupons, but would appreciate being advised if any difficulty arises.

The author would be delighted to receive your suggestions, comments and recommendations for the next edition. He can be reached at Berlitz Guides, avenue d'Ouchy 61, 1000 Lausanne 6, Switzerland.

© 1989 by Berlitz Guides, a division of Macmillan S.A., Avenue d'Ouchy 61, 1000 Lausanne 6
All rights reserved. No part of this book may be reproduced or transmitted in any form or by any means, electronic or mechanical including photocopying, recording or by any information storage and retrieval system without permission in writing from the publisher.
Berlitz Trademark Reg. U.S. Patent Office and other countries.

Marca Registrada. Library of Congress Catalog Card No. 88-64121

Printed in USA.

About More France for the $

Travel discounts

Ratings and Evaluations

Contents

Contents

Contents

Contents

Coupons

A 32-page road atlas is inserted between pages 16 and 17.
The sketch-map overleaf shows the geographical location
of each establishment reviewed.

About More France for the $

The hotels and restaurants in this book were selected solely for their fine quality, and not because of any discounts, gifts or benefits they may provide.

Ranging from small inns to stately châteaux, they all pride themselves on courtesy, charm, comfort, and—most important in France —good cooking. Even without the special incentives included in *More France for the $*, they offer outstanding value.

I have spent at least one night in each hotel and eaten at least one main meal in each restaurant, and there isn't one establishment I wouldn't gladly visit again.

Using your coupons

There are no strings attached to *More France for the $* coupons. You do not have to announce that you are entitled to a reduction or upgrading at the time you make your reservation. The only rule is that you must present your coupon when you check in or when you order your meal. You should also keep your book handy, just in case the hotel or restaurant manager asks to see it. Any restrictions on validity are mentioned clearly on the coupons themselves. If by any chance there's a language problem, show the person concerned the translation on the back of the coupon.

The agreements to provide the reductions, gifts or other considerations were made between the author and the owner or manager of the establishments concerned. All were pleased to participate in a program designed to take the edge off the high cost of travel; it's a way of saying "Welcome" that can be appreciated by all of us affected by the ups and downs of the dollar and the rise in hotel and restaurant prices.

Though neither the author nor Berlitz Guides can take any responsibility if coupons are refused, we would like to be informed of any difficulties you might possibly encounter. All your comments, in general, will be appreciated.

The ratings

Naturally, each hotel and restaurant has its own personality. The descriptions may help you decide which to choose. But for a rapid evaluation, to show at a glance what to expect, each establishment is rated for price and for quality. A few hotels and restaurants have been awarded a special ✳ symbol—they have an indefinable "plus" that cannot be incorporated into the rating system but means they are unique.

"$" ratings

Cost categories range from one dollar sign to four. For **hotels**, the system is based on the price of a standard double room. The $$$$-category hotels have no upper limit on cost, but in the off-season, they may have rooms available that fall into the $$$-category.

For **restaurants**, the ratings are based on the average price of a main course. In order to achieve a fair comparison, the cost of the most expensive dish on the menu was not included in the calculation—even the most modest restaurant might have one course with truffles, foie gras or caviar at a sky-high price which would distort the true picture.

Any room rates and menu prices mentioned are those of 1989; they do not take into account the reductions offered with the *More France for the $* coupons.

"A" ratings

Every **hotel with restaurant** has been rated from one to five points for beauty, comfort, service, and food. Only establishments scoring at least two points in each category have been included in *More France for the $*. I took the following items into consideration to evaluate the ratings:

Beauty

External appearance
Interior décor of lobby, lounges
   and public areas
Grounds
Immediate surroundings

5 breathtaking
4 very attractive
3 charming
2 pleasant

Service

Doorman
Porter to carry luggage
24-hour room service
Friendliness
Promptness
Attention
Smiles

5 irreproachable—they won't let
   you lift a finger
4 attentive and friendly—they
   will relieve you of your
   luggage at the hotel entrance
3 courteous and professional—
   luggage will be brought from
   reception to your room
2 cheerful but not servile—you
   will have to bring your luggage
   up yourself

Comfort

Size of room
Comfort of beds
General furnishings
Air conditioning
Closet space
TV, radio, Minitel
Direct-dial telephone
Minibar
Flowers and chocolates
Stationery
Soundproofing
Size of bathroom
Towels and robes
Toiletries
Extras

5 the ultimate in luxury
4 lavish
3 very comfortable
2 strictly functional, but adequate
   for a pleasant stay

Restaurant

Quality of cooking

5 inspired and inspiring,
   a revelation
4 wonderful, often inventive, food
3 excellent
2 usually good (prefer the house
   specialties)

A total score of 20 points is denoted by AAAAA
             17–19 points = AAAA
             14–16 points = AAA
             11–13 points = AA
               8–10 points = A

Restaurants are rated only on the quality of the food, though décor, comfort
and service are briefly described. Hotels without a restaurant are rated solely
on comfort.

A little French can make it nicer

No matter how well you might think you can pronounce French, unless you've lived in France for a very long time, they'll know right away you're a foreigner. There's no need to worry about it, for every hotel and restaurant mentioned in this book has someone who speaks English. But French is a beautiful language, and using it—even a little—is a gesture that's always appreciated.

S'il vous plaît (Please) and *Merci* (Thank you) will take you further than any other words. Calling *s'il vous plaît* is also the best way to get the attention of your waiter *(le garçon)* or waitress *(la serveuse)*. The head waiter should be addressed as *Monsieur*. In high-class restaurants, the waiter is more likely to be a *chef de rang*, which means he or she can prepare certain dishes and carve meat beside your table, as well as serve with a fine sense of style, according to very strict etiquette. The wine waiter is *le sommelier*.

Make a friend of the waiter, for ordering is not too easy. French chefs delight in concocting the most grandiloquently poetic names for their culinary creations, and even French people have to enlist the help of the waiter to decipher the menu.

The French section of the Berlitz *European Menu Reader* will help solve some of the mysteries of the menu, while the Berlitz phrase book *French for Travellers* has comprehensive chapters devoted to eating out, checking into hotels, and driving around; if you don't speak French, you'll find both books a big help. Several useful phrases are given below.

Checking in—Reception

My name is...	*Je m'appelle...*
I've a reservation.	*J'ai fait réserver.*
Do you have any vacancies?	*Avez-vous des chambres disponibles?*
I'd like a... room...	*Je voudrais une chambre...*
single	*pour une personne*
double	*pour deux personnes*
with a balcony	*avec balcon*
with a view	*avec vue*
facing the sea	*qui donne sur la mer*

How long?

We'll be staying…	*Nous resterons*
overnight only	*juste cette nuit*
a few days	*quelques jours*
a week (at least)	*une semaine (au moins)*
I don't know yet.	*Je ne sais pas encore.*

In the restaurant

I'd like to reserve a table for 2.	*Je voudrais réserver une table pour deux personnes.*
Could we have a table…?	*Pouvons-nous avoir une table…?*
in the corner	*dans un angle*
by the window	*près de la fenêtre*
outside	*dehors*
on the terrace	*sur la terrasse*
in a non-smoking area	*dans un coin non-fumeurs*
What are the chef's specialties?	*Quelles sont les spécialités du chef?*
What do you recommend?	*Que me recommandez-vous?*
Could I have a/an/some…?	*Pourrais-je avoir…?*
ashtray	*un cendrier*
cup	*une tasse*
fork	*une fourchette*
glass	*un verre*
knife	*un couteau*
napkin	*une serviette*
plate	*une assiette*
spoon	*une cuillère*
bread	*du pain*
butter	*du beurre*
pepper	*du poivre*
salt	*du sel*
coffee	*du café*
tea	*du thé*
spring water	*de l'eau minérale*
Nothing more, thanks.	*Je suis servi, merci.*

Finding your way

A large-scale, 32-page road atlas has been incorporated into this book; page and grid references are mentioned at the top of the hotel and restaurant evaluations, beneath the names of the town and region. In addition, detailed instructions are provided for driving to each establishment from the nearest expressway *(autoroute)* exit.

If you have to drive into a large town, you may be confused by one-way traffic (especially at rush hour). I have found that the best thing to do in these circumstances is to have a taxi cab show me the way. There's usually a cab stand on the fringe of the downtown area, and if there isn't, you can stop at a gas station and ask the attendant to call one for you. (Be sure to pay for the call, adding a few francs for the service.) You may even be closer to your destination than you think, in which case the attendant will give you directions. Keep in mind that the French often refer to streets by their route destination, rather than by the official name on street signs—*route de Verdun*, rather than *rue du Maréchal-Foch*.

To the attendant:

I'm looking for the... Hotel/Restaurant.
Je cherche l'hôtel/le restaurant ...

Could you tell me the way?
Pouvez-vous m'indiquer le chemin?

How many streets before I make a turn?
Combien de rues avant de tourner?

And if it still seems complicated ...

Could you call a taxi to guide me?
Pouvez-vous appeler un taxi pour me montrer le chemin?

To the taxi driver:

Could you guide me to the ... Hotel/Restaurant; I'll follow in my car.
Pouvez-vous me montrer le chemin jusqu'à l'hôtel/au restaurant ...; je vous suivrai dans ma voiture.

Have a nice trip—and *bon appétit!*

Alan Austin

TRAVEL DISCOUNTS

You will find the coupons corresponding to these offers at the end of the Coupon section, after the hotels and restaurants.

Hertz Chauffeur Service

Prestige Tours
182 boulevard Pereire
75017 Paris
Tel: (1) 45 74 77 12
Telex: 642 781
CC: AE, D, M, V

24-hour dispatcher in Paris; branch offices in Lyon and Nice. The pleasure of being picked up at your hotel by your own bilingual chauffeur in a luxury car adds a beautiful touch to any trip. Phone or telex ahead, and the driver will be waiting at the airport, ready to assist you with luggage and customs formalities. The fleet of cars ranges from four-passenger Renault to Rolls-Royce. Personalized tours are a specialty.

Europcar National

65 avenue Edouard Vaillant
92100 Boulogne-Billancourt
Tel: (1) 46 09 92 20
Reservations Center: (1) 30 43 82 82
Telex: 631 425
CC: major

Locations throughout France at airports, terminals, or through the porter at your hotel. Service includes maintenance and towing of the car in case of breakdown or accident, unlimited third party liability, and 24-hours emergency.

ROAD ATLAS

GREAT BRITAIN

Aberystwyth
Fishguard
Nottingham
BIRMINGHAM
Worcester
Coventry
Leicester
Great Yarmouth
Norwich
Cambridge
Swansea
Cardiff
Bristol
Oxford
London
Harwich
Exeter
Dorchester
Southampton
Portsmouth
Brighton
Eastbourne
Canterbury
Plymouth
Dartmouth

Groningen
Emden
Leeuwarden
Den Helder
Emmen
Osnabrück
Cloppenburg
AMSTERDAM
NL
Zwolle
DEN HAAG
Rotterdam
Münster
BR.
Oostende
Brugge
Gent
Antwerpen
Eindhoven
Venlo
Essen
Dortmund
Nijmegen
Dunkerque
Calais
St-Omer
LILLE
BELGIQUE
BRUXELLES
Liege
Namur
Düsseldorf
Köln
DEUTSCHLAND
Aachen
Bonn
Boulogne s.-Mer
Abbeville
Dieppe
Arras
Amiens
St-Quentin
Valenciennes
Charleville-Mézières
Koblenz
Wiesbaden
Mainz

La Manche

Cherbourg
Valognes
Bayeux
LE HAVRE
ROUEN
Beauvais
Compiègne
Caen
Evreux
PARIS
Soissons
Reims
Epernay
Châlons-Marne
Verdun
LUXEMBOURG
L
Saarbrücken
Pirmasens
Nancy
Metz
STRASBOURG
Freiburg i. B.
Colmar
Mulhouse
BASEL
BERN
SCHWEIZ

Brest
Morlaix
Paimpol
St-Malo
St-Brieuc
Dinan
Rennes
Fougères
Mayenne
Laval
Le Mans
Chartres
Etampes
Orléans
Montargis
Sens
Troyes
Chaumont
Langres
Dijon
Vesoul
Belfort
Besançon
Neuchâtel
Biel
Interlaken
Fribourg
Lausanne
Gstaad

6/7
8/9
10/11
12/13
14/15
16/17
18/19
20/21
22/23
24/25
26/27
28/29
30/31
32

Quimper
Lorient
Vannes
Redon
Châteaubriant
NANTES
St-Nazaire
Ancenis
Angers
Saumur
Cholet
La Roche s.-Yon
Châtellerault
Poitiers
Parthenay
Niort
la Rochelle
Rochefort
Saintes
Cognac
Angoulême
Ruffec
Bellac
Limoges
Aubusson
Clermont-Ferrand
Ussel
St-Etienne
LYON
GENEVE
Aix-les-Bains
Chambéry
Aosta
Annecy
Simplonpass
Brig
ITALIA
TORINO
Susa
Asti
Cuneo

Golfe de Gascogne

BORDEAUX
Arcachon
Libourne
Périgueux
Brive-la-Gaillarde
Aurillac
le Puy
Valence
Aubenas
Die
Grenoble
Briançon
Barcelonnette
Nice
Cannes

Mont-de-Marsan
Dax
Biarritz
S. Sebastian
Bilbao
Vitoria
Logroño
Pau
Lourdes
Tarbes
St-Gaudens
Auch
TOULOUSE
Montauban
Albi
Carcassonne
Foix
Andorra-la-Vella
Perpignan
Narbonne
Millau
Alès
Mende
Rodez
Figeac
Cahors
Villeneuve s. Lot
Agen

ESPAÑA
Pamplona
Jaca
Huesca
Barbastro
Zaragoza
Lérida
Manresa
Girona
Barcelona
Tarragona
Alcañiz
Castellón de la Plana

Nîmes
Avignon
Montpellier
Manosque
Digne
Castellane
Monte-Carlo
Aix-en-Provence
MARSEILLE
Toulon
St-Tropez
Nyons
Sisteron
Serres

Golfe du Lion

Méditerranée

Corse
Calvi
Bastia
Ajaccio
Bonifacio

© Hallwag

FRANKREICH
FRANCE

FRANCIA
FRANCE

Autobahn mit Anschlussstelle Tankstelle, Restaurant, Motel Autoroute avec échangeur Station-service, restaurant, motel	Ⓣ Ⓡ Ⓜ	Autostrada con svincolo Stazione di servizio, ristorante, motel Motorway with interchange Filling station, restaurant, motel
Autobahn im Bau mit Eröffnungsdatum Autoroute en construction avec date de mise en service	Ⓒ1988 Ⓒ1988 I - VI VII - XII	Autostrada in construzione con data d'apertura Motorway under construction with opening date
Autostrasse (international, régional) Route rapide à chaussées séparées (internationale, régionale)		Superstrada a carreggiate separate (internazionale/regionale) Dual carriageway (international, regional)
Grosse internationale Durchgangsstrasse Route de grand transit internationale		Strada di gran transito internazionale Major international throughroute
Sonstige internationale Fernverkehrsstrasse Autre route de transit internationale		Altra strada di transito internazionale Other international throughroute
Überregionale Fernverkehrsstrasse Route de transit interrégionale		Strada di transito interregionale Interregional throughroute
Regionale Verbindungsstrasse Route de liaison régionale		Strada di collegamento regionale Regional connecting road
Lokale Verbindungsstrasse Route de liaison locale		Strada di collegamento locale Local road
Strassen im Bau Routes en construction		Strade in construzione Roads under construction
Entfernungen in km Distances en km	10 3 5 5 3 7 2 2 3 5 10	Distanze in km Distances in km
Strassennummern: Europastrasse, Autobahn, Nationalstrasse Numéros des routes: route européenne, autoroute, route nationale	E7 A9 60	Numerazione stradale: strada europea, autostrada, strada nazionale Road classification: European road, motorway, national road
Pass, Berg, Ort mit Höhenangabe (m) Col, sommet, localité avec altitude (m)	1528 2967 ○Elm 648	Valico, vetta, località con altitudine (m) Pass, summit, locality with altitude (m)
Eisenbahn, Berg-/Luftseilbahn Voie ferrée; téléphérique/funiculaire		Ferrovia, funivia/funicolare Railway, mountain/cable railway
Autoverlad: per Eisenbahn Transport des autos: par voie ferrée per Fähre par bac	2h	Trasporto automobili: per ferrovia Car transport: by rail su chiatta by ferry
Flughafen Aéroport	✈ ✦	Aeroporto Airport
Schloss/Burg, Kirche/Kloster, Ruine Château/fort, église/couvent, ruine		Castello/fortezza, chiesa/convento, rudero Castle, church/monastery, ruin
Antike Stätte, Höhle, Leuchtturm Vestige antique, grotte, phare		Antichità, grotta, faro Site of antiquity, cave, lighthouse
Campingplatz, bemerkenswerter Ort Camping, localité intéressante	▲ ★	Campeggio, località interessante Camping site, place of interest
Staatsgrenze Frontière d'Etat		Confine di Stato National boundary

1 : 1 000 000

0	10	20	40	60	80 km
0	10	20	30	40	50 miles

Hallwag

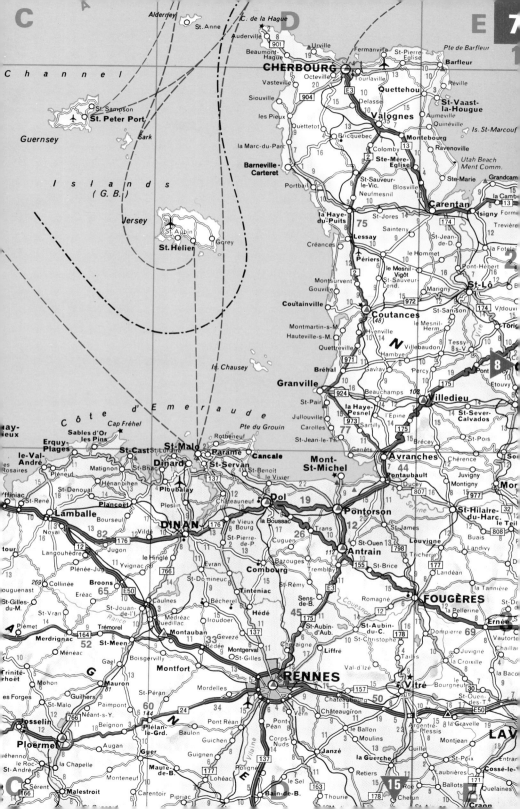

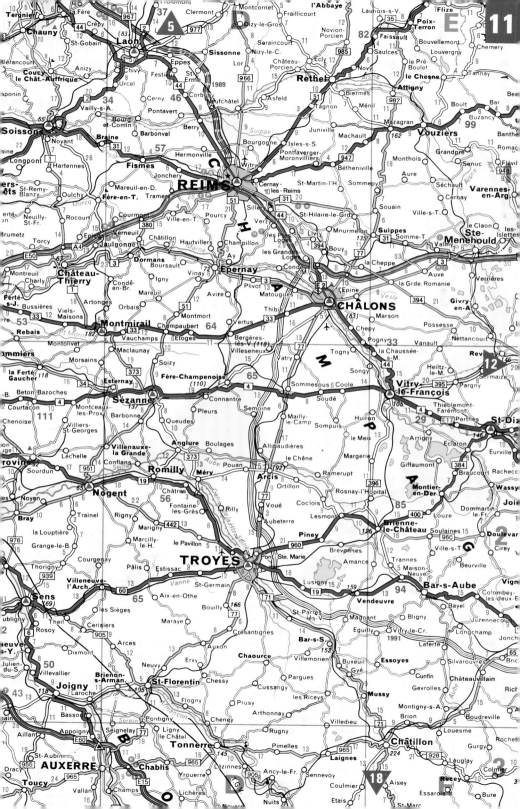

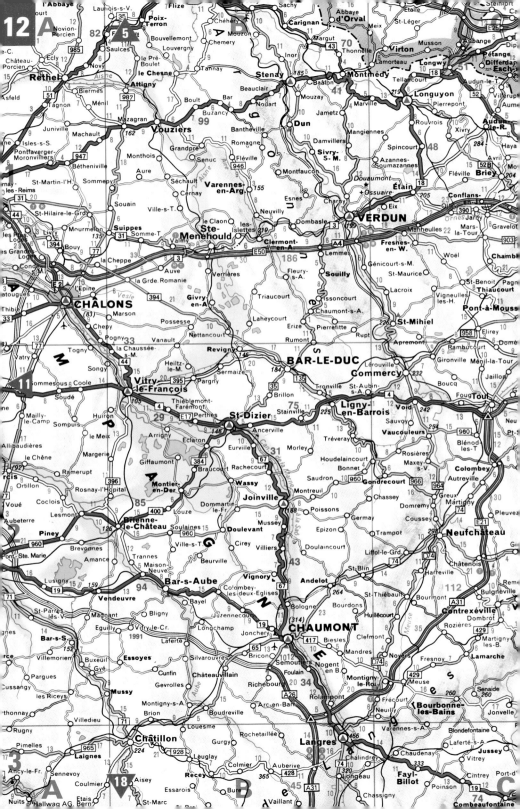

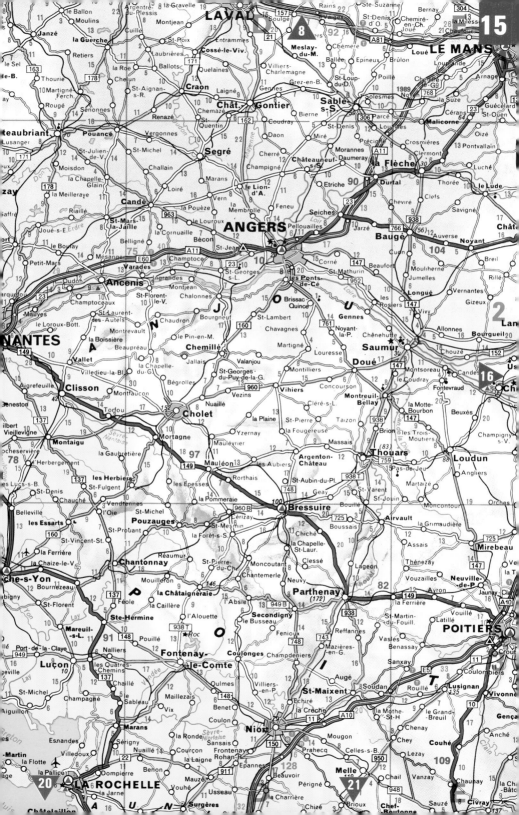

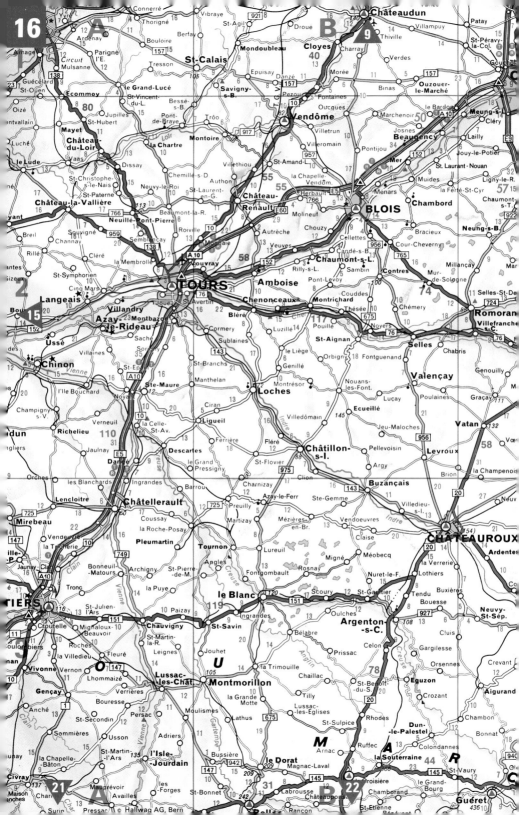

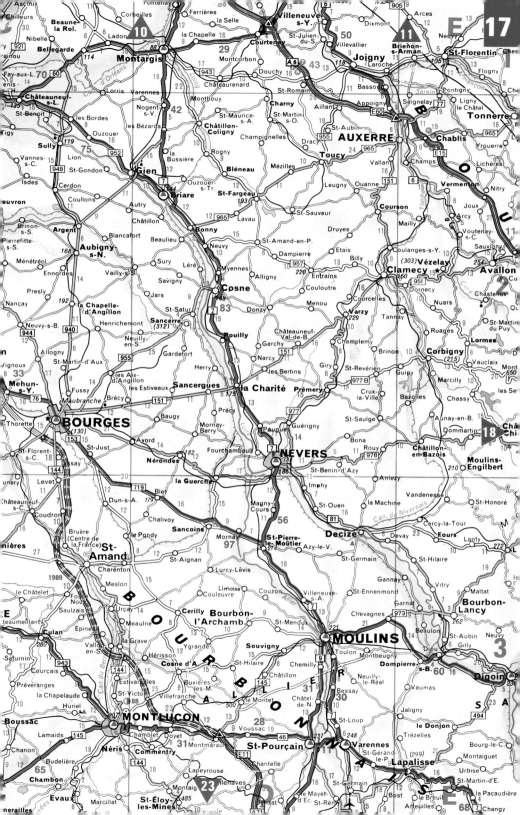

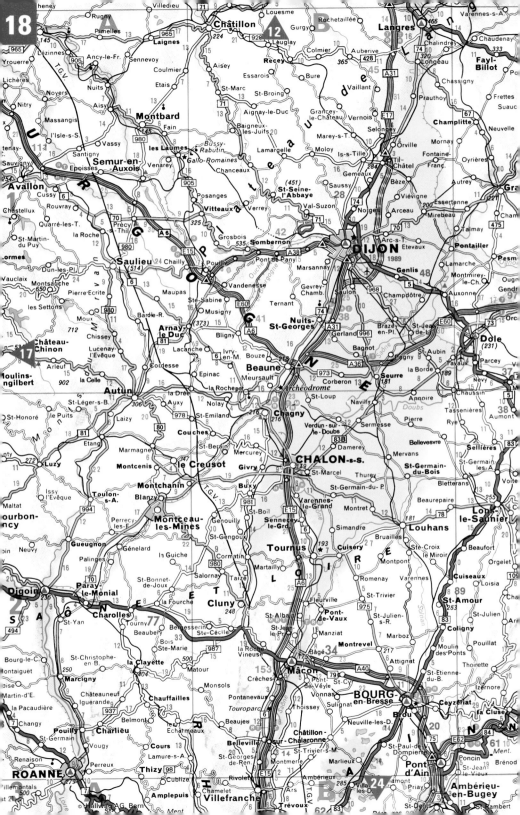

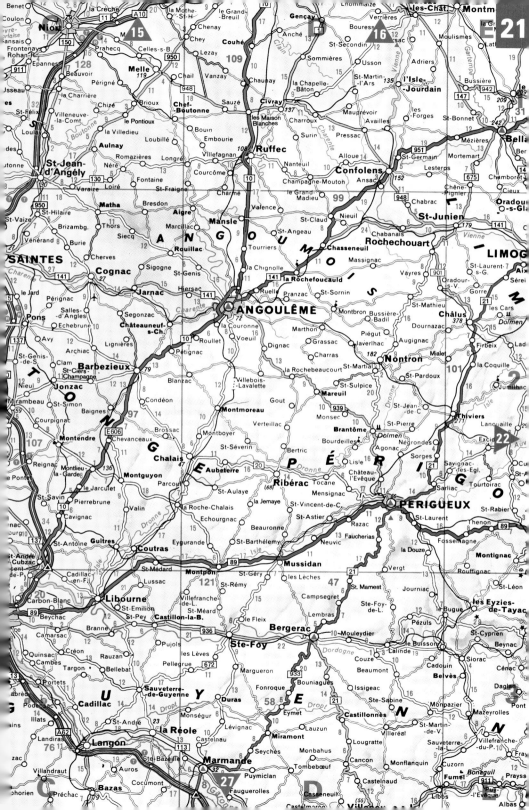

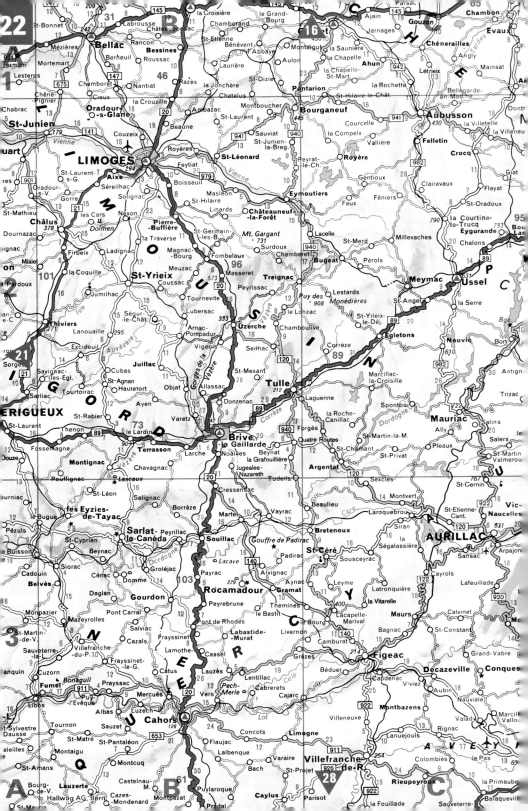

VICHY
Cusset
ROANNE
Charlieu
Pouilly
CLERMONT-FERRAND
Royat
Thiers
Feurs
Montbrison
ST-ÉTIENNE
Firminy
Riom
Issoire
Ambert
Brioude
la Chaise-Dieu
Yssingeaux
Tence
Murat
St-Flour
LE PUY
le Chambon
Chaudes-Aigues
Saugues
le Monastier
le Cheylard
Langeac
Langogne
Aubenas
Vals-les-Bs
Largentière
Marvejols
Mende
les Vans
Espalion
Ste-Enimie
Florac

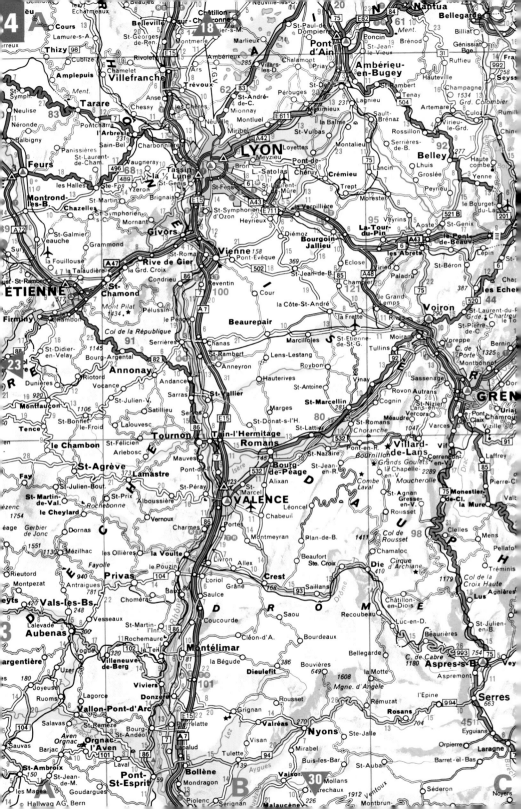

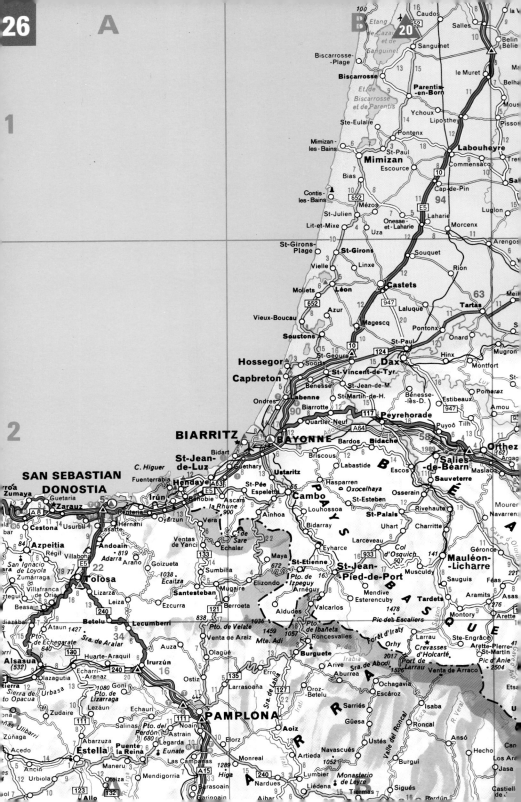

$ $

A A A

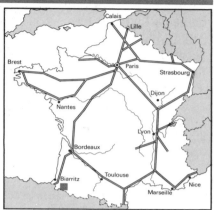

Hôtel Argi-Eder

64250 Aïnhoa
Tel: 59 29 91 04
Telex: 570 067

30 rooms, 16 suites
CC: AE, D, Eu, V
Open 10 April to 11 November.
Restaurant closed every
Wednesday except June through
15 September.

Location: leave the A63 at Bayonne Sud and follow directions for Cambo, then Aïnhoa. From St-Jean-de-Luz, follow signs for Ascain, Sare, then Aïnhoa.

A big Basque chalet in a picture-postcard setting of rolling hills and mountain peaks. The hotel was built less than 20 years ago, but the atmosphere is still one of rustic nostalgia: rough-hewn timber, stone trim, big fireplace, shiny brasses and antique farm implements adorn the reception area. The guestrooms are bright with bold-patterned country prints; heavenly views included.

It's a pleasure to hear the owner and chef, Jean-Pierre Dottax, rhapsodize about the right blend of steak tenderloin tips, foie gras, truffles and port for his *tournedos Rossini*. Everything comes fresh. The nearby river supplies the trout served with Bayonne ham in *truite de pays Aïnhoa*, his *axoa aux piments d'Espelette* is made from Basque beef, and the local ducks end up as *fricassée de canard Navarra*, cooked in regional wine. Just over the hills is the sea, and the *chipirons*, or squid, broiled with garlic or stuffed, steamed and served with a tomato and squid ink sauce. Country cooking straight from the heart, topped with a dessert of wild strawberries and red country wine. The four-course 175 F menu includes a glass of Piper Heidsieck rosé champagne.

RATINGS: beauty 4, comfort 4, service 3, restaurant 3.

Pool, tennis. All rooms with balcony.

$ $ $

A A A A

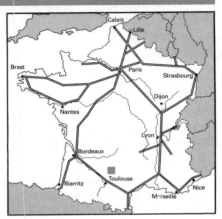

La Réserve

Route de Cordes
81000 Albi
Tel: 63 60 79 79
Telex: 520 850

21 rooms, 3 suites
CC: AE, CB, D, Eu
Open March to November.

Location: 76 km north-east of Toulouse on N88.
From Albi take the Cordes road, D 600, for 5 km.

La Réserve is a sprawling, red-tiled hacienda on the banks of the Tarn. A peaceful country club atmosphere prevails—the hotel is isolated from the rest of the world by a large park. Most of the rooms look out over the lawn to the river. The interior glistens with white stone floors and white leather furniture. All rooms have big tile and marble bathrooms, and the larger ones are furnished with antiques. Prices for a double start at about 500 F, but those fronting the river cost around 800 F.

The restaurant is spacious and light, with particularly cheerful and attentive service. The cuisine is classic: magret of duck served in a heavenly wine sauce, garnished with home-made fettuccini. A *cassolette d'escargots* with walnuts was equally impressive.

Extensive and reasonably priced wine list with emphasis on Margaux. Try the 1980 Château Siran.

RATINGS: beauty 5, comfort 4, service 4, restaurant 4.

Pool, tennis. Riding nearby. Most rooms with balcony.

$$

A A A

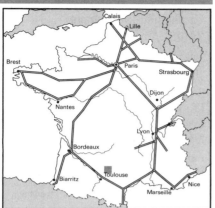

Hostellerie St-Antoine

17 rue St-Antoine
81000 Albi
Tel: 63 54 04 04
Telex: 520 850

56 rooms
CC: AE, D, Eu, V
Open all year.

Location: near Place Jean-Jaurès and across from
Lices Jean-Moulin, a small park in the centre of
town.

Albi is a destination for connoisseurs. One of the most attractive towns in France, with a fine red-brick Gothic cathedral, and the Toulouse-Lautrec museum in a bishop's palace—the Palais de la Berbie.

The Hostellerie de St-Antoine was founded in 1734, and the visitors' book reads like a who's-who of world history. But it has been modernized and borders on luxury. Only the antique furnishings and flower garden are reminiscent of times past. Most of the rooms are very spacious, with wall-to-wall carpeting, walls lined with fabric, and large, modern bathrooms. Rates are in the 500 F range.

The cheerful restaurant is famous for regional cooking. *Tripes à l'albigeoise* has been a house speciality from the start and follows a medieval recipe, using saffron from a type of crocus cultivated locally. Just as interesting is guinea-hen in a cream sauce flavored with juniper berries. Or the squab with beautifully cooked turnips in a wine sauce. Desserts include a meringue charlotte of fruit, an ice cream soufflé laced with Grand Marnier, and *crêpes flambées* with a splash of the same liqueur.

The wine list specializes in Bordeaux vintages, with exceptional buys of red Côtes de Bourg and St-Emilion.

RATINGS: beauty 4, comfort 4, service 3, restaurant 3.

Parking at rear of hotel. Garden. Pool and tennis court at La Réserve.

$ $

A A A

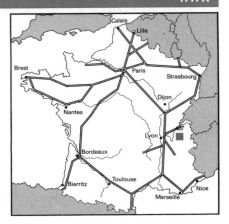

L'Abbaye

15 chemin de l'Abbaye
74000 Annecy-le Vieux
Tel: 50 23 61 08
Telex: 385 417

8 rooms, 3 suites
CC: AE, CB, D, V
Open all year. Restaurant closed
Mondays out of season.

Location: at Annecy, follow signs for Annecy-le-
Vieux until you come to avenue d'Albigny on the
lake front. Make a left turn opposite the public
beach at avenue de France and the second right at
rue du Mont-Blanc.

A 6th-century abbey steeped in charm. On a sunny day, the tree-shaded terrace at the back is a beautiful setting for lunch under pink and gray parasols. Dinner is even more romantic in what must have been the chapel, with vaulted ceilings, thick pillars, whitewashed walls, and a mural painted in more secular times depicting bare-breasted muses concertizing with flutes and lutes.

Unlike most abbeys and monasteries transformed into hotels, this one has quite large rooms, with big windows admitting plenty of clear Alpine air. Unusual religious art is displayed on the walls, while the appointments blend antique furniture and modern, muted fabrics.

The cuisine is light and inventive. A delicious trout tartare is served in two pancake pouches tied with a string of chive. *Canard à l'orange* is beautifully presented, the duck breast fillets forming a pyramid in the center of the plate over a ratatouille with mushrooms, framed by potato croquettes. The sauce is dark amber and pungent with the aroma of oranges and red wine. A ragout of veal sweetbreads in a pink peppercorn sauce, and veal with cranberries and *pleurote* mushrooms, are two more unexpected treats. The frozen mocha mousse dessert served in a demitasse looks good enough to drink.

The local wine, white Roussette de Savoie, made from the Altesse grape, is very fresh, fruity and light. Red Montmélian and Chignin, from the Mondeuse grape, are soft and go very well with gently spicy saint-marcellin cheese.

RATINGS: beauty 4, comfort 4, service 3, restaurant 4.

Large parking area in front of hotel.

$ $

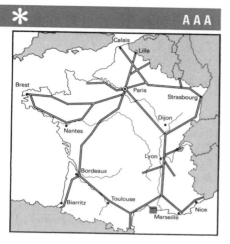

* AAA

Auberge La Fenière

Raphèle-lès-Arles
13200 Arles
Tel: 90 98 45 34
Telex: 441 237

25 rooms, 3 suites
CC: AE, D, M, V
Open all year. Restaurant closed
1 November to 20 December. Open for
dinner only, June through November.

Location: 4 km south-east of Arles on N 453.

A private road leads across grassy farmland to an ivy-covered 1868 farmhouse, within easy reach of lots of day-trip destinations.

The spacious public area. has a high beamed ceiling, checkerboard tile floor and comfortable Provençal antique furniture. The rooms are spacious too—even the smallest and lowest-price double was in no way claustrophobic. Priced at under 300F, it is one of the best travel values in Provence.

Madame Legros rules in the kitchen, while her husband takes care of reception. She executes regional specialities with a great deal of flair, for example *l'estouffade de boeuf camarguaise*—beef stew with onions, herbs, mushrooms, garlic and wine such as Coteaux des Baux. *Merlan à la provençale* raises hake to great heights with tomato, garlic and olive oil, plus special spicing. Mme Legros' rendering of another local ingredient, although in a style not confined to the south of France, is *encornets à l'armoricaine*—tasty rings of squid in a sauce of dry white wine, cognac, tomatoes, and shallots.

The mention of cognac also brings to mind young rooster broiled over a wood fire and flambéed, served with artichoke heart, green beans and crisp brown potato puffs that look like pine cones. Highest praise for the best *terrine maison* I've ever tasted: a blend of chicken, duck and goose liver with green peppercorns. Warm, freshly baked rolls are a considerate touch.

For a fragrant white Bandol without any acidity or roughness, try the 1985 Moulin des Costes.

RATINGS: beauty 4, comfort 3, service 3, restaurant 4.

Tennis and riding nearby. Five rooms with balcony.

21

Hôtel Mireille

2 place St-Pierre
13200 Arles
Tel: 90 93 70 74
Telex: 440 308

34 rooms
CC: AE, D, M, V
Open all year. Restaurant open
March 1 to November 15.

Location: just across the pont de Trinquetaille facing the old part of Arles. The hotel is signposted at the bridge.

The hotel is in two sections, separated by an attractive courtyard terrace and a swimming pool. Spacious, yet completely enclosed, it's a little world apart from the surrounding, not-too-elegant neighborhood. The pool is a nice touch, considering the Provençal summer heat. You can also take your meals beside it.

The rooms are modern but not devoid of personality. The minimum price for a double is 290F (*without the More France for the $ discount*). Minibar and radio are included, but not a TV. Nice tiled bathrooms.

The restaurant, **La Provence**, is also in two sections. You don't need to bring a lot of money, just a big appetite. Chef Jacky Carrairon can be reproached only for being too generous with his portions. The menu is changed often, but here's what you could have obtained for 95F the day I was there: a huge *aumônière de saint-jacques à l'estragon*—a pancake "purse" holding a large helping of scallops subtly flavored with tarragon, followed by *lapin sauce chaude moutarde*—tender roast rabbit in mustard sauce accompanied by a copious garnish of sautéed mushrooms and French beans, plus salad, cheese, and dessert. The à la carte menu includes duck in a sweet-sour orange sauce, and T-bone steak broiled over an open wood fire.

Very friendly service in the restaurant fits right in with the hotel's warm hospitality.

RATINGS: beauty 3, comfort 3, service 3, restaurant 3.

Pool. Private parking.

$ $

AAA

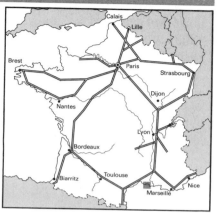

Hôtel Atrium

**1 rue Emile-Fassin
13200 Arles
Tel: 90 49 92 92
Telex: 403 903**

**89 rooms, 2 suites
CC: all
Open all year.**

Location: in the center of Arles, near the main post office.

A modern hotel, built over and around a small old one. Its mirror façade stands out on the Arles skyline. The entrance leads into a glass-roofed atrium with—of all things—an antique car at the top of the stairs. The overall effect is cheerful, light and pretty, and the same can be said for every room. The modern décor is mostly in pastels, with color schemes changing from room to room. In the old building, the rooms have balconies, but the interior décor in both buildings is similar. Prices for a double begin at 380 F.

There are two restaurants on the premises, under separate management from the hotel, but it was not possible to sample them in time for this edition of *More France for the $*. The rating is for rooms alone.

Pool, sauna. 35 rooms with balcony. Garage parking.

23

$ $ $ $

A A A A

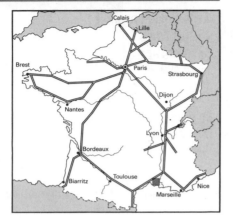

Restaurant Lou Marquès

Boulevard des Lices
13631 Arles
Tel: 90 93 43 20

CC: AE, D, M, V
Closed end of November to Christmas.

Location: in the center of town, at the Hôtel Jules César.

By popular and critical acclaim, the best place to eat in town.

As with most restaurants aiming for a high reputation, the à la carte menu illustrates the classic side of French cuisine: *consommé de langoustines aux truffes*; warm salad of scallops; *feuilleté* of morel mushrooms and asparagus tips; John Dory in a broccoli cream sauce; *panaché de veau cuit en papillote*— veal fillet, sweetbreads and kidneys baked in a paper case sealing in an aromatic melange of flavors.

Visitors interested in Provençal cooking should order the regional menu. Large portions served on bone china with flower motifs include *baudroie à l'aigo sau*—monkfish "bouillabaisse" with potatoes; *pieds et paquets de Camargue*—stuffed tripe and lamb trotters in a lemony herb sauce ... followed by cheeses and dessert.

Two good regional wines to try are Coteaux d'Aix Blanc de Blancs, and Coteaux des Baux VDQS, a fruity red rarely encountered elsewhere.

Authentic Provençal cuisine in an 18th-century convent.

24

$ $ $

A A A A

Hôtel de France

2 place de la Libération
32000 Auch
Tel: 62 05 00 44
Telex: 520 474

29 rooms, 1 suite
CC: AE, CB, D, Eu
Open all year. Restaurant closed Sunday
evening, Monday, and all January.

Location: 78 km west of Toulouse on N124; 71
km south of Agen on N21. In Auch, drive up the
hill to the center square; the hotel is on a corner,
near the town hall.

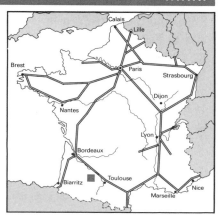

André Daguin's Hôtel de France is charmingly situated in a medieval hilltop town in the heart of Gascony. Many of the rooms look out over the rooftops. They are all different: mine was furnished with antiques; some have wood-burning fireplaces. The minibar is stocked with everything imaginable—including Daguin Colombard wine. Prices start at 450F.

The café next to the downstairs bar/lounge serves uncomplicated specialities like *poulet aux oignons* at low prices, and you can take your breakfast here, too—Daguin's breakfasts are renowned.

The ornate restaurant is a cathedral of Gascony cuisine, which is typified by the use of goose fat as a cooking medium rather than butter or oil. Ducks, geese, guinea hens, quail, and squab flock to Daguin's kitchen and emerge as an impressive array of rillettes, confits, terrines, magrets and foie gras. Stars on the menu are foie gras in a *feuilleté* with salmon, and scallops and foie gras cooked with basil *en papillote*. Lentils, crackling and gizzards are surprisingly combined in a delicious, light soup, and a delightful dessert is *le pastis gascon "estirat,"* using a method of *feuilletage* brought to Gascony by the Spanish Moors centuries ago: a paper-thin sheet of pastry is cut into discs, brushed with goose fat, soaked in armagnac, piled up and stuffed with slices of apple.

From the huge wine list, try the best local red, Madiran, or Daguin's own refreshing white Colombard. An amazing selection of armagnacs.

RATINGS: beauty 4, comfort 5, service 4, restaurant 5.

Garage parking.

25

$ $

A A A

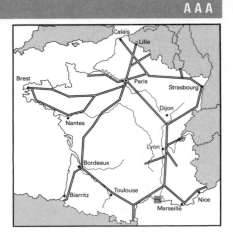

La Magnaneraie

**37 rue du Camp-de-Bataille
30400 Villeneuve-lès-Avignon**
Tel: 90 25 11 11
Telex: 432 640

14 rooms, 8 suites
CC: all
Open all year.

Location: directly across the river from Avignon. Directions for the hotel are placed at key intersections; it is on the high ground on the north side of the village.

One of the nicest places to stay in Avignon is this 15th-century house of cozy charm and character.

Each room shows the personal touch of Mme Prayal, the proprietor, and all have TV, radio, and minibar. Lush towels in the bathroom, designer fragrance soap and bath foam.

Lunch can be served in the pretty garden; the restaurant itself comprises several rooms furnished with country antiques. The cooking of M. Prayal attracts a big crowd of mostly French-speaking people. Some of the reasons they come: *la papillote de filets de poissons aux petits légumes* (fish fillets in a paper case with small vegetables), *le cœur de charolais en croûte* (tender beef baked in a pastry crust), *le coq de Guinée* (guinea fowl) *à la créole,* and *la tranche d'aloyau* (sirloin) in Roquefort.

The house wine is a superb Lirac made from the Syrah grape, grown at the southern end of the Côtes du Rhône.

RATINGS: beauty 3, comfort 4, service 3, restaurant 4.

Tennis, pool.

$ $

A A A

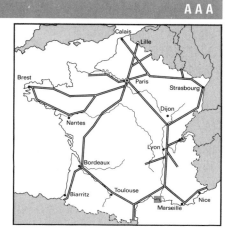

Auberge de France

28 place de l'Horloge
84000 Avignon
Tel: 90 82 58 86

CC: AE, D, Eu, V
Closed Wednesday evening,
all day Thursday, all January and
the second two weeks in June.

Location: in the center of Avignon, near the Palais
des Papes.

Yes, it is possible to eat superbly in Avignon without paying an arm and a leg. The austere appearance of this restaurant, owned by the Tassan family, belies the warmth inside. One brother in the kitchen provides delicious and inventive cooking, while another in the dining room makes sure the service is friendly and efficient.

The mussels *à l'avignonnaise* were a surprise, covered with *beurre d'escargots*—garlic and herb butter. *Filet de rascasse chemisé de laitue* was steamed in lettuce and presented with béchamel, framed with little ovals of melon. From the more traditional side of Provençal cooking, *pieds et paquets à la provençale* is something to write home about: mutton tripe rolled into small bundles, cooked with sheep's trotters in white wine, garlic and tomato.

Try the white Côtes du Rhône Villages Cairanne, produced only in small quantities. One of my favorite goat cheeses, Banon, soft, white, subtly flavored by its chestnut-leaf wrapping, is also a rare treat.

Feasting in the shadow of the Papal Palace.

$ $

A

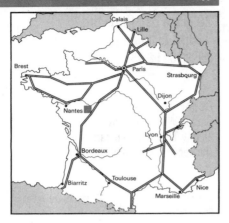

Le Grand Monarque

Place de la République
37190 Azay-le-Rideau
Tel: 47 45 40 08

28 rooms, 1 suite
CC: AE, Eu, M, V
Open all year. Restaurant closed
15 November to 15 March.

Location: 23 km south-west of Tours. The hotel is in the very center of Azay.

What this 18th-century relais is lacking in comfort, it makes up for in charm. Some time in the early 19th century, its owner extended the hotel by constructing a modest mansion directly behind it. The grassy space between the two buildings is just big enough to hold a couple of shade trees with tables underneath. Most of the rooms are now idealized reproductions of the perfect 18th-century "room at the inn" (some of those in the "new" building have not been restored)—heavy beams, antique country furniture, chintz curtains and bedspreads in pink and periwinkle. Each room has a TV and radio, and a modern tiled bathroom. Base price: 305 F.

The restaurant provides the best meal in town. Diners who want a light salad might be surprised if they order *la salade de homard Breton,* only to be served a half-pound lobster tail without a trace of greens. On the other hand, knowing this, the lobster can serve as an attractive—and attractively priced—main course.

The lamb fricassée was somewhat blighted by a long wait on the hot plate while I grappled with the lobster tail, but the fillets of red mullet were not a bit overcooked, and suffused in a tasty anchovy cream sauce.

Azay-le-Rideau produces a white Touraine which is not sweet (as some Touraine wines tend to be). Sainte-maure is the local goat cheese, well respected for its full flavor.

RATINGS: beauty 2, comfort 2, service 2, restaurant 3.

Garage across from the front entrance.

28

$ $

AAAA

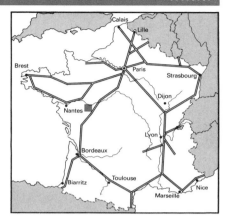

Auberge du XIIe Siècle

Saché
37190 Azay-le-Rideau
Tel: 47 26 86 58

CC: AE, D, V
Closed February and March.

Location: on route D17, about 7 km east of Azay-le-Rideau. The restaurant is in the center of the village, directly across from the town square.

The tiny village is a worthy attraction in itself—the small château where Balzac penned *The Human Comedy* is just across the street and open to visitors. The writer used to drop in to the 12th-century auberge for a glass of Vouvray and a chat. The restaurant looks so old that nothing much must have changed in the past 800 years. The stone steps leading to the front entrance are deeply worn; the huge roof beams are stained with age.

Jean-Louis Niqueux was *chef de cuisine* in a luxury hotel for ten years before finding a demure little place he could call his own. To make it pay, he keeps prices low, counting on the local clientele. It's wise to call in advance for reservations.

The most expensive à la carte item is *cœur de filet de bœuf Rossini*, in a sauce of foie gras, truffles and madeira, at 145 F. Everything else is priced far below. Simplicity prevails in his salmon in sorrel sauce, and roast saddle of lamb flavored with thyme. A matelote of eel in Bourgeuil wine and a *coq au vin* are two country dishes raised to epicurean standards. And *blanc de turbot aux huîtres et bigorneaux,* bright, white turbot fillet contrasting beautifully with a golden sauce of wine and Noilly Prat, studded with oysters and periwinkles.

The best local wine is Azay-le-Rideau-Saché, dry with only the merest hint of fruitiness. The red 1982 Touraine-Mesland, Domaine d'Artois, costs less than 100 F and tastes like a million. The 1978, 1982, 1983, and 1985 vintages were exceptional.

Public parking on town square.

29

$

A A A

Le Lion d'Or

71 rue St-Jean
14400 Bayeux
Tel: 31 92 06 90
Telex: 171 143

CC: AE, D, V
Closed 26 December to 20 January.

Location: on the N13 north-west of Caen. In the center of old Bayeux.

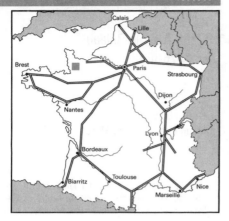

The Lion d'Or has been an inn since 1770. A small courtyard in front, where the carriages once trundled in, is now a car park. The exterior, like the adjacent houses and narrow streets, is largely unchanged and has a lot of atmosphere. The famous Bayeux Tapestry can be seen in the Centre Guillaume-le-Conquérant in rue de Nesmond, a short walk away.

Inexpensive by fine restaurant standards, the Lion d'Or has a harmonious décor of antique-style chairs, mirrors with inlaid stained glass, timbered ceiling and a wall of softly tinted glass panes facing the courtyard.

Whether the idea of eating skate wing and nettles sounds inviting or not, I hope the *raie Normande aux pointes d'orties* is given the chance it deserves. The white skate meat is suffused in a lemony butter-and-egg sauce distinguished by the fresh flavor of nettles. A light, delectable surprise. *Pigeonneau rôti et sa purée mousseline à l'ail* was worthy of star honors, not only for the squab cooked in its own juice—none of the stickiness many chefs try to disguise with red wine—but also for the delicate garlic flavor of the airy potato purée, lightly browned in the oven.

The house cocktail—Golden Dawn—is a potent mixture of orange juice, Calvados and apricot brandy!

Norman specialties with a delicate touch.

$ $

unrated

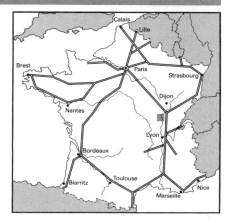

Hostellerie de Levernois

21200 Beaune
Tel: 80 24 73 58

12 rooms
Open all year.

Location: from Beaune autoroute exit, take the D970 for Verdun; after 4 km turn left for Levernois.

This 1750 château was in the process of being remodelled into a hotel and restaurant when I dropped by to inspect it. The new owner is Jean Crotet, proprietor and chef of the Côte d'Or in Nuits-St-Georges.

The stone building and stables are on a quiet gravel road, only minutes off the *autoroute*. The estate is surrounded by a large and verdant park, complete with babbling brook.

It is scheduled to open in early 1989, with standard double rooms priced at under 500F. By the look of the work in progress, we can expect great things.

Peace and quiet, and the promise of fine food.

31

$ $ $

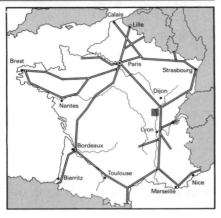

*   A A A A

L'Ermitage-Corton

21201 Chorey-lès-Beaune
Tel: 80 22 05 28
Telex: ERMICO 351 189

5 rooms, 5 junior suites
CC: AE, D, EU, M, V
Closed January to mid-February.
Restaurant closed Sunday evening
and Monday.

Location: On the N74, 4 km north of Beaune.

Chef and owner André Parra and his family almost overwhelm their guests with all the comfort and eating pleasure they can devise.

Room prices start at just over 500 F; there are no inferior or small rooms, only big and bigger. The doors and walls are upholstered with fabrics, and no two walls are the same! Stripes on one, paisley on another—it's not boring, to say the least. The fantasy extends to the bathrooms, but no matter how different, they all have robes and other considerate touches: big bottles of shampoo, pitchers of bath foam, almond-oil soap—even hair spray.

The restaurant outdoes itself, too. To nibble on while you're waiting: hard-boiled quail eggs, peppery country sausage, Provençal olives. The menus begin at 125 F with a daily special of one main course and a selection of cheeses. The 200 F menu offers a salad of white kidneys, chicken with aligoté wine sauce, pâtés, cheeses, and a plate of several desserts. The 325 F *Menu route des grands crus* goes all out with six courses, including warmed duck liver in a salad with walnut oil dressing, Swedish *gravad lax*, veal sweetbreads and kidneys in two sauces, duckling in blackcurrant sauce, cheese, and two desserts —and between courses, a green apple and Burgundy prune liqueur sherbet.

Two fine, not very expensive, wines out of the enormous list: white 1983 Ladoix, with an exceptional fruity aroma and very dry aftertaste; and a smooth, full-bodied red 1978 Santenay.

RATINGS: beauty 4, comfort 5, service 4, restaurant 5.

Extravagant décor, wonderful food—a memorable experience.

$ $ $

A A A

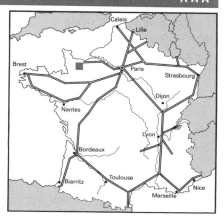

Le Manoir d'Hastings

14970 Bénouville
Tel: 31 44 62 43
Telex: 171 144

11 rooms
CC: AE, D, M, V
Open all year.

Location: on the Ouistreham road, 8 km north-east of Caen.

The hotel, **La Pommeraie**, and restaurant are in separate buildings on the same grounds. The manor house, which is now the restaurant, dates back to 1670, when it was built as a priory for the old church next door.

The rooms are spacious and comfortably furnished, with little extra touches such as pre-stamped postcards and envelopes, a basket of fruit—even a pants press which every man appreciates.

The stone-floored, thick-walled restaurant, where father and son Claude and Yves Scaviner reign over the kitchen, is one of the best in Normandy. Local lobster accompanies a seafood salad with sherry vinegar, or is boiled and served with a cider sauce, or broiled and topped with herb butter. *Le pigeonneau en caramel de gingembre* is an original, but don't forget to request it roasted at least medium, unless you like squab served *rosé*. Breast of duck is served with a cider sauce, and fillet of beef spiced with a sauce of five peppers.

Most interesting were *les œufs coque en surprise*—four eggs in the shell, topped with pastry: one with black caviar in cream sauce, one with oyster and smoked salmon in gelatin, one with truffles in duck aspic, and one with oyster and chives in a cream sauce.

Strong, soft and gold-colored Pont-l'évêque cheese from the nearby village is famous throughout France. Pungent, "fruity" La Bouille is another to ask for.

Many good buys on the wine list. The white Ladoix is dry enough to go with anything but a red wine sauce, and the very dry Graves—135 F—would be my choice for dishes with a Calvados sauce.

RATINGS: beauty 4, comfort 4, service 3, restaurant 4.

One of the best restaurants in Normandy.

$ $ $ $

A A A A A

Hôtel du Palais

1 avenue de l'Impératrice
64200 Biarritz
Tel: 59 24 09 40
Telex: 570 000

117 rooms, 24 suites
CC: AE, D, EU, V
Open 1 April to 31 October.

From the A63 follow the "centre ville" signs to the waterfront. Turn right, then a diagonal left into the hotel gates.

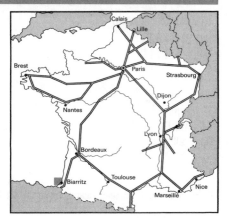

Formerly the Villa Eugénie, built in 1854 by Napoleon III for his wife, the Hôtel du Palais is a beach resort hotel and a palace in every sense of the word, with miles of marble corridors, gilded columns, rich carpeting and crystal chandeliers. Though the hotel fits into the highest price category, the standard, town-view doubles cost from 400 to 600 F less than the sea-view rooms, and you have a good chance of free upgrading with your *More France for the $* coupon. During the warm but windy months of May, June, September, and October, you can obtain complimentary use of a pool cabana, with access and view of the beach, private phone, and reclining lounges.

The three restaurants offer a free main course with any meal for two.

L'Hippocampe, an informal grill-room and seafood restaurant, specializes in simplicity. Dishes with a Basque flavour are served in **La Rotonde**, overlooking the ocean, and **Le Grand Siècle**, showy and more intimate: lobster in gaspacho sauce; *germiny d'ail vert* (sorrel and cream soup with garlic); baby lamb *"chouria."* Not to mention some exquisite paellas, depending on the season.

The wine list features the best Bordeaux, but don't overlook the local wines at a tenth the price: red 1983 Madiran, Domaine du Crampilh, dry white Jurançon *brut*, and a Spanish Basque Txakoli Txomin Echaniz, with a crisp, full flavor and a bouquet very similar to white Châteauneuf du Pape.

RATINGS: beauty 5, comfort 5, service 4, restaurant 4.

Pool, beach, sauna, fitness club. Most rooms with full or half-balcony.

$ $ $ $

A A A A A

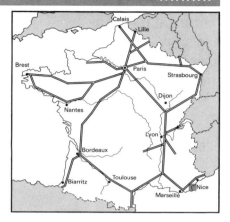

Hôtel Martinez

73 boulevard de la Croisette
06400 Cannes
Tel: 93 68 91 91
Telex: 479 708
Fax: 93 39 67 82

325 rooms, 25 suites
CC: AE, D, Eu, M, V
Open all year.
La Palme d'Or closed Monday.

Location: on the east end of La Croisette.

After complete renovation, the Martinez has an Art Deco sparkle. The lobby is a work of art, with mirrored ceiling, inlaid floor, leather armchairs, and big glass doors that let in the sun.

The rooms range from the far-out in tones of pink and gray, with Picasso prints on the walls, to the sedate. Bathrooms vary in opulence, but all rate a 5 for comfort. A standard double costs about 1,000F in summer and several hundred francs less in the off season.

The restaurant **L'Orangeraie** is exceptional value. Presided over by fabulously talented Christian Willer, it offers an à la carte menu with most dishes priced below 100F. For the entrée, try *pot-au-feu de cuisses de canette en gelée de fenouil*, duckling thighs and vegetables in a fennel aspic—or *soupe de poissons de la Méditerranée*—rockfish soup delicately flavored with peppers, garlic and saffron. The main courses do homage to classic salmon, sole, entrecôte, lamb and veal, plus some glorious variations on country food: *cuisses de canette confites croustillantes*—two crispy duck leg confits with Provençal vegetables; *osso buco à la mirepoix aromatique*—veal shank with diced vegetables scented with Provençal herbs.

Because its emphasis is on regional cooking, L'Orangeraie is like a country cousin to the glamorous **Palme d'Or** upstairs, where you'll get the most exquisite meal in town. An inspired pâtissier makes desserts for both restaurants: chocolate marquise with tiny grains of coffee; frozen lime soufflé; aniseed parfait with dark chocolate sauce...

RATINGS: beauty 5, comfort 5, service 5, restaurant 5.

Pool, private beach, tennis club, beauty salon, boutiques.

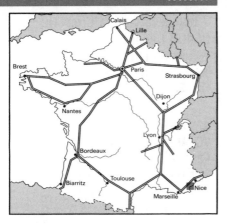

Hôtel Carlton
Inter-Continental

58 boulevard de la Croisette
06400 Cannes
Tel: 93 68 91 68
Telex: 470 720
Fax: 93 38 20 90

295 rooms, 30 suites
CC: AE, D, Eu, V
Open all year.

Location: in the center of La Croisette.

With its Belle Epoque wedding-cake façade and twin domed towers, the Carlton is the centerpiece of Cannes luxury. Its gleaming marble columns and crystal chandeliers, gold leaf capitals and ceiling frescoes are a reminder that the era of truly grand hotels is still with us. Its marble portals open to an arcade of boutiques, three restaurants, a central salon with grand piano, and a serendipitous sanctuary for intimate meetings over drinks, modestly named Le Petit Bar.

Upstairs, every room is equally luxurious. From November to April, the standard double price is cut by almost half. And complimentary upgrading is valid if a larger or sea-view room is available when you arrive.

There are three restaurants: **Café Carlton & Terrace** for cocktails and informal meals outside; **Le Relais-Grill**, with vaulted ceiling, Louis XIII décor, and stone walls, for international food; and **La Côte**, an elegant Edwardian room in pastel blue and beige, for classic French cuisine.

Specialties include *salade tiède de langoustines aux légumes barigoule*—warm prawn salad with mushrooms and artichokes; *raviolis de langoustines au beurre de truffes*—the ravioli rolled paper-thin; and a *pot-au-feu maraîchère minute*—a hotpot of veal, beef, chicken, and goose liver with herbs.

From the fine selection of Provençal wines, red Château Minuty is a wise choice.

RATINGS: beauty 5, comfort 5, service 5, restaurant 4.

Private beach. Tennis and golf by arrangement.

Hôtel Gray d'Albion

38 rue des Serbes
06400 Cannes
Tel: 93 68 54 54
Telex: 470 744

187 rooms, 12 suites
CC: AE, D, M, V
Open all year.
Restaurant closed February.

Location: half a block behind La Croisette and the beach.

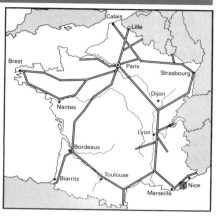

A very handsome, polished sandstone building. The spacious, elegant lobby was designed for modern efficiency, but takes nothing away from the feeling of luxury with a liberal display of flowers and deep, soft sofas. The main difference between the standard doubles and the deluxe rooms is a few extras in the bathroom and the saving of a few hundred francs. The east or west exposure makes it largely a choice between a sunny balcony at breakfast or a sunny balcony at cocktail time.

The restaurant, the **Royal Gray**, is more expensive than the hotel. Built on the reputation of Chef Jacques Chibois, the cooking is distinguished by its elegant presentation. Dishes range from the elaborate *rotonde de caviar aux noix de saint-jacques, à l'asperge et aux œufs d'escargots* (caviar, scallops, asparagus and— latest gimmick on the culinary scene—snail eggs) to the simple *agneau de lait rôti au cumin*—roast suckling lamb with cumin. There are three fixed-price menus at 320 F, 380 F and the 440 F nine-course *menu dégustation*; the à la carte menu shows no mention of price.

Best buys among the regional wines are 1985 Côtes de Provence Château Réal Martin Blanc de Blancs, and red 1984 Bandol Château Vannière, or, more in keeping with the *dégustation* level, white 1984 Châteauneuf-du-Pape Château Rayas, all under 200 F. Or you could chance the 1980 St-Emilion Grand Cru Château Vieux Pourret, and hope that it has mellowed after a doubtful start—it's a sporting proposition at 260 F.

RATINGS: beauty 4, comfort 5, service 5, restaurant 5.

Private beach, garage. All but 12 rooms with balconies.

$ $ $ $

A A A A

Hôtel Majestic

6 boulevard de la Croisette
06400 Cannes
Tel: 93 68 91 00
Telex: 470 787

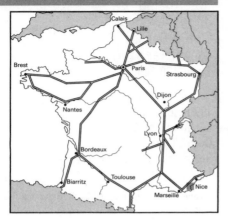

249 rooms, 13 suites
CC: AE, D, Eu, M, V
Closed 15 November to 15 December.

Location: on the west end of La Croisette.

The Majestic rules discreetly from the quieter end of the Croisette, with service as soft as the silk bedspreads. Despite a large number of rooms, the hotel is quite intimate, perhaps because of the personal, cheerful service.

The ultimate degree of comfort can be taken for granted, whether your room is big or small, with or without a sea-view. The upholstery is coordinated silk; the bathrooms have phone, robes, heated towel racks, designer fragrance soap and bath foam.

Off-season rates for a standard double are well under 1,000F. With complimentary upgrading, your room might be worth three times the price.

The restaurant is as majestic as the hotel, with food tending toward ornateness. Poached eggs with caviar in *sauce velours*; veal Marengo (with tomatoes, mushrooms, garlic and herbs); strawberry *millefeuille*... But you can enjoy simpler fare at **Le Grill** on the poolside terrace, especially at the bountiful beach buffet in the warm months.

RATINGS: beauty 5, comfort 5, service 5, restaurant 4.

Tennis and golf by arrangement. Pool, private beach.

$

A A

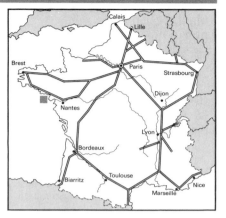

Lann Roz

36 avenue de la Poste
56340 Carnac
Tel: 97 52 10 48

13 rooms
CC: AE, CB, V
Open all year.

Location: leave the N165 at Auray. Follow the signs to the center of Carnac and continue past the church. The hotel is a steep-roofed Breton house surrounded by a garden.

Lann Roz feels more like a family home than a hotel. The name means "country rose" in Breton, and the garden is thick with rose bushes. The interior walls are of rough stone, alternating with knotty pine panels. The dining room has a big stone fireplace and wooden beams. Upstairs, the rooms are not large, but offer simple comfort—TV included.

Though it is charming, I chose this hotel for the restaurant, one of the best in Brittany. The atmosphere is informal and relaxed, and fairly inexpensive. The cooking is simple, but that doesn't mean that it's boring. *Marmite de moules en feuilletage* is really a savory tart bursting with mussels in a creamy broth. The almost obligatory *coquilles saint-jacques,* or scallops, of good French restaurants are prepared with apples in cider sauce. Salmon with coarse salt is broiled and served with a flan of asparagus and beans. The fillet of sole comes in a *coulis* (thick sauce) of tomato and artichoke hearts. The tournedos are served with *pleurotes*, a peppery species of fungus, while the more delicate morels accompany squab.

The 180 F menu "Entre Amis" entitles you to a complimentary bottle of wine from a very large and selective cellar. Your menu choices might include any of the dishes mentioned above, but of course, what is offered depends on the time of year. An ice milk of champagne and grapefruit between courses is a refreshing house tradition regardless of season.

RATINGS: beauty 3, comfort 2, service 2, restaurant 4.

Pool. Five rooms with balconies. Rose garden.

$ $

AAA

Château de la Salle

Montpinchon
50210 Cerisy-la-Salle
Tel: 33 46 95 19

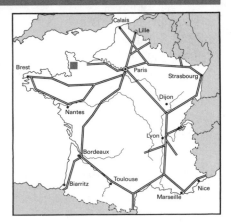

10 rooms, 1 suite
CC: AE, D, V
Open all year.

Location: on the Cotentin peninsula, south-east of Coutances. Take the D 972 between Coutances and St-Lô and turn off to Cerisy. The château is well-signposted locally.

One of the nicest of the old châteaux-hôtels, surrounded by an enormous park, in the pretty Soulle valley. The history of the estate goes back to the 11th century, and the huge hearth in the dining room is a vestige of that era. But the building's exterior suggests the 17th century, when it became the home of the Marquis de la Salle.

Furnished with exquisite antiques, the rooms contain fascinating collections of four-poster beds, hand-made oak wardrobes, and chairs upholstered in rich brocades. There are rough-hewn beams on the ceiling, big windows, and walls a foot thick. Prices for a double begin at 420F and edge their way upward according to room size. All are beautiful, regardless of price.

If La Salle were to return home today, he would be most pleased with the performance in the kitchen. Little bay scallops in a warm vinaigrette sauce, a shellfish *consommé*, a salmon steak with sweet peppers, and a saddle of hare baked in its own juice were absolute heaven. Pastry filled with apples and served with caramelized cider, and bittersweet chocolate charlotte in a thick chocolate sauce were noteworthy desserts.

Many outstanding wines for less than expected. A great example is 1982 Haut-Médoc Fort-Auvin for 118F.

RATINGS: beauty 5, comfort 4, service 3, restaurant 4.

Within easy reach of Normandy's top attractions.

$ $

A A A

Hostellerie des Clos

89800 Chablis
Tel: 86 42 10 63

26 rooms
CC: AE, D, Eu, V
Closed Wednesdays except in summer, and January.

Coming from the A6, drive into the village and take the first right turn. Watch for small signs for the hotel; it's on a corner with a tiny parking lot in front.

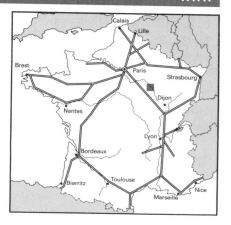

A visit to the Chablis vineyards is an excellent reason for stopping in this picturesque village; Michel Vignaud, chef and proprietor of the Hostellerie des Clos, will be happy to be your guide. His little hotel is a lovely place to stay in. It's an 18th-century inn, remodelled in a pleasant modern style. The rooms, priced at 260F, offer simple comfort and pleasant pastel décor.

The downstairs has a bright, unconfining reception area opening out to a large dining room. One wall is entirely of glass and overlooks a grassy courtyard with shade trees, where guests are invited to have their apéritif.

Michel Vignaud's cuisine is, by itself, worth the trip to Chablis. Reliance on local produce results in some delicate blends like ravioli *chèvre du pays* in a chive sauce with quail eggs, as well as in the classic escargots de Bourgogne.

Decidedly not local is the Mediterranean red mullet in an oyster sauce, artfully arranged with pods of baby peas and young scallions to resemble a branch bearing red fruit. Lobster, presented with orange-hued chanterelles, and gigot of baby lamb with a nice round aubergine stuffed with herbs and vegetables, taste as good as they look.

Try the local cheeses: fresh, white Soumaintrain; salty, soft, orange-dusted Epoisses; rare and strong Citeaux. A very heady wine, excellent with cheese, is a 1982 St-Romain from Beaune, bargain-priced at 109F. But in Chablis, no one will fault you for drinking white, whatever the course—prefer the 1986.

RATINGS: beauty 3, comfort 2, service 2, restaurant 4.

Magnificent vaulted cellar.

41

$ $ $

A A A

Le Royal Champagne

51160 Champillon-Bellevue
Tel: 26 52 87 11
Telex: 830 111

24 rooms, 1 suite
CC: AE, D, M, V
Closed January.

Between Reims and Epernay, on the N 51. From Epernay, follow the signs for Champillon and take the scenic Route du Vignoble. From Reims, watch on the right for the hotel sign, which will indicate the next left turn.

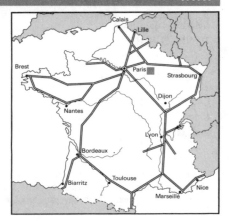

The *"belle vue"* from this hotel is an infinity of champagne vineyards, with Epernay in the center.

The reception and restaurant occupy the uppermost of three buildings. The smaller rooms, at slightly over 500 F, are in the middle building. They are almost too small for two people, although the double Murphy bed can be raised out of the way to create a sitting room. The larger—very large—rooms, in the lowest building, enjoy a totally unobstructed view and a small private patio, and cost around 1,000 F. Large or small, all the rooms have remote-control TV, radio, and robes in the bathroom.

A cheery waiter brings breakfast at the hour you want it; there is also a buffet in a small breakfast restaurant in the main building.

The restaurant is of high quality, good enough to have enticed Great Britain's Queen Mother out here for lunch.

Champagne accents most of Chef Jean-Claude Pacherie's cooking. Broiled lobster in a vinaigrette dressing is arranged in a ring, with champagne sabayon in the center. The same sabayon is served with fillets of pike *(brochet)* and walleye *(sandre)*. There's also veal sweetbreads with truffles in a fine champagne sauce, and several champagne fricassées.

The Royal Champagne seems to have every one of the 130 different brands of bubbly on its wine list. The menus, featuring three or four courses, start at 280 F and include a half-bottle of champagne, Mercier Brut Réserve.

RATINGS: beauty 4, comfort 4, service 4, restaurant 4.

Visits to champagne cellars in Epernay specially arranged for guests.

Château de Teildras

route de Juvardeil
49330 Cheffes-sur-Sarthe
Tel: 41 42 61 08
Telex: 722 268

11 rooms
CC: AE, M, V
Open April to November.
Restaurant closed Tuesday lunch.

Location: near Angers. Exit Seiches from A11, drive into the town and turn for Tiercé. Continue to Cheffes; the hotel is about 1 km north-west of the village.

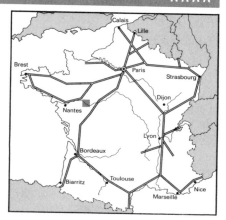

This château is small, cozy and charming, surrounded by an extensive estate with pastures, woods, and a river full of enormous pike.

An attractive drawing room is used as reception, and an adjoining salon with blue and gold furniture upholstered in velvet, 18th-century oil paintings, and an heirloom tapestry, serves as library and reading room, or the perfect setting for tea.

The bedrooms are furnished with antiques. They vary in size and appointments, but even the small one I had would be ample for two people who don't plan to spend much time sitting around in their room. Prices for a double start at 555 F.

The restaurant comprises several small and intimate dining rooms with wooden beams. The menu is equally small and absolutely first

rate. Pierrick Berthier deserves praise for his *terrine de homard et sauce cressonière*—each slice of terrine a study in three shades of orange. The *saumon farci, sauce au vin d'Anjou* was salmon rolled round a hard-boiled egg and covered in leeks, complemented by a sauce of rosé wine. Fillet of beef *en chevreuil* (cooked to taste like roe deer) came in an aromatic sauce of red wine and currant jelly.

Savennières is nearby. This inexpensive, dry, happy white wine made from the Chenin Blanc grape is one of my favorites. Aromatic Bourgeuil is a light, yet full-bodied red, not as rough as Chinon. One more local is Cointreau, distilled in Angers. The château used to bottle a rosé (this is Anjou country) which is still available if you ask for it.

RATINGS: beauty 4, comfort 4, service 4, restaurant 5.

Fishing, park. Tennis nearby.

$ $

* A A A A

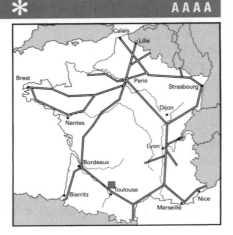

Le Grand Ecuyer

81170 Cordes
Tel: 63 56 01 03

14 rooms, 1 suite
CC: AE, CB, D, V
Open mid-March to November.
Restaurant closed Monday,
except July and August.

25 km north-west of Albi on D 600; between Ville-franche-de-Rouergue and Gaillac on D 922. Drive up and up to the old town, and park your car outside the citadel gate; the hotel is just inside.

Cordes commands a 360°-view of the Cérou valley. It was built by the Count of Toulouse in 1222 as a refuge for the Cathars. A collection of Gothic stone houses line the Grand'rue, the town's one and only street running all round the top of the hill. All of them are well preserved, but none better than the hunting retreat of Count Raymond VII, now the hotel Le Grand Ecuyer.

The wide stone staircase is lined with post-Renaissance paintings; suits of armor stand guard on the landings. No expense was spared to make each room a showplace, with four-poster beds, oriental rugs, oil paintings, Louis XIII furniture, and recessed niches holding medieval statues. The fixtures in the ultra-modern, marble bathrooms, are plated in gold. 450F will get you a room like this.

The owner, mastermind and chef is Yves Thuriès, who has turned Cordes into a gourmet heaven. While the restaurant is not as economically priced as the hotel, there's at least one good menu for the budget-conscious. For 160F you can try an appetizer of smoked goose breast with melon, then anglerfish spiced with coriander, followed by duck *confit* in a peppery *poivrade* sauce, and lastly, a *millefeuille* of paper-thin chocolate leaves sandwiched with mocha.

Thuriès' *menu douceur* will give you something to talk about back home: two supremely inventive starters, followed by *four* courses of dessert. The presentation is pure Cecil B. DeMille—ice sculptures holding sherbets and *granités,* spun-sugar figures and fabulous hot and cold dishes.

RATINGS: beauty 5, comfort 5, service 3, restaurant 5.

Heaven for the sweet of tooth.

$

A A

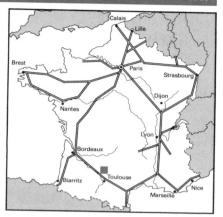

Hostellerie du Vieux Cordes

81170 Cordes
Tel: 63 56 00 12

21 rooms
CC: AE, D, Eu, V
Closed February.
Restaurant closed Wednesday,
except July and August.

Location: in the fortified top section of the village, on the left after you enter the citadel. Leave your car outside the gates.

The stone-walled building dates back to the Middle Ages, abounding with arched passageways, timbered ceilings and antique décor. The rooms are simple and often rather pretty, offering no-frills accommodations but spectacular vistas of the Cérou valley. Prices for doubles are as low as 250 F.

One of the joys of staying here is eating in the courtyard patio under a roof of wisteria vines that let through dapples of sunshine. There's also a country-style informal dining room, with tables carefully laid with crisp white tablecloths, pewter and fresh flowers. The food is inexpensive, and merits a special detour. I passed up the 70 F menu for the 95 F *menu de tradition*: a *bavarois* of smoked salmon with artichoke heart, followed by barbary duck in a jubilantly fruity orange and wine sauce, with gnocchis topped with a layer of browned, shredded potato.

Yves Thuriès of Le Grand Ecuyer is a consulting chef. With this in mind, it might be worth trying the eight-course 230F menu *les délices de Raymond VII*: warm foie gras parfait, two seafood dishes, two meat dishes, a warm cheese course, and two scrumptious desserts—strawberry flan with passionfruit coulis and a *croustillant* of green apple sherbet.

The à la carte menu has two dozen dishes united by low prices and imagination. The wine list is a who's-who of Gaillac and Bergerac châteaux—all priced below 100F. Try the 1984 Gaillac, Château Larroze, whose light, almost rosé color disguises a deep, slightly nutty, flavor.

RATINGS: beauty 4, comfort 2, service 2, restaurant 4.

Terrace. Sky-high views, down-to-earth prices.

$ $

A A A

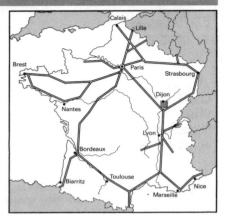

Hostellerie du Chapeau Rouge

5 rue Michelet
21000 Dijon
Tel: 80 30 28 10
Telex: 350 535

33 rooms, 1 suite
CC: AE, D, Eu, M, V
Open all year.

Location: in the center of town, near the archaeo-logical museum and just before the St-Bénigne cathedral.

The nicest hotel in town is named for a cardinal's red hat, because this was once the site of the cardinal's residence. The rooms are on the small side but pleasantly decorated, with oak beds, TV, radio, minibar; and a hairdryer in the bathroom. Fifteen of them have air-conditioning. Prices for a double start at under 400 F, good value without sacrificing anything but a little elbow room. Service is hospitable and helpful.

Downstairs you'll find a very cozy, pub-like bar, and a fine restaurant. After your house cocktail, a potent blend of gin, vermouth and cassis, be prepared for an excellent meal. It could begin with eggs poached in Burgundy wine, or a feuilleté of frog legs *aux fines herbes*. Then poached salmon in parsley cream, or Bresse chicken with morel mushroom sauce. And what would Dijon be without mustard? Try the *fricassée de rognons de veau à la moutarde,* veal kidneys in a mustard sauce.

Here in the old capital of the Dukes of Burgundy, you can be sure of a superlative wine list. In the reds, I found a 1980 Monthélie—nobody was happy about that year until now; the color was off and the taste a bit thin. But the wines that managed to age well are blossoming forth at bad vintage prices. If you do try it, let it breathe for 20 minutes. The aroma will come first, then a richness to rival Burgundy's best. In whites, the Rully Clos St-Jacques is a successful blend of tartness and fruitiness.

RATINGS: beauty 3, comfort 3, service 4, restaurant 4.

Park at a meter—the hotel will help you find a garage.

$ $ $ $

A A A A A

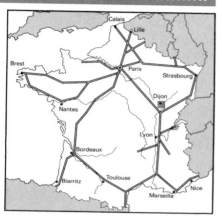

Jean-Pierre Billoux

14 place Darcy
21000 Dijon
Tel: 80 30 11 00

CC: AE, CB, D, Eu
Closed Sunday evening and Monday,
and all February.

Location: in the cellar of hotel La Cloche in the center of town.

This musty old wine cellar turned cheerful when the walls were painted white, vases filled with wild flowers and flowery china put on the tables. It turned into a great restaurant when Jean-Pierre Billoux took over the kitchen.

For epicurian appetites, this is the place to try *escalope de foie de canard chaud* (a thin slice of duck's liver) or *homard breton cuit au diable, sauce au beurre de pistache*—Brittany lobster with pistachio butter. Or the *paillasson de langoustines,* succulent prawns arranged on a soft bed of home fries, with julienne and parsley, or *filet de saint-pierre aux concassées d'olives,* John Dory fillets with a pungent aroma of crushed black olives.

Ordering à la carte may run into money—only the *bouquet de légumes à la grecque* was priced under 100F, the night I was there. So the four-course fixed-price menu at 200F is a wonderful bargain: you can have, for example, a cassolette of snails flavored with tarragon, guinea hen thighs with spring onions, and a cheese tray abounding with local cheeses such as *boulette de la Pierre-qui-Vire*, from the abbey of the same name, or the soft and creamy Montrachet chèvre. Plus dessert. The service is warm and friendly.

The wine list has a huge map of Burgundy from Montagny to Dijon, with every village and nearly every *appellation* indicated and available.

Lives up to its excellent reputation.

$ $

AAA

Hôtel Cro-Magnon

24620 Les Eyzies-de-Tayac
Tel: 53 06 97 06
Telex: 570 637

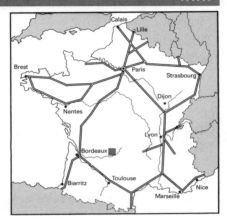

20 rooms, 4 suites
CC: AE, D, V
Open end April to mid-October.

Location: between Périgeux and Sarlat, on D 47.
On the west end of the village.

This hotel was built as a coaching station in the 18th century, and it has retained much of its old character in the original section housing the reception, lounges, dining room and some upstairs guestrooms. But the most appealing feature of the building is in a recent addition—though it is unnoticeable from outside, the solid rock face has been integrated as the back wall, providing the most appropriate décor for Les Eyzies, the Capital of Prehistory.

Intriguing as this is, it's fortunate that the décor of the rooms is not paleolithic, but paisley. Soft, charming and inviting, with country furniture and fluffy beds. Simple comfort, but in good taste.

Meals are taken in a garden under spreading chestnut trees, bounded by walls covered in Virginia creeper. The food is as lovely as the setting. Try the *escargots de grand'mère Anne*—a dozen snails in garlic butter with chopped walnuts and herbs. Or *les poissons de rivière fumés au velouté*—smoked perch, pike and walleye in a white sauce, garnished with turnips and broad beans. Local specialties abound, including *pommes sarladaises*, thinly sliced potatoes baked in goose fat with truffles. The chef, Xavier Davout, is capable of great delicacy—taste his pigeon pâté.

Bergerac white wines are crisp and inexpensive, but an outstanding value at the Cro-Magnon is a sweet and fruity 1976 Monbazillac for 140 F. Among reds, all the full-bodied Cahors.

RATINGS: beauty 4, comfort 3, service 3, restaurant 4.

Pool. Tennis nearby. Four rooms with balcony. Private parking.

$ $ $ $

* AAAAA

Château Eza

06360 Eze-Village
Tel: 93 41 12 24
Telex: 470 382

6 rooms, 3 suites
CC: AE, D, M, V
Open April to November.

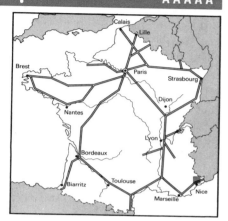

Location: from the A8, exit La Turbie from Nice, or Monaco from Italy. On the Moyenne Corniche, at the top of the village.

Cars must be parked at the bottom of the village. In a small, open shelter at the top of the public parking lot, there's a phone with a direct link to Château Eza reception. Once they know you're there, a porter will come leading a donkey to carry up your luggage, while you follow at your own pace up the cobbled pathway, past houses that have been leaning into each other for centuries.

The cluster of houses that forms the hotel was once the residence of a Swedish prince, and overlooks a magnificent panorama, with Cap Ferrat and Villefranche Bay far below. The present owner took six years to transform it into a hotel. The suites have huge private ter-races; all rooms have stone walls, exposed beams, and Spanish Renaissance furniture. The bathrooms are enormous, thoughtfully equipped with a complete toiletries kit. Prices start at 1,000 F.

The restaurant is undergoing a change of chefs, but the standards set by M. Rochat, the owner, prevail. When I visited, subtly flavoured noisettes of lamb with curry and *ail douce* were served with a light, delicately herbed couscous. This was preceded by John Dory and scallops in Sauternes sauce—simply French, simply wonderful. Dessert was a *marbré de chocolat chaud sur sa crème d'amande*—to be ordered at least 20 minutes in advance.

RATINGS: beauty 5, comfort 5, service 5, restaurant 5.

Cocktail terrace with glorious view.

$ $ $ $

A A A A A

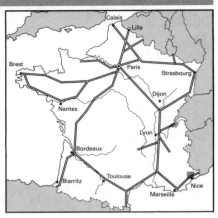

Château de la Chèvre d'Or

06360 Eze-Village
Tel: 93 41 12 12
Telex: 970 839

11 rooms, 3 suites
CC: AE, D, V
Open March to December.
Restaurant closed Wednesdays
until Easter.

Location: same as Château Eza, but slightly lower
on the cliffs of the Moyenne Corniche. Courtesy
phone at the bottom of the village.

In a glorious setting overlooking the sea, the Chèvre d'Or straddles several tiers of the cliffside. A narrow cobbled pathway about halfway up the village leads to reception, restaurant, and bar, in a series of 9th–12th-century stone houses on both sides of the street. The hotel is almost a village in itself. Some of the rooms are in a 12th-century house on a level above the reception, while others are in stone cottages on lower tiers amidst olive trees and bougainvillea. You may have to stoop to enter the doorway, but inside the rooms, care has been taken to ensure that the charm doesn't infringe on comfort.

The restaurant has glass walls for a good view of the Côte d'Azur. Elegant service makes the atmosphere both formal and festive.

The chef, Elie Mazot, is—conservatively speaking—a genius. An example of his talent is his wonderful *suprêmes de pigeonneau en salade tiède*: two crisply roasted squab drumsticks, boned then stuffed with chopped thigh meat and vegetables, with three delicate little *millefeuilles* of steamed leek and minced breast of squab—one of the best dishes I have ever tasted.

Le Grill at street level offers the same grand view, a smaller menu and a more casual atmosphere.

A white wine to keep in mind throughout your stay in the south of France is Palette Château Simone. Inexpensive Sancerre from the Loire is another good choice. From the enormous selection of cheeses, try the local goat cheese, Tovet-aux-herbes.

RATINGS: beauty 5, comfort 5, service 5, restaurant 5.

Pool, terrace.

$

A A

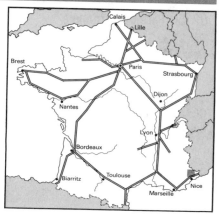

L'Hermitage du Col d'Eze

La Grande Corniche
06360 Eze-Village
Tel: 93 41 21 11

14 rooms
CC: all
Closed mid-December to early January.
Restaurant closed Wednesday lunch
and all day Monday,
and from 12 November to March.

Location: on the Grande Corniche, D 46. Can also
be reached from the Moyenne Corniche from Eze
center up the hill to Col d'Eze, then left.

A small hotel on a wide curve in the Grande Corniche, in uncrowded surroundings, with a bird's-eye view of Nice on the western horizon. The young proprietors, M. and Mme. Bérardi, will give you a warm welcome, and a clean, simple room with private bathroom and telephone for the astonishing price of 140 to 210 F.

The restaurant is spacious, bright, and completely relaxed. Gaspard Bérardi is as proud of his sparkling kitchen as of his light-as-air dauphine potatoes and his secret *civet* recipe.

The fixed-price 80 F menu gives you a choice of *terrine du chef à l'armagnac* or shrimp salad, followed by the deliciously rich blood-thickened *civet de porcelet Gaspard*, stewed suckling pig, or *lapin au pistou*, rabbit wih garlic and basil pesto.

RATINGS: beauty 4, comfort 2, service 2, restaurant 3.

Pool. Parking in front.

$ $ $ $

A A A A

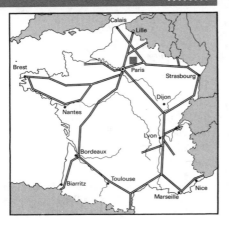

Hostellerie du Château

02130 Fère-en-Tardenois
Tel: 23 82 21 13
Telex: 145 526

14 rooms, 9 suites
CC: AE, D, M, V
Closed January and February.

Location: exit Dormans on the A4 south-west of Reims. Turn right at the one and only traffic light in the village; after a few kilometers you'll see a sign for the hotel.

The ancient castle, dating mainly from the Renaissance, is now no more than a ruin—only the bridge over the moat is intact, and the main portico with many bas-reliefs still visible on the arches. It comes into view when you drive to the reception of the hostellerie, an imposing 16th-century building full of odd-shaped rooms and zig-zag corridors. Each room differs not only in shape and size, but also in décor, with Louis XV predominant.

The kitchen is in the hands of Christian Blot; his cooking rates high marks for inventiveness and wonderful flavor. *Sous-presse de saumon et anguille fumée* not only blends two exquisite tastes—salmon and eel—but looks like something painted by Miró. His originality is also apparent in unusual combinations of main ingredients. Quail breast and frogs legs may sound an odd couple, but in the *suprême de caille en grenouillade*, both are light enough to complement each other without overpowering the delicate cream sauce.

The young chef excels in enhancing the natural taste of food while preparing it in a simple way—his roast rack of lamb served with sweet garlic was a revelation.

A chilled bottle of Bouzy grand cru Jean Vesselle, a Pinot Noir varietal from the neighboring Champagne district, is a fitting companion for Brie cheese or a soft-textured and sharp-flavored boulette d'Avesnes, a herb cheese from the Ardennes.

RATINGS: beauty 4, comfort 4, service 4, restaurant 5.

Golf, tennis, jogging trails.

52

FONTVIEILLE
Provence   30 B 2
Hotel-Restaurant

Auberge La Régalido

rue Frédéric-Mistral
13990 Fontvieille
Tel: 90 97 60 22
Telex: 441 150

14 rooms
Closed December and January.
Restaurant closed Monday and lunch
Tuesday, except July through September.

Location: 10 km north-east of Arles. If coming
from A7, exit Cavaillon; follow signs for St-Rémy,
Maussane then Fontvieille. In the center of the
village.

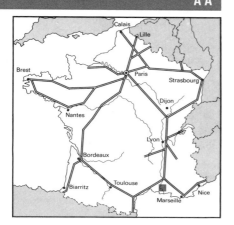

This luxurious 18th-century house with pretty garden is a haven of peace. The rooms, all named after herbs, vary in size but not in comfort. But no matter how nice the atmosphere or how comfortable the beds, the main reason to come here is for Jean-Pierre Michel's cuisine.

Leave the *menu gourmand*—at 380F—to those celebrating a wedding anniversary, and choose a regional menu. *Spécialités Régalido* gives free expression to the chef's poetic sensitivity to pure flavor, and leaves no doubt that Provençal cooking is his love. Try the *mous-*

seline de loup des Saintes-Maries-de-la-Mer, a frothy blend of sea bass, hollandaise and cream, with a subtle touch of fennel. Or the *gratin de moules*, mussels and spinach baked golden. Provençal main courses give you the choice of tender lamb grazed on wild thyme and rosemary, *tranche en casserole et à l'ail*—steak in a casserole with garlic, or breast and thigh of duck with green olives.

The wine list is crammed with reasonably priced local vintages. The Côtes de Provence has its best red in Château Minuty, and the best white in Château de la Bégude.

RATINGS: beauty 3, comfort 4, service 2, restaurant 4.

Seven rooms with balcony or private terrace.

AA

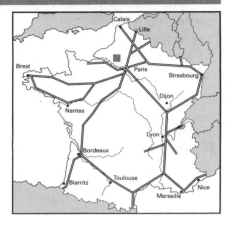

Château de la Rapée

Bazincourt-sur-Epte
27140 Gisors
Tel: 32 55 11 61

10 rooms
CC: AE, D, V
Closed 15 January to 1 March
and the last two weeks in August.
Restaurant closed Wednesday.

Location: north-west of Paris on D915. From the square in front of Gisors' old castle (*château féodal*), take the route de St-Paërs and follow it for about 4 km through the forest, until you see the signs for the hotel. Do not follow signs for Bazincourt.

This château is a member of Relais du Silence, and silence is what you will find. The road from Gisors passes through a thick forest to emerge into a clearing with a gingerbread mansion in Anglo-Norman style. The warm reception from the proprietors, M. and Mme. Bergeron, and the rural atmosphere are the ideal antidote to modern stress.

Room prices for a double start at 230F, and for that you can count on a fairly big room, with tall windows overlooking the fields. In case the silence gets too deafening, there's a TV in every room.

The à la carte menu includes a number of Norman specialties. For 85F, a *matelote*, or stew of eel, in dry Norman cider—gloriously aromatic. Duck breast braised with cider vinegar, and *marmite dieppoise*—sole, turbot, monkfish, mullet, scallops, shrimp, and mussels, cooked with leeks, onions, white wine, and cream—are similarly low-priced.

If you sample the local fare and top it off with *crêpe délice normand, sabayon au Calvados*, you'll be very glad you came here.

Normandy is not wine country, but white Mâcon Villages for 110F and red Rully for 85F seemed very reasonable. Both are also available in half-bottles.

The local cheese is from Neufchatel—small cylinders with a smooth texture and mild taste. Gold-colored Livarot is strong and spicy, with a semi-hard texture. Those who like a good runny Brie should try the Norman Brillat-Savarin, a treble-cream cheese with a flavor as proud as its name.

RATINGS: beauty 3, comfort 3, service 2, restaurant 3.

Riding nearby. Peace and quiet in a country setting.

$ $ $

A A A A A

Château de Locguénolé

Route de Port-Louis
56700 Hennebont
Tel: 97 76 29 04
Telex: 950 636 CHATEL

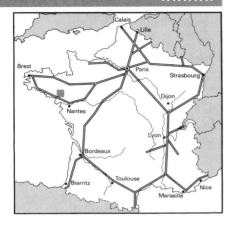

21 rooms, 3 suites
CC: AE, D, Eu, M, V
Open all year.
Restaurant closed in winter.

Location: exit Port-Louis on the N165; drive in the direction of Port-Louis. The château is clearly signposted.

The Château de Locguénolé comes very close to perfection. It must be admitted that the granite mansion built in 1810 is esthetically less appealing than the graceful 17th-century carriage house and stables. But taken together with the estuary shimmering just beyond the lawn and the surrounding forest, it is a uniquely beautiful place.

The rooms are furnished with luxurious antiques and exquisite tapestries. A kind touch is a bottle of mineral water and a basket of fruit. No minibar, only a 24-hour "your-wish-is-our-command" service. The bathrooms are large and well appointed.

Chef Denis le Cadre is totally original. Unusual, to say the least, was his ragoût of oysters and leeks in cider-flavored broth. Contrived, but

successful, his *meunière de plie aux mousserons frais et jus de volaille* (sole with wild mushrooms). Daring and provocative, his *poularde en papillote, bouillon de tapioca en timbale et fettucini aux truffes*. And unafraid to be simple with a sprinkle of cockles and a dash of champagne added to *blanc de turbot*. Finally, the "odd-couple" dish: *filet mignon* of pork with a curry and pineapple sauce, together with a quail drumstick—boned, wrapped in its skin, roasted, served with a cream sauce and spring vegetables.

The wine list has bottles like 1966 St-Estèphe Château Montrose for 1,200F. But if that's too rich, a robust red Saumur Champigny or cold, crisp Savennières from the Loire remind us that the best things in life are *almost* free.

RATINGS: beauty 5, comfort 5, service 5, restaurant 5.

Tennis, pool, waterskiing. Riding and sailing nearby.

$ $

A A A A

✳

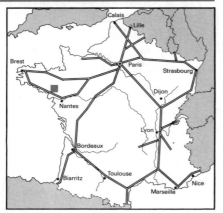

Les Chaumières de Kerniaven

Route Plouhinec
56700 Hennebont
Tel: 97 76 29 04

12 rooms
CC: AE, D, Eu, M, V
Open all year.

Location: Take the first left on the route de Port-Louis after the Château de Locguénolé; turn right to Plouhinec beach, then left after 1.5 km.

This big stone farmhouse with thatched roof was built in 1650. The Château de Locguénolé took it over and converted it into a vacation residence of big bedrooms with beamed ceilings, antique country furniture, big modern bathrooms, in a hushed rustic setting. Breakfast is served on the premises, but guests must go out for lunch or dinner. Prices for a double start at 350 F and go up to 557 F for a huge room with sleeping loft. The 50% discount included with *More France for the $* will, of course, slash that in half!

Not only is the standard of comfort extremely high, but guests have full use of all Château Locguénolé facilities. A beach is a few kilometers away, and Carnac is less than an hour's drive. Hennebont, too, is a beautiful tourist attraction.

A haven of peace not far from Brittany's most interesting towns.

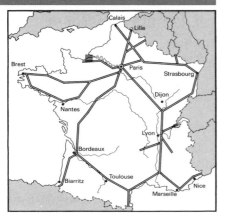

Ferme Saint-Siméon et son Manoir

rue Adolphe-Marais
14600 Honfleur
Tel: 31 89 23 61
Telex: 171 031 SIMEON
Fax: 31 89 48 48

38 rooms, 5 suites
CC: Eu, M, V
Open all year.

Location: follow the coast road out of Honfleur harbour in the Trouville/Deauville direction; turn left at the green lighthouse.

Only the timbered main building that houses reception and the restaurant remains to remind us that this was once a farm. The only things cultivated here today are luxury and the pursuit of pleasure. And it's hard to think of any place more luxurious or pleasurable for a Normandy vacation. From the deep wool carpeting to the thick pastel terry robe, no aspect of comfort is missing from any room.

The restaurant has a sea view and a rustic atmosphere. The menu is big and provocative, begging a guest to come several times. Consider this for variety: rock lobster and mussel fritters with ginger tartare sauce; sea bass tartare served with quenelles of fresh farm cheese with herbs; turbot *feuilleté* in creamy lime and pink pepper sauce; broiled lamb from the salt meadows near Mont-St-Michel; poached Bresse chicken cooked in coarse salt... the preparation by Jean-Pierre de Boyssière is near perfect. His *feuilleté de champignons sauvages* with chanterelles, boletus and not-exactly-wild baby buttons, was rich with flavor and lavish with Norman butter. The *cassolette de crustacés au calvados* was as light as a feather, with just the merest hint of calvados.

The wine book lists 1,000 vintages. If price is no object, a 1971 Château Pétrus Pomerol at 6,000 F is for you. For the less fortunate, a 1955 Château Ripeau St-Emilion is 490 F, and closer to my level, 1968 Château Croizet-Bages Pauillac, 220 F and as dry as an Arizona summer.

RATINGS: beauty 5, comfort 5, service 4, restaurant 4.

Tennis, indoor pool.

$ $ $ $

* A A A A

Résidence de la Côte St-Jacques

14 faubourg de Paris
89300 Joigny
Tel: 86 62 09 70
Telex: SAINJAC 801 458

23 rooms, 7 suites
CC: AE, CB, D
Closed January.

Location: about 1 km west of the center of Joigny and the bridge over the Yonne.

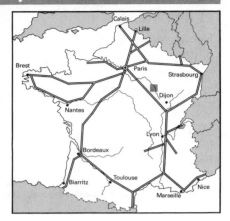

One of the most celebrated chefs of France is the proprietor of a fascinating place to stay. La Résidence de la Côte St-Jacques is on two sides of the street, with an underground tunnel joining the two buildings. The one fronting the river, full of sumptuous rooms remodelled in modern style and priced from 875 F per night, has all the comfort and elbow-room anyone could ask for. The older building has the reception, the restaurant and 15 rooms for half the price, with enough comfort for anyone for whom it's not essential to have the ultimate in luxury.

You can only stay here if you intend to have dinner, and frankly, considering Chef Michel Lorain's talents, why else would anyone come? Madame Lorain selects the wines and oversees hospitality.

There is enough on the menu to fulfil anyone's ambition to taste the last word in French cuisine: red mullet fillets with coriander-spiced vegetables and *mousseline de piments*; cassolette of *foie gras* with small fruit; duckling with Puy lentils and spring onions. And Lorain's most famous specialty, *le dos de saumon en vessie*—salmon fillet cooked in a pig's bladder, an adaptation of an ancient method for cooking chicken and duck. Even the traditional *bœuf bourguignon* in Irancy wine turns out something unexpected.

The red Irancy has a bouquet unlike any other Burgundy. The 1988 is fresh, aromatic and inexpensive.

RATINGS: beauty 4, comfort 3/5, service 4, restaurant 5.

Indoor swimming pool. Balconies. Boat dock.

$

*   A

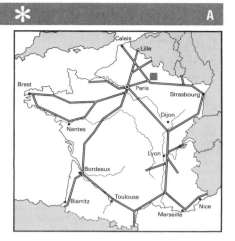

Hôtel de la Bannière de France

11 rue Franklin-Roosevelt
02000 Laon
Tel: 23 23 21 44

19 rooms
CC: AE, CB, D, M, V
Closed mid-December to mid-January.

Location: On the A26 between St-Quentin and Reims. In the center of the upper town, near the cathedral. Follow signs for "plateau".

This medieval town is on a hill, 300 feet above the surrounding countryside. Once you glimpse it in the distance, it's hard to resist.

There are no luxury hotels in Laon. But for charm, character and that certain mystique very old places have, nothing can beat the Hôtel de la Bannière de France. It might be the oldest hostelry in continuous service in France, having first thrown open its doors in 1685.

Beyond the installation of electricity and plumbing, not so much can have changed since the 17th century. Don't go searching for an elevator—the wide, slightly listing stairs still serve well enough. And the room price is commensurately low.

The restaurant surpasses the room standard, but the cost is still reasonable. Consider the 92 F menu which offers an avocado and shrimp salad, followed by seafood brochette with an orange-colored *rouille* of peppers, garlic and saffron. Plus a choice of cheese or dessert.

The 125 F menu allows both cheese and dessert, with a wider selection of courses, for example frog legs provençale followed by lamb steak with bacon and mushrooms. You might also have a sirloin steak with sauce Bercy, young guinea-fowl with pears, or an *émincé* of veal with parsley and mushrooms. Your dessert choice could be *profiteroles au chocolat*.

Any building that has been a French hotel for 300 years is likely to have a big wine cellar; here it occupies three levels and is replete with vintages going back to 1949—St-Estèphe Château Cos d'Estournel, 900 F. On the other end of the price range are wines sold by the carafe.

RATINGS: beauty 2, comfort 2, service 2, restaurant 3.

Thirteen rooms with private bathroom. Covered parking.

$ $ $

A A A A

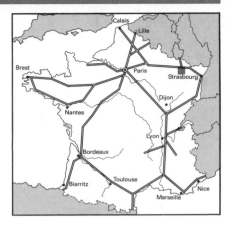

Les Vannes

6 rue Porte-Haute
54460 Liverdun
Tel: 83 24 46 01

CC: AE, D, Eu, V
Closed Monday and all February.

Location: 15 km from Nancy. Exit Frouard on the Nancy–Metz autoroute (A31). Follow directions for Liverdun; take the road up the hill from the lower village.

With only five rooms above the restaurant, Les Vannes is not rated as a hotel. Consider it an extraordinary restaurant worthy of an excursion from Nancy, or a detour off the *autoroute*. Its location in a tiny fortified medieval village is pleasant enough, and the restaurant's added attraction of a panoramic view of the Moselle River winding placidly below makes it doubly romantic. While it's a bit more expensive than a typical place rating $$$, the offer of a complimentary main course takes the edge off the price. The food preparation, however, is of a high gourmet level.

Turbot in Burgundy wine sauce is one of those classic dishes that depends on slightly undercooked, firm fillets and a generous, carefully reduced sauce redolent with wine essence. No one cooks it better than the chef of Les Vannes. Other skilful preparations include sea bass in parsley cream; roast guinea hen with a gâteau of its liver; roast lamb with rosemary; squab glazed with vanilla and honey, then steamed in almond milk; and smoked salmon in a wine-flavored cream sauce of mushrooms and shallots.

Warm desserts must be ordered at the start of the meal. A *millefeuille* of red fruit might make a rosy ending.

The local red wine, Côtes de Toul, is robust in all but price.

Fabulous food spiced with fabulous views of the Moselle.

$ $

AA

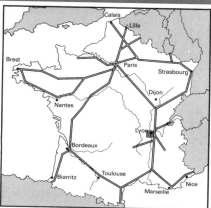

Grand Hôtel Concorde

11 rue Groslée
69002 Lyon
Tel: 78 42 56 21
Telex: 330 244

140 rooms, 3 suites
CC: AE, D, Eu, M, V
Open all year.
Restaurant closed Sunday.

Location: in the old town, on the banks of the Rhône.

The hotel was built in 1870 and has high ceilings, tall windows and wide corridors. All the rooms have undergone remodeling to include soundproofing, air-conditioning, remote-control TV, minibar, built-in radio... and modern, if not much more than utilitarian, bathrooms.

The staff is very friendly and helpful, making you feel you're staying in a much smaller hotel.

Its restaurant, **Le Fiorelle,** cannot compete with the best of the restaurants in the culinary capital of France, but the cooking is better than expected, with the additional advantages of low prices and speedy service.

The 25% reduction in rates for travelers with *More France for the $* certificates makes it all an unbeatable bargain.

RATINGS: beauty 3, comfort 3, service 3, restaurant 3.
Garage parking. Rhône river views.

$$$$

AAAAA

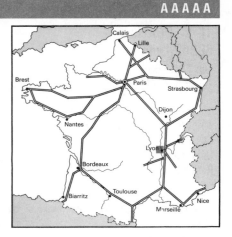

Restaurant Orsi

3 place Kléber
69006 Lyon
Tel: 78 89 57 68
Telex: 305 965

CC: AE, CB, Eu
Closed Sunday.

Location: at the end of cours Roosevelt, on the east bank of the Rhône.

In a country full of great chefs, it's foolish to think which one may be the best, but if my mind drifts in that direction, the name of Pierre Orsi comes up.

Leaving aside the elegance and charm of a nostalgic dining room with old paintings on the walls and pretty flowers on the tables, presided over by attentive waitresses in floor-length granny dresses, plus the infectious festive feeling that permeates the place, let's think only of the pleasure of eating—salmon baked in a hard salt crust and served with chive butter, saddle of hare *en cocotte* with thyme, or baked fillet of walleye in wine and marrow sauce.

Some things are total invention, like *minestrone de homard décor-tiqué, nage au Pouilly-Fuissé,* others pure flight of fancy: *pêche Bretonne au homard, loup et rouget barbet,* or *saint-pierre à la vapeur sur un lit de poirettes.* But you can come down to earth and still say the taste was heaven with a *cœur de bœuf charolais, beaujolais à la moelle,* which is simply a steak worth taking a trip across the Atlantic.

For dessert, if *crêpes Suzette au beurre d'oranges* sounds too prosaic, Orsi's *feuillantine* with caramelized pears is the talk of Lyon.

The Côtes du Rhône start just south of Lyon at Vienne, and the local wine, Côte Rôtie, made from a blend of red Syrah and white Viognier grape, has an unforgettable bouquet. 1983s are ready and perfect.

A short cab ride from the center of town.

$ $ $

A A A A A

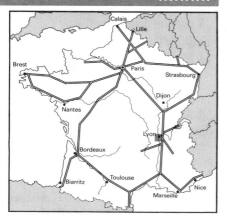

Restaurant Henry

27 rue de la Martinière
69001 Lyon
Tel: 78 28 26 08

CC: AE, D, V
Closed Saturday lunch and Monday.

Location: in the center of town, not far from the Hôtel de Ville (City Hall).

An elegant and totally modern environment. Mirrored walls topped with huge impressionistic paintings by Lyon painter Truphémus, futuristic stainless-steel ceilings—the décor is almost a distraction from Pierre Balladone's cooking.

Like all the best chefs, he prefers simple—though not necessarily easy—combinations. An example is the *feuilleté* of snails with the most delicate and flavorful of forest mushrooms, chanterelles, in a mild garlic cream sauce. Or the *gratin d'huîtres chaudes Candice,* three oysters on the half-shell placed on a bed of dark seaweed, covered with a creamy oyster and lobster sauce and baked golden brown. Salmon in a lobster coulis, or breast of duck with pears further illustrate his talent. Truly simple, and if not inspired, then inspirational: *le filet de sandre simplement braisé à la fleur de thym*—walleye braised with thyme flowers.

This is the place to try *cervelle de canut*, an old Lyon specialty—fresh white cheese, shallots, herbs and chives, mixed with cream, white wine and a dash of oil—named for the *canuts*, or silk weavers who worked in Lyon's Croix-Rousse district.

One of the best Mâcon whites comes from the village of Viré, and you'll find it here. Hermitage, from the left bank near Valence, is the best red Côtes du Rhône. But less expensive and well worth trying is Cairanne Côtes du Rhône from further south, made from the Grenache grape...not too subtle, but a full body and good aroma.

An elegant dining room with dining to match the fame of Lyon.

63

$$

A A A

$ $

A A A

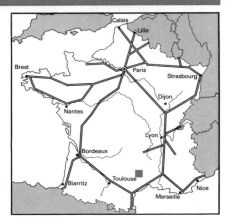

MILLAU
Rouergue   29 D 2
Hotel-Restaurant

La Musardière

34 avenue de la République
12100 Millau
Tel: 65 60 20 63

13 rooms
CC: AE, D, V
Open April to November.
Restaurant closed Monday,
except in August.

Location: about two blocks north of the train station,
on a graceful old street opposite a small park.

The stateliest mansion in a row of 19th-century houses, a cream-colored building with cobbled driveway and sheltered portals, is a luxurious little hotel, run like a family guesthouse. In Paris, a room in such a hotel would cost at least 1,500F. But here in Millau, a quiet town that once earned its living from the manufacture of kid gloves, you can have one of Mme Canac's exquisite chambers for as little as 400F. The rooms are furnished with authentic 19th-century pieces, the wall coverings and décor delicately coordinated with the colors of the marble mantelpieces. The bathrooms are big and sparkling, with huge bath sheets.

Breakfast is beautifully served on porcelain, with silver pitchers, flowers on the tray, and big, flaky crois-

sants that taste better here than anywhere else in France. A young chef, Fabrice Contanceau, rules over the small, reasonably priced restaurant. The 190F menu includes a starter of rabbit and vegetable terrine, followed by a Roquefort crêpe, and an airy, hot chocolate *fondant* with walnuts.

Roquefort-sur-Soulzon, where the famous ewe's-milk cheese ripens in caves, is only 24 kilometers away.

The wine list is small but varied, with many Languedoc wines for around 50F, and a red, ripe vin de pays de l'Hérault, Domaine St-Martin de la Garrigue, for 60F. If price is no obstacle, one of the supremely great Bordeaux wines, a 1951 Graves from Château Haut-Brion, can immortalize your evening for 800F.

RATINGS: beauty 4, comfort 5, service 3, restaurant 4.

Garden. All rooms with half-balcony. Private parking.

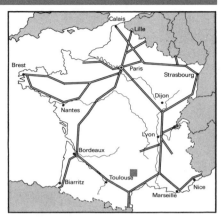

International Hotel

1 place de la Tine
12100 Millau
Tel: 65 60 20 66
Telex: 520 629

110 rooms, 7 suites
CC: AE, D, Eu, V
Open all year.
Restaurant closed Sunday evening.

Location: south-east of Rodez on D911. The hotel
is in the center of town.

A town lost in time might not seem the right setting for a modern hotel, but the International is a special place. In both room and restaurant quality, it's a great travel bargain: room prices range from 250 to 435 F —four-star comfort for a two-star price. All rooms have wall-to-wall carpeting; the upper-story rooms look out over the rooftops to the outlying Causse hills.

Pierre Pomarède is the only chef I know who can offer a four-course menu for 98 F—and not just any menu. A choice of *mérou* (grouper) *au citron vert*, or *salade de moules* (mussels), followed by *piccatas de lapereau à la fleur de Meaux* (young rabbit with mustard sauce), or *civet de caneton* (duck stew), or *mulet au beurre d'anchois* (mullet with anchovy butter), then cheese, and a scrumptious baked kiwi, strawberry and orange dessert covered with sabayon.

Only one item on the à la carte menu exceeds 100 F—crayfish flambéed with old whisky. Even his award-winning *papillote de saumon et foie gras* costs less.

You can sample one of a dozen regional specialites, including fresh trout from Rouergue streams, a blanquette of lamb, or *le corfidou*—the local beef ragoût made grandma's way.

The wine list features some 500 wines from the Dordogne. White Gaillac and red Cahors—1983 Château du Cayrou, specially recommended. Monbazillac is a softly-sweet, fruity dessert wine. The 1975, sold here for 125 F, is worth shipping home.

RATINGS: beauty 4, comfort 4, service 3, restaurant 5.

Rooftop lounge. 50 rooms with balcony. Garage parking.

$ $

A A A A

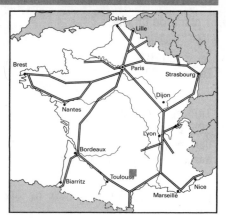

La Braconne
8 place du Maréchal-Foch
12100 Millau
Tel: 65 60 30 93

CC: AE, D, Eu, V
Closed Monday.

Location: in the old part of Millau. Park your car at the Place de la Fraternité, and follow the rue de la Capelle to place Maréchal-Foch.

A 13th-century room built from stone blocks, with vaulted ceiling, stone archways, iron chandeliers, and the aroma of ducks and chickens roasting on a spit in a blazing fireplace.

Prepared with *herbes du Causse* by Madame Sola and her mother, the birds are as tasty as only farm fowl that scratch and peck for grain can be. Wild trout, cooked *en papillote*, is seasoned with herbs from the surrounding hillsides. Goose and duck liver entrées are served with a wine-flavored cream sauce with shallots.

Try the sirloin steak broiled over the open fire, flambéed with cognac and served with morels. Or one of the local specialties such as *trénels à la millavoise*—sheep's tripe cooked with white wine and tomatoes, much better than it sounds. And my favorite specialty, very simple and bursting with ripe flavor—*feuilleté au roquefort*.

The most expensive set menu for 140F begins with *cou d'oie farci* —goose neck stuffed with a mixture of minced goose meat, foie gras and truffles, cooked in goose fat like a confit. Among the four courses that follow, you might try the flame-roasted duck breast. When the smiling waitress brought mine, she said, "Voilà, Monsieur. Bon appétit!" Truer words were never spoken.

Open-hearth cooking in the heart of old Millau.

$ $

A A

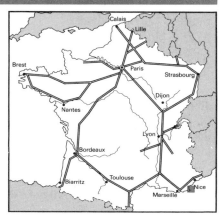

Hôtel St-Christophe

066590 Miramar-par-Théoule
Tel: 93 75 41 36
Telex: 470 878
Fax: 93 75 44 85

40 rooms
CC: AE, D, Eu, V
Open mid-March to mid-October.

Location: on the Massif de l'Estérel. Exit A 8 at Mandelieu and follow signs for Théoule then Miramar. The St-Christophe is on your left.

A pink stucco mini-highrise half-hidden by seaside cliffs, dedicated to sea and sun worship. Tiers of terraces and balconies face south, with the Mediterranean lapping at the rocks below. A long, wide rock shelf at the water's edge, aptly named Red Roc, serves as a private beach; higher up on a rock ledge is a large, oval swimming pool. Lunch is served on a large terrace with buffet and barbecue, so you can spend the whole day in swimwear if you like.

The rooms are simply furnished, either in white fiberglass or brown walnut. Every room has a balcony. Since you will be spending most of your time outside anyway, the rooms facing away from the sea offer the best value at less than 500 F.

The food in the indoor restaurant is above average. Specialties include oysters in champagne, fillet of sole and trout *feuilleté*, and seafood of the day, simply prepared.

RATINGS: beauty 4, comfort 3, service 3, restaurant 3.

Pool, private beach. Tennis nearby and golf 8 km away.

$ $ $

A A A A

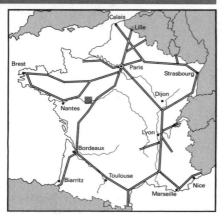

Château d'Artigny

Route d'Azay-le-Rideau
37250 Montbazon
Tel: 47 26 24 24
Telex: 750 900

46 rooms, 7 suites
CC: CB
Open second week in January
to late November.

Location: 13 km south of Tours on N10, on a high
plateau overlooking the Indre valley. The entrance
to the château is clearly marked.

Any 17th-century princeling would have been proud to call this palace his own—from its rococo grandeur you would never guess it was built in the 1920s by perfume magnate François Coty. Each room outshines the other in elegance and opulence. A second building in the same style has rooms economically priced at under 500F, with the bonus of a view of the Château d'Artigny itself.

The dining room is a magnificent circular affair with gilded columns, gold-leaf trim, delicate chandeliers, and French doors opening onto a terrace with a view reaching out for miles.

The food is on a similarly grand scale. *Ravioles de homard et truffes au basilic*—lobster and truffle ravioli, delicately flavored with basil; *confit de pigeon et foie gras*; broiled flank steak with veal sweetbreads and a tarragon and mint sauce. Or, even grander, roast beef in a Chinon red wine sauce with croûtons topped with marrow and truffles. It all costs a pretty penny, as you might expect. The restaurant is in a higher price-category than the hotel (except for the biggest rooms and the suites).

The wine cellar has 50,000 bottles, presided over by a sommelier who is just as happy to select a fresh and cheerful Montlouis, a small *appellation* on the south bank of the Loire, as a 1919 Vouvray that has finally come of age. The white Bonnezeau is a good choice for a light course or dessert—a successful blend of dry and sweet with a fragrant bouquet.

Weekends October through March feature musical evenings and very special prices.

RATINGS: beauty 5, comfort 5, service 5, restaurant 4.

Tennis, pool, putting green.

$ $ $ $

A A A A A

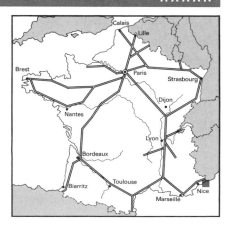

Hôtel Hermitage

Square Beaumarchais
98000 Monte-Carlo
Tel: 93 50 67 31
Telex: 479 432
Fax: 93 25 59 17

260 rooms, 16 suites
CC: AE, CB, M, V
Open all year.

Location: in the center of Monte-Carlo, one block from the casino.

Built in 1900, the Hermitage is a palace of marble and crystal, oriental carpets and sumptuous living. The rooms offer every degree of luxury and a glorious view of the harbor; in the low season, prices start at 1,100 F. The maid service is meticulous and frequent—you'll always find fresh towels in your marble bathroom, which is scrubbed twice a day.

The bar/café has a large terrace overlooking the world's most ostentatious yachts bobbing in the harbor. There's a terrace swimming pool club, and all guests enjoy free entry to the casino, as well as a big reduction on golf and tennis facilities. A little yellow bus provides a non-stop shuttle service to the Monte-Carlo Beach Club.

The **Restaurant Belle-Epoque** lives up to its name with marble columns topped with gold leaf, crystal chandeliers, velvet curtains and ceiling frescoes. The à la carte menu lists some 30 main courses, all with an original touch: lobster bisque made with old armagnac and served with lobster ravioli and lobster pâté; *paupiette de saumon* cooked in paper with diced baby vegetables; a delectable *piccata de rognons de veau sur feuilles d'épinards*—veal kidneys between layers of spinach, surmounted with a mustard grain sauce and served with pleurotes.

The 250 F luncheon menu features chicken breast and thigh with morels and a truffle cream sauce, and a wine selection for 125 F the bottle, or 75 F for a half.

RATINGS: beauty 5, comfort 5, service 5, restaurant 5.

Pool, beach. Golf and tennis nearby. Private parking.

$ $ $

A A A A

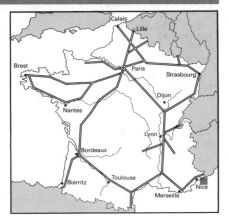

Hôtel Beach Plaza

Avenue Princesse-Grace
98000 Monte-Carlo
Tel: 93 30 98 80
Telex: 479 617

315 rooms, 9 suites
CC: AE, D, M, V
Open all year.
Le Gratin closed 15 November
to 15 December.

Location: on the sea front, just east of the town center.

A complete beach resort that allows some economy, without your having to give up anything significant in comfort or style. The building is modern, with balconied rooms facing the sea or the town. The town-view rooms cost around 300 F less than those fronting the sea, but otherwise they are identical. All modern comforts are included.

The beauty of the hotel is its outdoor setting on a crescent beach with facilities for all water sports.

The terraced restaurant serves light, inexpensive fare; it's a nice place for a *salade niçoise* or simply prepared seafood. **Le Gratin** is more formal, but not stuffy; a piano player on a small revolving platform keeps the atmosphere cheery. The food is unambitious but beautifully prepared. For example, a consommé lightly perfumed with garlic. Or a delicious crab salad in the shell, the claws still attached. A friendly waiter deftly shells them for you. The veal escalopes are accompanied by a delicate lemon sauce.

The house wines are red and white Côtes de Provence Commanderie de Peyrasol. Very little red wine is produced under the Côtes de Provence *appellation*; this one is particularly smooth and full-bodied.

RATINGS: beauty 5, comfort 4, service 5, restaurant 3.

Two pools, private beach, scuba diving. Balconies.

$ $ $ $

A A A A A

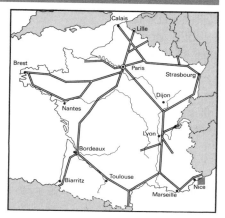

Restaurant Louis XV

Place du Casino
98000 Monte-Carlo
Tel: 93 50 80 80
Telex: 469 925

CC: AE, D, Eu, V
Closed Tuesday and Wednesday,
and from November to mid-December.

Location: in the Hôtel de Paris, across from the casino.

It could be called the grandest restaurant in France, were Monaco not a principality. Sky-high ceilings with frescoes, a ceiling-high mural, Louis XV period furniture, porcelain vases, mahogany paneling, and the glitter of gold plates and gold-plated silver ware.

Only a chef as great as Alain Ducasse could create dishes to match the dazzling surroundings. Deft, friendly service from an inspired maître d'hôtel and aspiring chefs du rang add to the spectacle.

The menus here allow no restrictions on creativity. Your soup might be *velouté léger de crustacés en infusion de cèpes et morilles au cerfeuil*—an indescribable blending of shellfish, morels and boletus mushrooms with chervil. Veal sweetbreads are baked with vegetables, topped by a creamy covering of cardoons, truffles and marrow. Not all the dishes are complicated, but everything has an unusual touch. One of a dozen wonderful desserts is a warm *gratin* of wild strawberries and pine kernels in thyme-flavored sauce, with lavender-honey ice cream.

Wines sold by the glass to go with dessert include a ruby-red Banyuls with a natural sweetness from the Grenache and Malvoisie grapes.

A dining experience to dazzle the senses.

$ $

A A

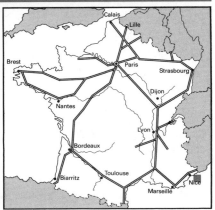

Restaurant Polpetta

2 rue Paradis
98000 Monte-Carlo
Tel: 93 50 67 84

**Closed Tuesday, and all February.
Reserve in advance.**

Location: on the upper sections of central Monte-Carlo. Follow avenue de Roqueville up the hill to the corner of rue Paradis, a fairly steep climb.

Frank Sinatra's been there, and so has Prince Rainier, united by their love of Italian cooking, and that "crowded little Italian restaurant" atmosphere.

The Polpetta is owned by two lively brothers, Enzio and Leo Guasco, who rush around all over the place calling friendly greetings, moving tables apart or together, affably squeezing in one more guest.

The atmosphere is completely informal, and the prices match. The heaps of food are better described as "how much" rather than "how." Ravioli, lasagna, spaghetti, veal piccata... traditional, and lots of it. Whatever you order, Enzio or Leo will come round to make sure you eat all of it.

Everyone's favorite Italian restaurant in Monte-Carlo.

$ $ $ $

* A A A A A

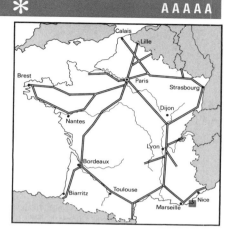

La Ferme de Mougins

10 avenue St-Basile
06250 Mougins
Tel: 93 90 03 74
Telex: 970 643

CC: AE, D, Eu, V
Closed Saturday lunch, all day Thursday,
and February.

Location: 7.5 km north of Cannes, at the bottom of
Mougins village.

In this little village of great restaurants, the greatest is a big, white stucco farmhouse, with timbered walls and beams, and a large flagstone terrace by a stream complete with rushing waterfall. Even if the à la carte prices are almost as steep as Mougins hill, the six-course 190 F menu offers a lot for the money.

The chef, Patrick Henriroux, trained at some of the most famous restaurants in France. He now flies on his own with superb, unusual dishes: *foie gras et aile de caille en surprise*, two equal slices of goose liver and boned quail wing, herbed and peppered, wrapped in bib lettuce and cooked together; *pistou de daurade rosé*, dorado with chick peas and black beans with a basil pesto; *carré d'agneau mariné en tapenade à l'huile d'olive*, lamb chops marinated in a black olive, caper and anchovy purée; veal kidney *au jus de truffes*, sliced thin and arranged in an overlapping circle, brought sizzling to your table.

Two fine, inexpensive wines from the Nice area are white Cassis—1985 or 1986 Clos St-Magdaleine—and red Bandol 1985 Domaine Tempier. Both are full-bodied and smooth. The house cocktail is a delicious heady concoction of champagne, sweet Muscat and akvavit.

My favorite restaurant in Mougins is second-to-none.

$

AA

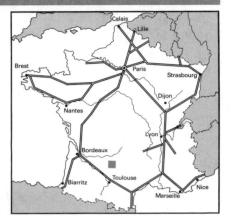

Hôtel Belle Rive

12270 Najac
Tel: 65 29 73 90

42 rooms
CC: AE, CB, D, V
Open April to November.

Location: Halfway between Villefranche-de-Rouergue and Cordes, on D 922. At La Fouillade, take D39 for Najac. Continue past the village, following the river, to the other side of the castle hill.

This peaceful hotel nestles on the bank of a wide, shallow river teeming with trout, under the dramatic shadow of Najac castle. No one could ask for a more beautiful setting. Drinks and meals are served on the terraces surrounding the hotel, to the sound of rushing water.

The rooms are simple but adequate, with pleasant views. The proprietor, Jacques Mazières, is a consummate chef, determined to keep his creations within affordable bounds. The four-course fixed-price menu features rabbit *en gibelotte*, but it's better to take the 95 F five-course menu: asparagus in vinaigrette, or melon; *thon à la provençale*—tuna in a tomato sauce with lots of garlic; duckling in a cherry sauce; then cheese and dessert.

Everyone loves the kind of food that Mazières cooks. Particularly commendable are his *matelote d'anguilles au vin de Cahors*, a delicious eel stew, and *magret de canard et sa poêlée de cèpes*, crisp roasted duck breast with boletus mushrooms. And a dessert that takes years to learn to make: *le pastis quercinois à la vieille prune*—a cake of wispy shreds of pastry, spiced up with plum brandy.

The wines are very reasonably priced, especially the 1982 Cahors, Château Haute-Serre for 78 F. For 65 F you can sample a 1985 Madiran Château Montus. It's a wine from the Pau district, usually found further south—hearty and full-bodied, mellowing after half an hour and taking on some very sophisticated nuances.

RATINGS: beauty 4, comfort 2, service 2, restaurant 4.

Pool, fishing; tennis and riding nearby.

$$

AAAA

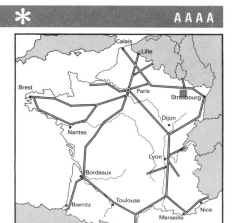

Grand Hôtel de la Reine

2 place Stanislas
54000 Nancy
Tel: 83 35 03 01
Telex: 960 367

52 rooms, 6 suites
CC: AE, D, Eu, V
Open all year.

Location: on historic place Stanislas, a short taxi ride from the station. If you're driving, look carefully for the direction signs; they are well placed, but it's easy to miss them in congested traffic.

King Stanislas Leszczynski of Poland, Duke of Lorraine, changed Nancy into a glittering town of rococo palaces. Place Stanislas and the Grand Hotel were his capstone. While the hotel has changed since Marie-Antoinette stayed there, the façade is still remarkably beautiful, and if not quite as palatial inside, it's still a wonderful place to stay.

The rooms are appointed in a style that we might say is Louis XV, almost grandiose, with all modern conveniences, big beds, and big bathrooms with robes (if you ask for one).

For as little as 400F for two, this hotel offers exceptional value, and the discount with *More France for the $* makes it even more of a travel bargain.

Restaurant **Le Stanislas** provides another chance to get more for your money. The night I was there, the *menu gourmand* was priced at 190F and featured a salad of asparagus tips with melon, walleye baked with bacon in a white wine sauce, a *granité* of small yellow mirabelle plums, thin slices of breast of duck baked in its own juice and served with cannelloni, a cheese course, a napoleon of pancake layers interspersed with various red fruit, petits fours, and coffee. Even if the à la carte menu is much more expensive, some things are hard to pass up: the *strudel de cuisses de pigeon en vinaigrette d'asperges; croustillant de pommes de terre au foie gras*; or John Dory with beans and wild mushrooms in a sweet-sour sauce.

RATINGS: beauty 5, comfort 4, service 4, restaurant 4.

The hotel will help with parking.

$ $ $

A A A A

Le Goéland

24 rue des Ponts
54000 Nancy
Tel: 83 35 17 25

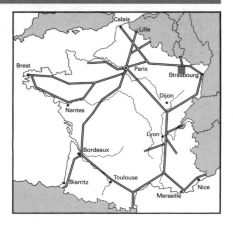

CC: AE, D, V
Closed Monday lunch, Sunday,
and the second two weeks in July.

Location: in the center of town near the Palais des Congrès. Ten minutes' stroll from place Stanislas.

A very attractive modern dining room perched on the second floor of an inconspicuous building. But the inside, made pleasant by soft classical music, natural woodwork and bright paintings, is still no match for the fabulous cuisine of Jean-Luc Mengin.

Seafood predominates, but the meat dishes are just as excellent. Try *filet d'aloyau rôti avec sa moelle,* a lean, tender and perfectly broiled sirloin—*bleu* for rare, *saignant* for medium-rare—served with marrow and shallot sauce. Or the fricassée of squab stewed with veal sweetbreads, or duck breast with sweet and sour sauce.

But oysters, clams and lobster are the house specialties. For example, a salad of oysters in lime aspic. Or *les six huîtres spéciales cuites à la* *vapeur d'algues, poivrade de bigorneaux*—oysters steamed open over sea-water with seaweed, served on the half-shell in a light sauce of pepper, wine vinegar and vegetable broth, with tiny periwinkles sprinkled on top. This delightful entrée was priced at 84 F. There are so many good reasons for ordering à la carte, it might be hard to order the 124 F or 185 F four-course menu. Both can start with oysters on the half-shell—either nine or a dozen, depending on price. A bouillabaisse for two at 185 F has a salt-air aroma and all the authentic flavor of Marseilles.

A fine wine list at down-to-earth prices features fragrant 1983 Muscat d'Alsace Réserve and youthful but hearty 1985 Côtes du Rhône St-Joseph for slightly over 100 F.

Imaginative seafood in the heart of Lorraine.

$ $ $ $

* A A A A

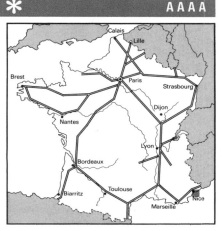

Hôtel Négresco

37 Promenade des Anglais
06000 Nice
Tel: 93 88 39 51
Telex: 460 040
Fax: 93 88 35 68

140 rooms, 18 suites
CC: AE, D, M, V
Open all year.

Location: on the seafront, near the town center.

A historical monument, and one of the greatest hotels in the world. For all its grandeur, it is not necessarily top-of-the-line expensive. Prices start at under 1,000F, and a deluxe room with sea-view can be double that. But with the possibility of an upgrading at no extra cost, the Négresco rises to the top for value.

Everyone who's anyone has stayed here, and it's easy to see why. The central rotunda has the world's largest Aubusson carpet and biggest crystal chandelier. Pillars, busts, tapestries, modern paintings, beautiful antiques, and a king's ransom in gilding—and the décor is constantly changing thanks to the unceasing efforts of Mme Jeanne Augier, chairwoman.

The main restaurant, **Le Chantecler,** achieved national fame years ago, and might be headed for even greater glory, newly renovated and now supervised by young Dominique Le Stanc, formerly of Château Eza. The other restaurant, **La Rotonde**, is also well worth a visit. Merry-go-round horses prance to the sound of fairground music; smiling waitresses in bloomers and petticoats dance around bringing meals. The menu is simple, well prepared and inexpensive. La Rotonde has its own entrance off the Promenade des Anglais, so non-hotel guests needn't be intimidated by having to go through the lobby. Though the Négresco is one of the friendliest places I know of, and a short tour of the ground floor is part of the fun for everyone.

RATINGS: beauty 5, comfort 5, service 5, restaurant 4.

Some rooms with balconies and sea views.

$ $ $

A A A A

Hôtel Beach Regency

223 Promenade des Anglais
06200 Nice
Tel: 93 83 91 51
Telex: 461 635
Fax: 93 71 21 71

308 rooms, 14 suites
CC: all
Open all year.

Location: on the sea front, five minutes from the airport, ten from the town center.

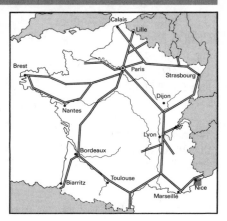

A very big hotel offering plenty of resort amenities on the uncongested end of the Promenade des Anglais.

The rooms are bright and cheerful, with king-size beds and big bathrooms. They are all similar, but those valid for your *More France for the $* upgrading have balconies facing the Baie des Anges and are worth around 200 F more than the 650 F standard doubles.

A special feature is the rooftop swimming pool and restaurant with terrace bar, summer barbecues, and live band music.

The hotel's best restaurant, **Le Regency**, deserves honorable mention for cooking far surpassing that of the typical big hotel. Worthy of high praise: snails in garlic butter with basil in a light *feuilleté*; *goujonnettes de chapon de la Méditerranée en papillote*—rascasse fillets with pesto, baked in foil; lobster with green pasta; and duck breast and thigh in an olive fricassée. Service is deft and friendly.

RATINGS: beauty 4, comfort 5, service 5, restaurant 3.

Pool, fitness center, boutiques, beauty salon. Underground garage.

$ $

unrated

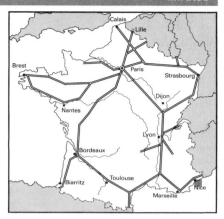

Le Gourmet Lorrain

7 avenue Santa-Flor
06100 Nice
Tel: 93 84 90 78

11 rooms
CC: AE, D, V
Open all year.
Restaurant closed Sunday evening,
all Monday and August.

Location: in the northern part of town, just north
of Place Charles-de-Gaulle.

This little hotel was undergoing total renovation, and is therefore not rated in this edition of *More France for the $*. It will offer charm and personality—and considerable savings—for anyone willing to stray off the beaten track, even with a round-trip by cab to the center of town added to the 400 F price of a double room.

Each room will have a modern bathroom, TV, and the personality typical of a family-owned *auberge*. Sound-proofing in this quiet neighborhood is totally unnecessary.

M. and Mme. Leloup will give you a warm welcome. The restaurant is well recommended; quite a few achievements and awards attest to chef Leloup's prowess in the kitchen. The prices are almost unbelievably low—an 85 F menu gives four courses, including fish soup and roast quail. The *menu gastronomique* is just 150 F, featuring the cooking of Lorraine. The restaurant's claim to fame is the world's greatest quiche—which must be ordered 30 minutes in advance. There's a good selection of cheeses, listed by category, region and name.

Wash it down with 100-year-old armagnac, compliments of the house.

A homey atmosphere in a Nice auberge.

$ $

Hôtel de Lausanne

36 rue Rossini
06000 Nice
Tel: 93 88 85 94
Telex: 461 269

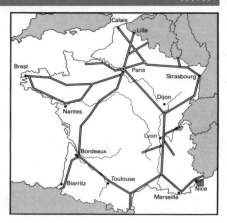

40 rooms
CC: AE, D, Eu, V
Open all year.

Location: near the center of town.

The pride of the Perez family shows in this small hotel with lots of character. Situated in a corner building with a Belle Epoque flavor— French windows and half-balconies with iron grillwork and balustrades, a cozy interior with birdcage elevator, comfortable lounge, small bar, and big-windowed breakfast room.

The rooms are not large, but attractively furnished in rattan, with varying color schemes. There's a hairdryer in the bathrooms. All *More France for the $* patrons are entitled to robes in the bathroom, so don't hesitate to mention it.

Breakfast is another element of family pride, served in the finest French tradition with baskets heaped with fresh-baked croissants and brioches.

Cozy charm and friendly personality. Parking available.

$ $

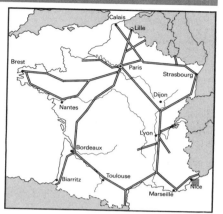

Hôtel Pullman

28 avenue Notre-Dame
06000 Nice
Tel: 93 80 30 24
Telex: 470 662

201 rooms, 9 suites
CC: AE, D, M
Open all year.

Location: center of town, not far from the railway station.

A modern, streamlined hotel, well situated and offering efficient and attractive rooms for under 500 F.

The service is not very personal, so don't expect anyone to greet you and ask how you are. But the atmosphere is cheery, and the rooms are bright. All are air-conditioned, sound-proofed, and equipped with TV, radio, minibar, and automatic alarm clock. There are hairdryers and big towels in the bathroom.

On the 8th floor, there's a sauna and rooftop swimming pool overlooking the city, sea and mountains. No restaurant, but room service offers hot and cold dishes between 7 and 11 p.m.

Pool. 50 rooms with balcony. Garage parking nearby.

$

AA

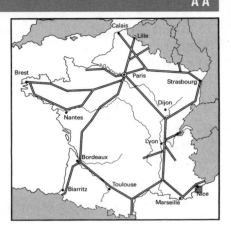

Neptune Plage
Promenade des Anglais
06000 Nice
Tel: 93 87 16 60

Open 1 May to 30 September.

Location: on the beach, directly in front of the Négresco.

The general manager of the Négresco recommended this beach restaurant as a good place for lunch. It *was* good, and I'm glad to pass it along.

The restaurant is on a terrace overlooking the beach, a private property·where admission fees are charged and mattresses rented—a necessity on a gravel beach. The

Neptune Plage has blue and white parasols, blue-carpeted walkways and chaise-lounges with adjustable backrests, all available free of charge with your *More France for the $* coupon, if you have lunch.

Luncheon on the terrace offers inexpensive seafood dishes and wonderful salads, including the best *salade niçoise* in Nice.

Good food and the most fashionable beach.

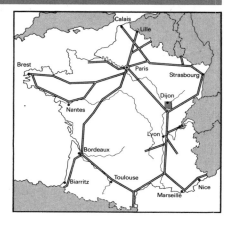

La Côte d'Or

1 rue Thurot
21700 Nuits-St-Georges
Tel: 80 61 06 10

6 rooms, 1 suite
CC: CB, V
Closed Sunday evening, Wednesday,
and the first three weeks in July.

Location: halfway between Dijon and Beaune, on
the N 74.

The rooms are very attractive, furnished with antiques, quite large and reasonably priced at 320 F and up for a double. The restaurant is noted for its good food, and is also reasonably priced, considering the level of cuisine, but in a higher price category.

The day I visited, there were three fixed-price menus: 220 F, 300 F, and 420 F. And à la carte, such luxury courses as *le pigeon poêlé au foie gras et à la truffe grise de Bourgogne* for 180 F—flavorful and piquant white Burgundy truffles, goose liver and roast squab, united by a red wine sauce. On the 220 F menu we encounter one of my favorites, *le blanc de volaille en croustille de pomme de terre*, breast of chicken stuffed with spinach and coated with shredded potatoes before being roasted.

A wonderful appetizer included in the 300 F menu is *les petits escargots de Bourgogne en cocotte lutée*. Picture a small porcelain tureen with a soufflé rising out of it—a volcano about to erupt. Poke a hole in the top, and the wonderful aroma of a garlic, shallot, cream and wine sauce rises up to meet you.

My favorite desserts were nougat with minced candies on a bed of blackcurrants. And a black-as-night chocolate cake on an orange sauce.

The wine list is a 100-page book. Two wines you might not find in many places are the 1985 white Savigny Vergelesses for 150 F and the 1982 red Savigny-lès-Beaune for 165 F, a wonderful value. And suppose you did order the squab with white truffles, what wine would you choose? I suggest a dark red full-bodied 1982 Chambolle-Musigny.

RATINGS: beauty 3, comfort 3, service 3, restaurant 5.

Among the best in Burgundy.

$ $ $

A A A A

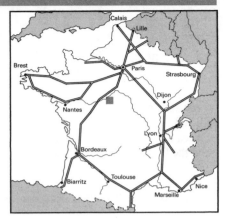

Domaine des Hauts-de-Loire

Route de Herbault
41150 Onzain
Tel: 54 20 72 57
Telex: 751 547

23 rooms, 4 suites
CC: AE, D, M, V
Closed December and January.

Location: from Blois, take the N152 to Onzain, then follow directions for Herbaut for about 2 km.

This elegant, three-story mansion was originally built as a hunting lodge in 1840, and though it has been completely modernized, and now looks more elegant than sporting, you can still imagine the old hunting preserve when you drive through the gates into an ancient forest and park your car under trees as tall as a church steeple.

The rooms are luxuriously decorated in bright colors. Bathrooms are lined with marble. A recently constructed building, which you could mistake for the rustic hunting lodge itself, has rooms of the same luxury standard, but with private terraces on the ground floor.

The restaurant in the main building has one of the most cheerful and attractive dining rooms I've ever seen, with bright yellow walls, white cane chairs, wooden beams and a stone fireplace. The food is equally attractive. For example, fillets of duck breast with red fruit, or white fillet of walleye *(sandre)* in an orange sauce. A salad of red Verona and green bib lettuce, surrounding two fried quail eggs on toast, topped with a sprinkling of red cranberries, also made a pretty picture.

Sauvignon de Touraine is an excellent local dry white wine. Superb Touraine-Mesland red is produced in neighboring domaines.

RATINGS: beauty 4, comfort 5, service 5, restaurant 4.

Tennis, fishing. 36-hole championship golf course at Les Bordes.

$ $ $ $

AAAA

Hôtel Lotti

7 rue de Castiglione
75001 Paris
Tel: 42 60 37 34
Telex: 240 066
Fax: 40 15 93 56

126 rooms, 5 suites
CC: all
Open all year.

Location: close to Place Vendôme.

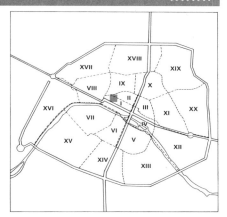

The Lotti has enjoyed a good reputation since 1910 when the Duke of Westminster put up the money for Mr Lotti, maître d'hôtel at the neighboring Hôtel Continental, to establish something smaller, more intimate and nicer nearby. Though the hotel passed out of family hands long ago, it is still hailed as the grandest of the small hotels.

The lowest price category at the Lotti is for a group of 33 singles and tiny inside doubles. The mid-price designation offers excellent value—silk-upholstered rooms overlooking one of the most beautiful streets in Paris. No two are alike, though all are decorated and furnished in Louis XV or Louis XVI style. The building was renovated recently but the rooms still retain some old-fashioned touches, such as a little closet in the wall to leave your shoes for shining overnight.

The restaurant—**Le Lotti**—has an à la carte menu. Since your hors d'oeuvre is complimentary, a glimpse at the choices might be interesting: *salade périgordine*, which includes duck or goose liver; half a dozen Burgundy snails; a salad of artichoke hearts and shrimp; duck terrine with pistachios.

This is the only menu I have ever seen in France that labels main courses "Entrées" as we do in America. They are classic and uncomplicated, judging by the *côtes d'agneau vert-pré* I sampled—thinly sliced lamb, suffused in a sauce of butter, parsley and lemon. Finish with a celery sherbet for a different treat.

RATINGS: beauty 4, comfort 5, service 5, restaurant 3.

Elegant atmosphere in the grandest of the small hotels.

$ $ $ $

A A A A

Hôtel Westminster

13 rue de la Paix
75002 Paris
Tel: 42 61 57 46
Telex: 680 035
Fax: 42 60 30 66

84 rooms, 18 suites
CC: AE, CB, D, Eu, V
Open all year.
Restaurant closed Saturday and Sunday.

Location: between Place Vendôme and the Opéra.

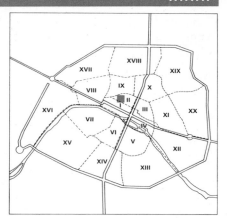

At the turn of the century, the owner of this small hotel had a penchant for collecting clocks, and these are still the main decorative motif throughout. Although it's been renovated several times, rich wood paneling, molded ceilings, marble mantelpieces, and many Louis XIV antiques remain.

All guestrooms are equipped with a minibar, color TV, radio, and air conditioning, and each bathroom is in marble. And the bigger the room, the greater the value. The antiques, silver clocks and marble are particularly noticeable in the suites, where you'll also find deep, bold-colored sofas, oil paintings and beautiful porcelain vases.

The restaurant, **Le Céladon**, is fairly small and modern, with soft lights and an intimate, elegant atmosphere. A bit on the pricey side, but close to greatness and a good value overall. The same can be said for the wine list, with many good wines available for less than 200 F— for example, 1983 Château Guibeau St-Emilion or 1986 Domaine La Roche Chablis.

The young chef, Joël Boilleaut, is inventive to the point of being poetic; his cooking is as delicate as the green Chinese porcelain vases for which Le Céladon is named. Anglerfish in a light veal sauce on an airy bed of leeks. Fried walleye *(sandre)* in *beurre nantais.* And most impressive: *râble de lapereau farci de son foie, jus poivré*—saddle of young and tender rabbit, stuffed with its own liver, in a peppercorn-scented sauce. A French original to change anyone's mind about ordering rabbit.

RATINGS: beauty 3, comfort 4, service 5, restaurant 5.

Comfortable piano bar. Lively atmosphere.

$ $ $

AAAA

Le Miravile

25 quai de la Tournelle
75005 Paris
Tel: 46 34 07 78

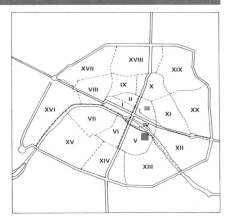

CC: AE, D, V
Closed Sunday.

Location: on the left bank of the Seine, a short stroll from Notre-Dame.

When I asked the celebrated chef of the restaurant Louis XV in Monte Carlo, Alain Ducasse, to name his favorite "undiscovered" restaurant in Paris, the Miravile was his choice. If you visit this intimate little eatery on the banks of the Seine, you won't be disappointed.

The appetizer of clams in a curry broth was my first hint that whatever followed would not be commonplace. The next appetizer was baked goose liver wrapped in a thin piece of goose skin scraped of all fat, and arranged to look like a tiny bird. One could have a fabulous meal here concentrating on appetizers alone:

zucchini flowers filled with ratatouille; tomatoes and baby vegetables in *pistou* (a sauce of garlic, basil, cheese, and olive oil)... But of course you'll want to go on to greater things. John Dory *(saint-pierre)* with eggplant caviar, or salad of sea bream with sweet pimentos, or broiled steak with *sauce Foyot* (béarnaise with tomato), or veal in marrow sauce and ratatouille, or sautéed baby lamb. You can taper off with a special selection of cheeses, or fritters of goat cheese *au porto*. End with one of eleven exquisite desserts.

The wine list includes twelve fine vintages priced under 200 F.

A memorable discovery on the Left Bank.

Hôtel Lutétia

**45 boulevard Raspail
75006 Paris**
Tel: 45 44 38 10
Telex: 270 424
Fax: 45 44 50 50

300 rooms, 17 suites
CC: all
Open all year.
Le Paris restaurant closed Sunday,
Monday and August.

Location: in the heart of the left-bank district, on
the corner of boulevard Raspail and rue de Sèvres.

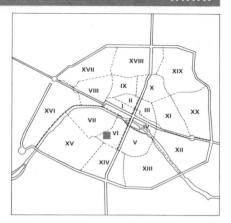

After top-to-bottom renovation, this left-bank landmark is probably more beautiful today than when it first opened its doors in 1910. Paul Belmondo, father of Jean-Paul, sculpted the garlands, grapes and goddesses of the white façade.

The Lutétia is both Parisian and international in atmosphere; the décor pure Art Deco. In the spacious, high-ceilinged rooms, the orignal style has been retained, with inlaid wood furniture, mahogany wardrobes and octagonal headboards, enhanced by new wall-to-wall carpeting. High marks for comfort.

If you eat in the brasserie or sidewalk café-restaurant, "the simpler the better" might guide your choice. The hotel's intimate restaurant, **Le Paris,** is next door. Seating only thirty, it was redecorated by Sonia Rykiel in 1930s "sleeping-car style".

The chef's specialty, *saumon frais norvégien en homardine*, won him the Bocuse d'Or award. But with the 250F menu, you might try red mullet fillets with caviar, followed by a *panaché* of seafood with sea urchin coral, or an assortment of broiled red meats with *marmelade de courgettes* (zucchini relish), followed by cheese and dessert—why not *soufflée à l'orange*? The wine cellar boasts 30,000 bottles, with a good selection of noble wines priced under 150F. But the complimentary bottle of Taittinger champagne is sure to please.

Round-the-clock room service, as well as cheerful concierges, doormen, porters and maids, round out the picture of a grand hotel at not-so-grand prices.

RATINGS: beauty 5, comfort 4, service 4, restaurant (Le Paris) 4.

Upper-story rooms with half-balcony and view of the Eiffel Tower.

$ $ $ $

AAA

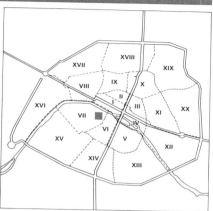

Hôtel Pont-Royal

**7 rue de Montalembert
75007 Paris**
Tel: 45 44 38 27
Telex: 270 113

75 rooms, 5 suites
CC: AE, D, V
Open all year.
Restaurant closed Sunday and August.

Location: off rue du Bac, between boulevard St-Germain and the Pont Royal.

A flapper-era hostelry, with a lot of character. Tiny balconies sprout all over the exterior, looking out over a small square.

A ramp to an underground parking garage practically in front of the hotel does intrude on the nostalgic atmosphere, but inside, the feeling of other times is largely retained.

A very warm reception will be waiting; the Viennese concierge in a natty dark blue uniform has just the right mix of informality and aplomb.

Upstairs there are two kinds of rooms: the kind I like and the kind I don't. The latter have flowered carpets and heavy walnut furniture. The ones I do like have muted solid-tone carpeting, light Regency furniture, recessed sleeping alcoves, antique day beds and settees, floor-to-ceiling windows, and half-bal-conies. Luckily, these make up about half the hotel.

All rooms are air-conditioned and equipped with TV, minibar, radio, and a safe. They're priced right at the 1,000 F mark.

The bar downstairs is that low-key type of place that feels right for a rendezvous or for a drink after work, apparently popular with editors and writers.

The restaurant is called **Les Antiquaires** because of all the antique shops in the welter of little streets between here and the Seine. It has the atmosphere of a formal restaurant spilling over into a glass-enclosed sidewalk café. The food, like the hotel, is dressy but basic. The 170 F menu, wine and service included, is good value for better-than-average eating in a very pleasant setting.

RATINGS: beauty 4, comfort 3, service 3, restaurant 3.

Three rooms with roof-top view of Paris.

$ $

*   A A

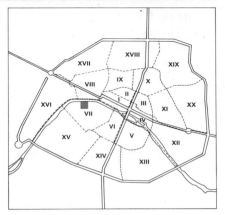

Hôtel St-Dominique

62 rue St-Dominique
75007 Paris
Tel: 47 05 51 44
Telex: 206 968
Fax: 47 05 81 28

38 rooms
CC: all
Open all year.

Location: on the left bank, near the Esplanade des Invalides.

On one of the prettiest and most historic of Paris streets, in a 17th-century building with an ancient wine cellar and garden where you can have breakfast, the Hôtel St-Dominique is a very pleasant place to save on expenses in Paris. At the end of 1988, the lowest-price double was 350F—around 300 less than at a similar left-bank hotel not far away on rue St-Simon. The rooms are not very large, but furnished with antique stripped-wood period pieces. Each room has a TV, minibar, and direct-dial phone. Small but modern bath-rooms.

No surprise that this hotel is heavily booked much of the year. Reservations as far in advance as possible are recommended.

Charming, economic, and conveniently located.

$ $

*   A A A A

La Ferme St-Simon

6 rue de St-Simon
75007 Paris
Tel: 45 48 35 74

CC: V
Closed Saturday lunch, Sunday,
and August.

Location: near the intersection of boulevard St-Germain and rue du Bac.

One of the best restaurants in Paris, for any price, so reservations are a must. And no wonder this intimate and elegant left-bank restaurant is usually full—the cooking is inspired and the execution flawless. Just take the *salade de rouget* for starters— red mullet fillets marinated in lime juice and tender greens, with a dressing that combines the fish livers, oil, vinegar, and mustard for a unique and intriguing flavor. And almost as great, in the same group of first courses, you'll find small, paper-thin ravioli filled with meat of giant crab *(tourteau)*. Don't hesitate to try the *petite lotte rôtie au lard, au pomerol*—monkfish wrapped in smoked bacon, served with a wine sauce. Just one more example of unexpected things that go well together is *émincé de langue et grenouille*, a peaceful coexistence of tongue and frog legs in a light cream sauce. It is academic to say that the food was delicious. Don't forget to leave room to sample the panoply of desserts.

Favorite venue of the députés from nearby Palais-Bourbon.

$ $ $ $

Hôtel Concorde St-Lazare

108 rue St-Lazare
75008 Paris
Tel: 42 94 22 22
Telex: 650 442
Fax: 42 93 01 20

342 rooms
CC: AE, D, Eu, V
Open all year.

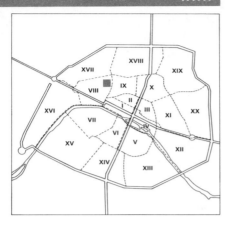

Location: near the Place de l'Opéra.

The lobby has been designated a national monument, worth seeing for its two-story-high ceilings of intricate tile mosaics reminiscent of a Moorish palace, marble columns topped with gold leaf, marble walls and marble portals, a galaxy of crystal chandeliers... The Edwardian billiards room adjacent to the lobby looks like something from a film set.

To be sure, the bedrooms have seen better days, but a major renovation is underway, and those rooms that have been refurbished don't lack for much. Minibars, color TVs and direct-dial phones have been installed, plus indirect lighting and a soft, if impersonal, décor.

The hotel's "Paris Plus" program offers all guests a complimentary cruise along the Seine in a *bateau mouche*, half-price cocktails between 5 and 6 p.m. in the Golden Black lounge, no charge for children under 12 in a room with their parents, and a visit to a fashion show with breakfast included.

The **Café Terminus** is the hotel's restaurant, an informal place with a glass façade facing the sidewalk, fine for people-watching and simple meals.

RATINGS: beauty 4, comfort 4, service 4, restaurant 2.

American bar and billiards.

$ $ $ $

A A A

Hôtel Royal Monceau

37 avenue Hoche
75008 Paris
Tel: 45 61 98 00
Telex: 650 361
Fax: 45 63 28 93

180 rooms, 40 suites
CC: AE, D, V
Open all year.

Location: near the Arc de Triomphe.

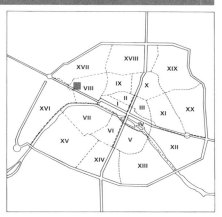

After passing through a period of staidness, this classic luxury hotel now caters to a younger crowd who like the indoor fitness center with jazzercise, pumping iron, and nautilus machines. A steam room, sauna, and heated indoor swimming pool in a lounge-like setting with adjacent weight-watchers restaurant also pull in beautiful people from Paris and the world.

It is stylish without being garish, yet it's the kind of place where your newspaper is tucked into a see-through envelope before being placed on your breakfast tray. Where you wouldn't hesitate asking the concierge to have your Montblanc filled if it runs dry. Although it has taken women longer to claim the job of hotel concierge than to become airline pilots, the Monceau got the first and the best.

In most hotels, courtyard rooms mean a desolate view; here, however, they overlook a pleasant outdoor restaurant. Front rooms face the wide and relatively quiet avenue Hoche. In either case, there are no bad rooms. And no compromise on comfort—fresh towels twice a day.

In case you want to mix business and pleasure, there is a business club and full secretarial service.

RATINGS: beauty 4, comfort 5, service 5, restaurant 2.

Piano bar. Fitness center.

$ $

A A A

Baumann Marbeuf

15 rue Marbeuf
75008 Paris
Tel: 47 20 11 11

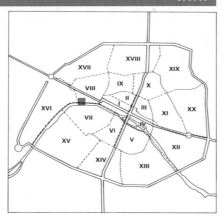

CC: AE, D, V
Open every day.

Location: off the Champs-Elysées, about one block south.

This festive restaurant with marble-top tables is owned by one of the great chefs of Alsace, Guy-Pierre Baumann of the Maison Kammerzell in Strasbourg. Not surprisingly, there's quite a bit of Alsace represented on the à la carte menu. But M. Baumann, who spends a few days a week here, is as Parisian as he is Alsatian.

If your appetite is hearty enough, try the classic Alsatian *choucroute strasbourgeoise*, featuring five different kinds of sausage on a bed of delicately spiced sauerkraut. Or from M. Baumann's Parisian side, sample the braised fillet of beef in green pepper sauce, or a *feuilleté* of steak served with a Roquefort sauce. Steak tartare is the great specialty of the house—six on the menu from *tartare Attila*, flavoured with peppers, to *tartare aux herbes d'été*, with mint, chives, basil, parsley, chervil, and tarragon. Each one is a generous helping of prime lean steak with a lavish green salad. Priced at less than 90F, it pays to come hungry. Also ample, but very light, is my favorite Baumann first course: *l'escabèche de sardines*. The little fish are fried crisp, then marinated in white wine, vinegar and lemon juice with tomato, shallot, cumin, and coriander.

The best wine values are red Saumur-Champigny and white Alsace.

The taste of Alsace in the center of Paris.

$ $ $

A A A

Restaurant Napoléon

38 avenue de Friedland
75008 Paris
Tel: 42 27 99 50

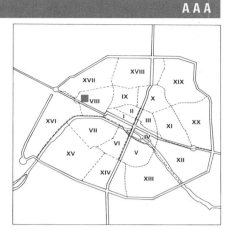

CC: AE, D, Eu, V
Open every day.

Location: near the Arc de Triomphe.

A classy little restaurant a few minute's walk from the Champs-Elysées presided over by two fine chefs. Guy-Pierre Baumann, the owner and founder, made his reputation here, and Philippe Serre brings his own high style to the menu. *Raviolis de crabe aux cornes d'abondance*, feather-light ravioli filled with crab meat and presented in a sauce of wild mushrooms, or a *blanc de volaille*, breast of chicken stuffed with mushrooms and baked to a crisp finish with a coating of shredded potato, served with béarnaise, or lean chops of young lamb sautéed with three kinds of pepper. M. Baumann's *choucroutes*, especially the one made with fresh salmon, also deserve note. Some brilliant desserts—orange and almond ice cream, bitter-sweet chocolate cake, and *feuilleté aux poires caramélisées, coulis de framboises.*

A warm welcome and perfect service from Philippe Moncheny, maître d'hôtel and director.

Stylish and central.

95

$ $ $ $

A A A A

Hôtel Scribe

1 rue Scribe
75009 Paris
Tel: 47 42 03 40
Telex: 214 653
Fax: 42 65 39 97

217 rooms, 11 suites
CC: AE, D, V
Open all year.

Location: near the Opéra, just off the Grands Bou-
levards.

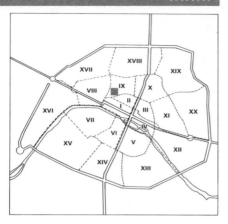

The Scribe is an absolutely perfect luxury hotel. Not a hair out of place, not a flaw anywhere. The building dates back to 1863; a plaque outside commemorates the Lumières brothers' showing of the first motion pictures in the same building in 1895.

Though it has more than 200 rooms, the Scribe seems much smaller—because of its quiet atmosphere and low-profile exterior. The lobby is pure Napoleon III Grand Epoque style, and the bedrooms are furnished in Louis XVI or Louis-Philippe, with maximum comfort even in standard category rooms. Should you avail yourself of the Scribe's offer of room upgrading, you'll have a bigger bedroom and slightly more luxurious bathroom with thick robes. (You gain a bottle of fine champagne in any case.)

The Scribe is a civilized place, to say the least. Once a week there is a musical soirée at 8 p.m. sharp in a downstairs reception room. It costs 100F, including champagne, and features renowned guest artists.

The night I ate in the restaurant, **Les Muses**, the hotel was playing host to an ensemble from Belgium. The Scribe's chef, Christian Maissault, prepared to perfection some of the specialities of Roger Souvereyns, one of the greatest Belgian chefs—goose liver sautéed with endives, a pastry shell of brill flavored with rosemary, veal sweetbreads in a schnaps sauce with nutmeg-scented asparagus.

RATINGS: beauty 4, comfort 5, service 5, restaurant 4.

In the heart of the theater and shopping district.

$ $ $ $

A A A

Hôtel Ambassador Concorde

16 boulevard Haussmann
75009 Paris
Tel: 42 46 92 63
Telex: 650 912

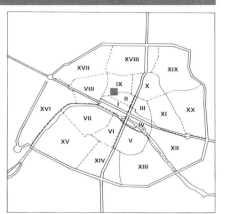

300 rooms
CC: AE, D, Eu, V
Open all year.

Location: near the Place de l'Opéra.

The lobby and public areas are attractive, even palatial, with wood veneers and gold trim, crystal chandeliers and marble floors. The rooms have been renovated. New mattresses, bright décor, radio, TV, minibar, direct-dial phones, nice bathrooms. And the location is very central.

A pleasant surprise was the restaurant, **Le Lindbergh**, named in honor of Lucky Lindy because his celebratory banquet was held there. The dining room is big, bright and pleasant, with friendly and attentive service.

The cuisine of Gilles Pineau is easy to recommend for its inventiveness and lightness. Thin slices of raw salmon marinated in lime juice with ginger, alone, would be worth the visit. Carpaccio de canard (air-dried duck), is a special treat; it must be ordered a day in advance, but the price was only 75 F. The *papillote* of trout and spinach was another delectable bargain at the same price. Or broiled brochette of anglerfish with anise-flavored butter.

The prices are very reasonable—you could compose a luncheon menu for under 100 F with a delicate omelet for 26 F, a cassolette of snails with garlic- and anise-flavored butter for 48 F, or a trout and watercress salad for 42 F. And if you crave for a really great steak, a thick one broiled the way you like it, with béarnaise, is the most expensive thing on the menu at 122 F.

The wine list is small but selective. Typical, and rarely found abroad: red Graves 1983, for 125 F. Pouilly-Fumé for 135 F.

RATINGS: beauty 4, comfort 4, service 3, restaurant 3.

Hairdresser, boutiques.

97

$ $ $ $

A A A A

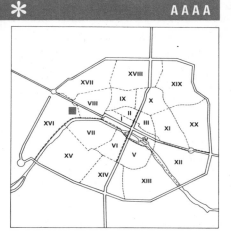

Hôtel Raphaël

17 avenue Kléber
75116 Paris
Tel: 45 02 16 00
Telex: 610 356
Fax: 45 01 21 50

46 rooms, 45 suites
CC: AE, D, MC, V
Open all year.

Location: near the Arc de Triomphe.

You might not notice the Raphaël on a street full of Belle-Epoque buildings, but once inside, you'll be fascinated by its grand *palazzo* style and overwhelming profusion of oil paintings, oak panels, oriental carpets, marble arches, and antique furniture.

The Raphaël is quite small, with an atmosphere more leisurely than businesslike. If you're in a hurry to get to your room, you might as well walk up the staircase, rather than wait for the small, overworked brass "birdcage" elevator. The staff will give you a warm reception and are always willing to please, so you don't feel uncomfortable asking for any special service.

With as many suites or junior suites as there are rooms, and free upgrading with your *More France for the $* coupon, the Raphaël is great value. Whatever room you occupy, it will be high-ceilinged, airy, full of antique furniture, with every comfort including minibar and remote-control television. Plus a huge, old-fashioned bathroom of glistening white tile, equipped with lush towels and bathrobes.

The star-quality restaurant is worth the trip, even if you're staying elsewhere (one main course offered free). Absolutely stunning were the *raviolis au fumet d'oranges sanguines*—an invention of young chef Philippe Delahaye, who deserves acclaim. Another original was the scallops and salmon with *jus de truffes* and crab sauce. Almost too good to be true.

RATINGS: beauty 5, comfort 4, service 5, restaurant 4.

All rooms with balcony or half-balcony.

$ $ $

A A A A

Hôtel Centre-Ville Etoile

6 rue des Acacias
75017 Paris
Tel: 43 80 56 18
Telex: 206 968
Fax: 47 66 74 14

16 rooms
CC: all
Open all year.
Restaurant closed Sunday
and public holidays.

Location: near the Arc de Triomphe.

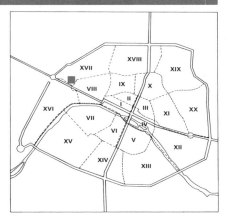

A stay in this bright and comfortable hotel, slightly off the beaten track in a residential area, is a nice way to halve the price of a room in Paris. If you make use of your *More France for the $* coupon, the extra 50% saving will make your stay in Paris a formidable bargain indeed.

The hotel is on a very quiet little street, only a few minutes' walk from the Champs-Elysées. Each room is tastefully, if simply, fitted with black lacquer furniture; you'll find a big easy chair and a king-size bed, plus minibar, TV with American and British satellite service, and a Minitel. The pristine bathroom is equipped with good quality soap and bath foam; robes are provided.

Although there is no doorman or concierge, reception is very warm and friendly. Service at breakfast is equally pleasant; fresh juice and fluffy croissants delivered with a friendly smile.

The restaurant, **Le Cougar**, in a separat building opposite the hotel, comes close to gourmet greatness. The chef, Taira Kurihara, came to Paris from Japan to study architecture and fell in love with French cuisine. He combines the subtleties of basic French cooking—chicken sautéed with mushrooms, gently spiced roast leg of lamb—with a touch of the Orient—*assiette de poissons crus* (thinly sliced raw fish); warmed *crottin* cheese covered with slivers of coconut.

The service in the small dining room is careful and elegant; the young waiters in starched white jackets very eager to please.

RATINGS: beauty 3, comfort 4, service 3, restaurant 4.

Stylish, comfortable, and economical.

$ $ $ $

A A A A

Le Manoir de Paris

6 rue Pierre-Demours
75017 Paris
Tel: 45 72 25 25

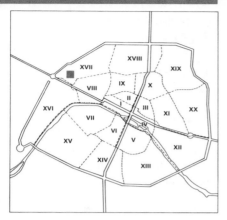

CC: AE, D, Eu, V
Closed Saturday and Sunday,
and the last two weeks of July.

Location: west of Place des Ternes, between
avenue Niel and boulevard Pereire.

When two great chefs put their toques together, anything can happen, especially when Francis Vandenhende, Maître Cuisinier de France, and Philippe Groult, Meilleur Ouvrier de France 1982, are behind the burners.

Before you set out for the heights of cuisine in this elegant eatery, try the simpler and less expensive "grandmother's style home cooking", for example *pieds d'agneau mijotés grand-mère*, lamb shanks simmered with a little sugar, red wine and bread. Twice as light are the scallops poached with ginger and lemon. Main courses include a suprême of duck in a truffle and cream sauce, roast suckling pig (a rarity in French restaurants), not to mention the classic leg of lamb and *pièce de bœuf à l'émulsion d'échalotes*, beef with creamed shallots.

A 310 F four-course luncheon menu includes a half-bottle of wine per person from a fairly wide selection, including Quincy, St-Véran and Pouilly-Fumé among the white, and Graves and Haut-Médoc among the red.

Fine food combined with Parisian elegance.

100

$ $ $

AA

Terrass'Hôtel

12 rue Joseph-de-Maistre
75018 Paris
Tel: 46 06 72 85
Telex: 280 830

93 rooms, 13 suites
CC: AE, D, JVC, V
Open all year.
Restaurant closed August.

Location: in Montmartre, across from the cemetery.

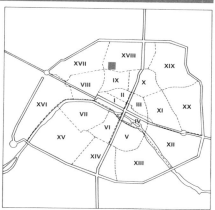

A somewhat modest hotel, and not exactly cheap. But this is Paris, after all, and the Terrass has enough charm—and a great location—to make people want to come back again.

One particular attraction is the roof terrace, with a grand view of Paris all the way to the Eiffel Tower. The lobby is cheerful and inviting, with a wood-burning fireplace at one end and plenty more warmth from the friendly reception.

The 24 deluxe-category rooms have particularly rich bathrooms with modern shower stalls sprouting several jets in strategic places. All the rooms feature a decent standard of comfort; those numbered 02 are fitted with a Minitel.

In the morning, you can have a French-style continental breakfast brought up to your room, or dig into an American-style buffet in the restaurant, **Le Guerlande.** Here simplicity rules. The 160F menu is good value, offering three choices in three courses. A typical meal could include fish terrine with sorrel sauce, mixed grill and *sauce diable* (hot'n spicy), a selection of five cheeses, or a tartelette of sherbets in a fruit sauce. The chef takes great pride in the presentation: asparagus arranged like a wreath around a thick steak tenderloin on a green-peppercorn sauce; home-fried potatoes surrounded by a green border of cucumber slices.

The most interesting wines on the list were a Gevrey-Chambertin and a Château Haut-Brion for around 250F, making doubly attractive the offer of a complimentary bottle of wine with lunch or dinner for two.

RATINGS: beauty 3, comfort 3, service 3, restaurant 3.

Two rooms with balcony and 30 rooms with half-balcony.

101

Les Hospitaliers

26160 Le Poët-Laval
Tel: 75 46 22 32

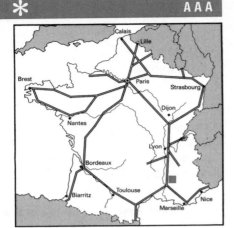

19 rooms, 1 suite
CC: AE, D, V
Open March to November.

Location: exit A7 at Montélimar and follow signs for Dieulefit. The village of Le Poët-Laval is about 10 km down the road. Les Hospitaliers is well signposted; it's an ancient castle looming over the village.

This is much more than an overnight stop, it's a destination in itself, a unique place for leisurely poking through battlements and chapels, following the winding streets that once resounded with the footsteps of the armor-clad Knights Hospitalers of St. John, after whom the hotel is named. It's hard to stay here without feeling touched by the hospitality of M. and Mme. Morin, and the historic charm of their hotel.

The rooms have standard comfort, but considering they have been constructed and reconstructed out of the age-old stones and rubble of the castle village, that's quite impressive. The bathrooms are generous, with lush towels, scented soaps and bath foam. A few of the rooms don't have a private bath, so it's better to specify.

The food is just as interesting as the environment—country fare for the sophisticated palate. I love the *pot au feu d'agneau à la sarriette* —the herbs and lamb in this simple dish create an aroma that raises it to glory. Quail and guinea-fowl are two other regional specialties raised to unexpected heights.

Try the soft, mellow Picodon Alpine goat's cheese with one of M. Morin's Burgundy varietals.

RATINGS: beauty 5, comfort 3, service 3, restaurant 4.

Pool. Tennis and riding nearby. Mountain views.

$ $ $

AAAA

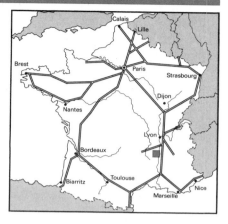

Michel Chabran

avenue du 45e-Parallèle
26600 Pont-de-l'Isère
Tel: 75 84 60 09
Telex: 346 333

12 rooms
CC: V
Open all year.
Restaurant closed Sunday evening
and all Monday,
and from October to March.

Location: exit Valence on A7; Michel Chabran's
hotel and restaurant is about 3 km north on N7.

This small hotel is 100 years old and has been in the hands of the Chabran family since 1935. But nothing shows of the past except the misleadingly plain exterior. Inside, everything is as ultra-modern and chic as could be. Room prices start at 500F.

Michel Chabran has climbed to the stellar heights of French culinary fame. His is a quest for new flavors, tempered by a dedication to lightness, spontaneity—plus a lot of talent.

It seems almost unfair to suggest that anyone can get an idea of Chabran's skill with a 110F luncheon *menu rapide*. In addition to salad and dessert, there is a choice of main course: the day I was there, it was mussels with a *bohémienne* of vegetables, or a fricassée of chicken in an Hermitage wine vinegar sauce.

Dinner menus range from 190F to 390F. The most expensive might include Chabran's remarkable *mille-feuille* of duck livers, baked with leaf-thin layers of squash and artichoke heart. Or red mullet fillets with artichokes on a tomato fondue with Nyons olives; or garlic-flavored lamb noisettes served with chanterelles and eggplant baked with a topping of Gruyère cheese.

Hermitage, the greatest of the Côtes du Rhône red wines, grows on nearby slopes. Its first cousin, the St-Joseph Tournon, is no poor relation, though the red needs to breathe a good while before the family ties assert themselves. Not so, the white St-Joseph. Even a youthful 1987 was robust and flavorful from the first sip.

RATINGS: beauty 4, comfort 4, service 4, restaurant 5.

Outdoor terrace and garden. Enclosed parking.

$ $ $

A A A A

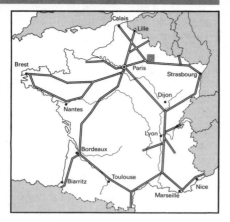

Le Chardonnay

184 avenue d'Epernay
51100 Reims
Tel: 26 06 08 60

CC: AE, D, Eu, V
Closed Saturday lunch and Sunday,
all January and the last two weeks
of July.

Location: south of the A4; nearest exits are Reims
Cathédrale and Reims Tinqueux.

A bustling restaurant that draws a big crowd for lunch or dinner. The menu gives a wide choice, and the prices, while not cheap, are more than fair. The most inexpensive menu, 185 F, offers four courses and the 250 F, five. These include *vinaigrette tiède de rouget au fenouil* (warm red mullet salad with fennel); *ravioli de homard au sauternes,* one huge pastel green ravioli stuffed with lobster tail meat, the claws arranged on the plate; then the demurely named *noisettes d'agneau grillées à l'huile d'olive*—broiled lamb completely covered by an aromatic ratatouille with some innocent-looking baked cloves of garlic on the side. Garlic lovers, this is *l'ail nouveau!* For those who really enjoy the taste of garlic raised to its most sublime.

And just to show how much variety there is here, the à la carte menu has a terrine of salmon in aspic with oysters and caviar, a *feuilleté* of local white asparagus with champagne sabayon, and a savory tart of vegetables flavored with basil together with frog legs. The baked rock lobster with squash flowers is an epicurean delight. Enormous cellars feature 150 specific champagnes, with 36 bruts for under 200 F. Also, wines by the glass.

A cheerful restaurant of gourmet standard, not far off the autoroute.

$ $ $

A A A A

Le Florence

43 boulevard Foch
51100 Reims
Tel: 26 47 12 70

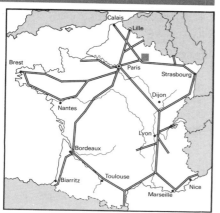

CC: AE, D, Eu, V
Closed Sunday evening and Monday,
all February,
and from mid-July to mid-August.

Location: in the center of Reims, near the railway station.

This fine 18th-century town house with tall windows and gold-trimmed ceilings is the scene of elegant—although not necessarily formal—luncheons and dinners. The cooking of Chef Yves Méjean has much delicacy. A gold star for originality goes to his *pot-au-feu de foie gras à la purée d'ail doux*. This is no rustic pot-au-feu. Here, the bowl placed in front of you contains a study in pastels—a delicate, fragrant, light yellow broth with spring onion, carrot slices, scallion, and goose liver—aromatized with herbs, garlic, and a sprinkle of sea salt.

And of course, this is Champagne country, and there's no escaping from it. As vinegar in *salade de queues de langoustine au vinaigre de champagne*. And champagne butter forms the base for a *marinière de crustacés et poissons*.

The variety of inventiveness impressed me. *Boudins de saint-pierre panés* saw John Dory fillets rolled, breaded and infused in a light cream and shellfish sauce. A *crépinette* filled with roast squab thigh meat and mushrooms. Duck meat poached in Bouzy wine.

A plate of regional cheeses includes an interesting fresh and light Chaource, and a very ripe Maroilles. Top it with a raspberry sabayon—red dots on a field of yellow.

A beautiful mansion dedicated to beautiful cooking.

Hôtel Beau-Site

46500 Rocamadour
Tel: 65 33 63 08
Telex: 520 421

50 rooms
CC: AE, D, JCB, V
Open 1 April to 1 November.

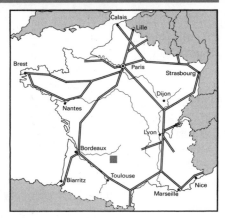

Location: south of Brive-la-Gaillarde on N20, then D140 at Cressensac. Only cars going to the hotel are permitted through the medieval gate into the town.

The medieval character of Rocamadour remains intact, its houses and streets stacked one upon the other beneath an overhanging cliff. Floodlit at night, the town takes on an eerie, almost entrancing beauty.

The location of the hotel is no less spectacular for being at the bottom of the town—every room looks out over the river valley and steep hills. A 15th-century building houses reception and some rather austere rooms, while across the street, another building, 300 years younger, contains brighter rooms with décor and furnishings evocative of medieval times, apart from the TV and private bath.

Also in the "new" building, the restaurant, **Le Jehan de Valon,** has a modern dining room strangely out of keeping with the milieu, though it's cheerful and bright. If weather permits, dine on the terrace and enjoy the view. Everything except *truffe sous pâte* and chateaubriand with béarnaise is priced under 100 F. Regional fare includes *potée quercinoise,* a wonderfully aromatic country vegetable soup made with smoked ham, or a *civet de canard au vin des coteaux* (rich duck stew). Fixed-price menus begin at 79 F.

The least expensive local wines are from Cahors; the best buy is 1985 Château de Haute-Serre for 82 F. Of the whites, Gaillac Perlé is light, neither dry nor sweet, and slightly sparkling.

The goats frisking around the surrounding hillsides provide milk for Cabécou cheese, whose nutty flavor is brought out nicely in the oven—ask for it *chaud.*

RATINGS: beauty 4 (in the "new" building), comfort 3, service 2, restaurant 3.

22 rooms with balcony. An attendant will park your car.

$ $ $

AAAA

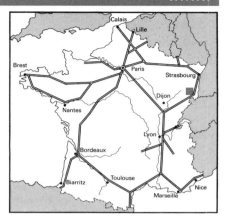

Château d'Isenbourg

68250 Rouffach
Tel: 89 49 63 53
Telex: 880 8198 ISBOURG

37 rooms, 3 suites
CC: CB, Eu, V
Closed January and February.

Location: about 20 km south of Colmar on the N 83.

Perched on a hilltop, this château is as magnificent as it is inviting. It has a graceful, 18th-century air, though its origins are much older, as shown by the stone corbels, curved lintels and worn stone steps in the cellar. The rooms and terraces look out over a sweep of vineyards and the village.

Every room is different, but with a similar standard of luxury. The Louis XV furniture, headboards and even walls are upholstered in silk brocade. The bathrooms are small, but that's understandable in a building that was never intended for modern comfort.

The restaurant, **Les Tommeries**, is in an interesting cellar, which is only partly underground. The cooking here is justly acclaimed. The pike and crayfish mousseline, the sweetbread escalope with orange and avocado, the supreme of squab, and the pear *millefeuille à la williamine* impressed me on my first visit, years ago. This time, a delicate escalope of warmed goose liver, supreme of chicken with two cabbages, and an unbelievable cheese soufflé with fruit won my affection.

Good riesling grapes grow on the château's slopes, but a Tokay d'Alsace is my first choice. The sommelier here was awarded the title of Best Sommelier of France; you can be sure your complimentary bottle of wine won't be anything less than excellent, whatever it may be.

The charm of the managers, the Dalibert family, infects the entire staff.

RATINGS: beauty 5, comfort 4, service 4, restaurant 5.

Pool, tennis. Some rooms with balcony. Park.

107

$ $

A A A

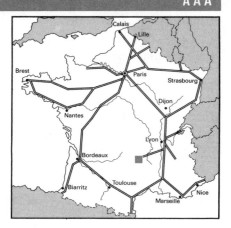

Hôtel Radio

43 avenue Pierre Curie
63400 Royat-Chamalières
Tel: 73 30 87 83
Telex: 530 955

27 rooms, 1 suite
CC: all
Open all year. Restaurant closed
Sunday evening and all Monday.

Location: 3.5 km west of Clermont-Ferrand. Exit
Chamalières on A71 from Paris. The hotel is on a
hill, near Royat railway station; follow avenue des
Thermes.

When the hotel was built in 1940, the word "radio" had connotations of all that was modern. Today the hotel is a lovely testament to the Art Deco period. It sparkles like new. The rooms have been refurbished in keeping with the original concept, more delicate than luxurious. Most have a nice southern exposure and a view of Clermont-Ferrand. Bathrooms are rather small, but attractively tiled. The starting price of a double is 390 F.

The hotel is owned and managed by Michel Mioche, Maître Cuisinier de France. Like the dining room, the food he prepares also has a touch of Art Deco—even if unintentional. The appetizer, a terrine of Puy lentils and Auvergne *saucisson*, is a square of pastel green framing a deep rose-red circle. The *menu dégustation* is regal, with foie gras salad, lobster civet, baked salmon and lamb filet mignon with coriander seeds, somewhat regally priced at 390 F. More down-to-earth, at 190 F, the five-course *menu du terroir* includes salmon with Puy lentils and a regional specialty, *petit salé de porc dans son embeurré de choux* —salt pork on a bed of buttery cabbage.

From the excellent selection of cheeses, try the nutty-flavored Cantal d'Auvergne, and a sharp blue Fourme d'Ambert. The Clermont-Ferrand area is the home of VDQS Côtes d'Auvergne, from the Gamay grape, similar to Beaujolais but with a distinct, full-bodied character, not unlike the more expensive Fleurie.

RATINGS: beauty 4, comfort 3, service 3, restaurant 5.

Pool nearby, garden. Three rooms with balcony.

$ $

A A A A

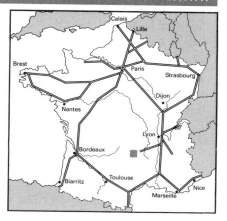

La Belle Meunière

25 avenue de la Vallée
63130 Royat
Tel: 73 35 80 17

CC: AE, D, Eu, V
Closed Sunday evening
and all Wednesday, and three weeks
in November and February.

Location: on the upper reaches of Royat, past the
casino and spa.

On a granite gorge with fast-rushing stream, this Belle Epoque restaurant can't have changed much since the 1880s, when General Georges Boulanger came here to forget his political worries and to tryst with his mistress, Marguerite de Bonnemains —"La Belle Meunière." The crystal chandeliers, gilt-framed mirrors, delicate woodwork, 19th-century oil paintings, and velvet drapes all recall a bygone era, as does the traditional cuisine of Jean-Claude Bon.

Fixed price menus at 127 F, 200 F and 250 F feature delicacies like duck liver marinated in Sauternes, tomatoes stuffed with mushrooms and flavored with *beurre d'escargots*, salmon with lentils and cream sauce, and *panaché de poissons à la vapeur d'herbes*.

An overwhelming array of desserts that take 40 minutes to prepare— order in advance. The choice Côtes d'Auvergne wines are moderately priced.

A lovely Belle-Epoque restaurant in a romantic setting.

$ $

A A A

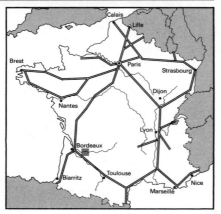

Hostellerie de Plaisance
Place du Clocher
33330 St-Emilion
Tel: 57 24 72 32

11 rooms, 1 suite
CC: AE, D, M, V
Closed January.

Location: 39 km from Bordeaux. Turn off N 89 at Libourne. The hotel is at the top of the village, next to the clock tower.

Formerly an executive for a big hotel chain, Louis Quilain one day decided to run a hotel of his own. He bought a small medieval cloister in St-Emilion, on the uppermost plateau overlooking the entire cobble and red-tile village, and turned it into a comfortable hotel. The day his chef quit, he took over the kitchen himself. If the number of people enjoying themselves in the restaurant is anything to go by, he has made a success of the venture.

Foie gras heads the list of entrées on his five-course, 204 F *menu gastronomique*. The most popular dishes are those that go best with the famous local red wine. Leg of lamb, beef brochette, duck breast—even fish *(filet de maigre)*—are served with a sauce of St-Emilion.

Any St-Emilion wine is such a fine balance of bouquet and flavor that the cheese you choose to go with it should never be overpowering. La Besace du Berger, a goat cheese from Dordogne with a blue-mold rind but fresh inside, works very well.

The wine list will teach you a lot about the best châteaux and vintages in the region. You'll find all the *Premier Grand Cru Classé* châteaux. Cheval Blanc is possibly the greatest, and the easiest to remember, followed by Ausone, Figeac, Canon, and Magdaleine. The most exceptional years were 1964, 1971, 1975, and 1982. But all the 1980s have been good years in St-Emilion. Château Cap de Mourlin 1982, for 240 F, and Château Haut-Vilet 1985, 112 F, are recommendable.

RATINGS: beauty 5, comfort 4, service 3, restaurant 3.

Public parking in front of the Syndicat d'Initiative.

110

$ $ $ $

A A A A

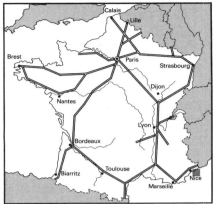

Grand Hôtel du Cap-Ferrat

06290 St-Jean-Cap-Ferrat
Tel: 93 76 00 21
Telex: 470 184
Fax: 93 01 62 49

58 rooms, 7 suites
CC: AE, D, V
Open April through October.

Location: between Nice and Monte-Carlo, at the tip of the Cap-Ferrat peninsula.

This hotel built its reputation by catering to the aristocrats of the Belle Epoque who flocked here in the winter season. Though today's guests are more interested in swimming than strolling, the ambience is still the same.

A four-story white-stone building spreads its wings from a central rotunda. Every room is spacious and stylish, and all have big marble bathrooms. A vast lawn, landscaped with flowerbeds and emperor palms, slopes gently down to the edge of a cliff, where a funicular takes guests down to the Club Dauphin and a large terrace with heated saltwater pool on the rock face, one edge spilling over into the sea for a truly spectacular effect.

The **Club Dauphin** features a lavish 190 F buffet, or the elegant cooking of Jean-Claude Guillon: *salade de volaille exotique*—sliced breast of chicken with mango and avocado; broiled prawns in butter flavored with pastis; or just a *sandwich gourmand*, bursting at the seams with smoked salmon, lobster, and shrimps.

The hotel restaurant is a big salon looking out to sea, a place where a white silk jacket would not be taken amiss. Many dishes have a regional flavor, such as *soupe de légumes de Nice au pistou*—pesto-flavored vegetable soup, or a warm salad of red mullet fillets with *ailloli*. But the chef is inventive, too: poached sea bass with grapes, and breast of Barbary duck enhanced by a tangy sour cherry sauce.

There are many fine regional wines, priced just over 100 F: dry white Cassis La Ferme Blanche, and red and white Côtes de Provence.

RATINGS: beauty 5, comfort 5, service 5, restaurant 4.

Pool, tennis. 18 rooms with half-balconies, 7 with full balconies.

111

$ $ $

A A A A

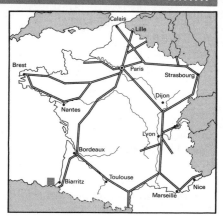

Grand Hôtel

43 boulevard Thiers
64500 St-Jean-de-Luz
Tel: 59 26 12 32
Telex: 571 487

50 rooms, 3 suites
CC: AE, D, V
Closed January, February,
first three weeks in March.
Restaurant closed Sunday evening
and all Monday.

Location: 15 km south-west of Biarritz. On the
beach, just past the casino.

From the street, it looks rather staid. But from the beach, you see a stately Belle Epoque building, the nicest hotel in the row.

Upstairs, there's a charming, airy café and breakfast room, with a full view of the sea. Room comfort borders on top luxury. But the most pleasant surprise is the beautiful, high-ceilinged dining room in a bay-windowed rotunda. Its panoramic view of the bay and the hills beyond is only part of its attraction, for the chef, Patrick Michelon, is among the most talented and versatile along the whole Atlantic Coast. He makes the most of local ingredients, adding Basque flair to classic cuisine. The *frito de poularde aux truffes, fricassée de rognons et crêtes de coq* is out of this world, even if an analysis of the components might make you hesitate (chicken wings, truffles, white kidneys and cocks' combs). Try also the squab: one thigh served in a nettle cream sauce with garlic, the other with sweetbreads and an endive and foie gras salad.

The highest-price menu at 220 F could include two such courses, followed by a warm gratin of wild strawberries with orange butter.

The local cheese, Belloq, is made from ewe's milk and has a mild, nutty flavor and a firm texture.

Sample the interesting local white Pacheranc du Vin-Bilh, but be sure to specify dry or semi. There are several regional reds, which pale in comparison with my favorite, ruby-red 1983 or 1985 Madiran, Domaine de Bouscasse.

RATINGS: beauty 4, comfort 4, service 4, restaurant 5.

Pool, beach. Most rooms with full or half-balcony. Public parking.

$ $

A A A

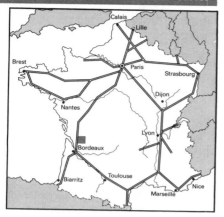

Relais du Bois St-Georges

rue de Royan
17100 Saintes
Tel: 46 93 50 99
Telex: 790 488

30 rooms, 2 suites
CC: V
Open all year.

Location: exit Saintes from the A10. Follow the signs for Royan; you'll see a small sign for Relais St-Georges where the road forks.

Just a few minutes from the *autoroute*, a 21st-century hotel in a little microcosm, complete with swan lake, duck pond, and 11th-century keep. The castle remnant forms a stone cloister on one side, while sliding glass walls opposite give access to a large terrace. This dramatic restaurant setting connects with the indoor pool and sun terrace.

The rooms themselves are amazing, each with a completely different personality. A narrow, thickly carpeted spiral staircase led to my room in a tower. On the first level was a lavish, circular black-tiled bathroom. The next flight of steps ended in a burst of sunlight from the balcony door opposite the bedroom. The loft above it had transomed windows and beamed ceiling. The other rooms are just as original—the receptionist will show you a picture album so you can choose according to your wildest fantasy. Whichever you take, it will offer a luxurious standard of comfort, and a lot of fun, for a price starting at 390 F.

Stay on the lighter side of the menu at the restaurant with broiled sea bass, or *tournedos flambé fine Cognac*.

The featured Bordeaux wines are Graves and Pomerol.

RATINGS: beauty 4, comfort 5, service 3, restaurant 3.
Park, indoor pool; tennis nearby. All rooms with balcony.

113

$ $ $ $

*   A A

Mas de la Fouque

Route d'Aigues-Mortes
13460 Stes-Maries-de-la-Mer
Tel: 90 47 81 02
Telex: 403 155

12 rooms, 2 suites
CC: AE, D, M, V
Closed January to mid-March.
Restaurant closed Tuesday.

Location: from Arles take D570 towards Stes-Maries, then D38 until you see a sign for the hotel at the bottom of a private unpaved road.

This place is unique, providing an unforgettable view of the Camargue. Most of the rooms are set at the edge of the marsh, with terraces looking out over the water. The only sounds are the splashing of fish and sea birds. The rooms are all junior suites in size and arrangement, with the bathroom filling half the space, featuring a sunken tub big enough for two, where you can have a good soak and watch the wildlife doing the same outside. But beware, the prices are as spectacular as the environment—doubles start at 1,170 F.

The pretty restaurant's high point is leg of lamb broiled over a charcoal grill (for a minimum of two people). The charcoal-broiled chicken might not be for all tastes, as it's been dipped in honey. A fish course, *gigot de mer*, is nicely firm but bland monkfish served with a very subtle *ailloli*, almost bereft of garlic. Number one on the menu is delicate pink shrimp-fed *truite saumonée*, sliced thin and marinated in lime juice with coriander.

The house wine has a rich, full-bodied flavor and a lean price.

RATINGS: beauty 4, comfort 4, service 2, restaurant 2.

Pool, tennis. Private terraces.

$ $ $

A A A A

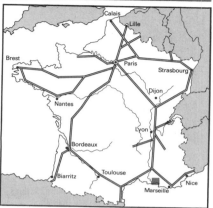

Abbaye de Sainte-Croix

Route du Val-de-Cuech
13300 Salon-de-Provence
Tel: 90 56 24 55
Telex: 401 247

19 rooms, 5 suites
CC: AE, CB, D, V
Open March to November.
Restaurant closed Monday lunch.

Location: on the heights overlooking Salon. Exit A7 at Salon Nord, head for the center of town, but watch for the small hotel sign to turn left and continue up the hill.

Too often considered just a stopover on the way to the south, this ancient abbey is well worth a longer stay. The tiny villages in the hills to the north and east are lovely to explore, as are the abbey's immediate surroundings. On the bluffs above the property, you can see dwelling cairns made by hermits in the 9th century or even earlier. The abbey's 3-foot-thick walls were erected in the 12th century.

Stone walls and ancient cells may not sound like luxury, but the only thing I found lacking was a robe in the bathroom. The prices, starting at 570F, are reasonable, especially considering the 20% reduction with *More France for the $*.

Chef Yves Souret shows flair and originality, even in regionally inspired dishes such as a salad of warmed lamb's tongue *confit* in a vinaigrette with honey. His *filets de rouget à la vanille et au citron vert*—red mullet fillets in vanilla and lime sauce—seem like a throwback to *nouvelle cuisine*, but there is no getting away from the wonderful blending of three delicate flavors. Equally inventive, his *blanc de poulette farci à l'oseille et foie gras*—breast of young chicken stuffed with sorrel and goose liver, in a chervil, spinach and tarragon mayonnaise. A strawberry *feuilleté* in a red fruit *coulis* tops everything.

Fine selection of regional wines. Red Côtes de Provence Château de Calisanne is light, and a nice companion for a slighty spicy and piquant Grenoillant goat cheese.

RATINGS: beauty 5, comfort 4, service 4, restaurant 4.

Pool. Tennis club very close, and riding nearby. Panoramic views.

$ $ $

*   A A A A

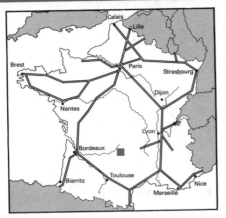

Château de la Treyne

Lacave
46200 Souillac
Tel: 65 32 66 66
Telex: 531427

14 rooms, 2 suites
CC: AE, M, V
Open Easter to 31 December.

Location: between Brive and Cahors, on the banks of the Dordogne. Take N20 as far as the small D43, 5 km south of Souillac. Follow directions for Lacave. The entrance is clearly marked.

This is the most perfect of all the châteaux I have ever seen, a gem so meticulously restored, so beautifully placed, that no visitor can ever forget it. It is lovingly tended by Mme. Michèle Gombert-Devals.

The interior is most remarkable for its exquisitely furnished Louis XIII drawing room. The bedrooms are individually decorated with period pieces from the same era—four-poster beds, oriental carpets, antiques worthy of a museum. Whether you take breakfast outside under an ancient cedar, on the terrace near the river, or in your room, it will be brought on a silver tray with elegant silver pitchers and fine porcelain.

A brilliant chef is charge of the kitchen. His specialties include a truffle *feuilleté* baked in ashes; salmon marinated with juniper berries; and a *feuilleté* of Cabécou goat cheese (from nearby Rocamadour) gently laced with aged plum brandy. Hot raspberry soufflé, or a made-in-heaven chocolate *marquise* with pistachio sauce, followed by coffee and an after-dinner drink in the drawing room by the fire, to the strains of live music, add the perfect ending to the perfect day.

Luncheon guests are invited to use the pool, tennis court and changing facilities. 250F added to the price of the room covers dinner and breakfast.

RATINGS: beauty 5, comfort 5, service 4, restaurant 5.

Pool, tennis, sauna, fishing. Hunting in season. Riding nearby.

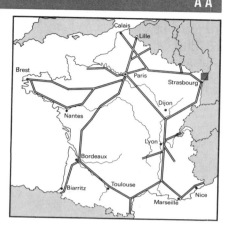

Hôtel Monopole-Métropole
16 rue Kuhn

67000 Strasbourg
Tel: 88 32 11 94
Telex: 890 366

94 rooms
CC: AE, CB, D, M, V
Closed Christmas through New Year's
Day.

Location: in a quiet neighborhood, near the railway
station.

Built in 1890 and in the very personal hands of the Siegel family since 1919. The staff is warm and friendly, the rooms simple, clean, and mostly furnished with Alsatian antiques. TV, radio and minibar are in each room. It is just a notch short of rating AAA for comfort, and a notch up on value, with the minimum price for a double well under 400 F.

The bathrooms are fairly large and feature a robe for each guest (rare in this price-category). Main floor public rooms are paneled in dark oak or mahogany. There is a cozy bar. And at the time of my visit, an indoor pool, jacuzzi, sauna, and fitness room were under construction.

Breakfast is a choice of room-service continental, or an eat-all-you-want Alsatian buffet.

Bicycles for rent. Garage parking. Short stroll to most attractions.

$ $ $ $

A A A A

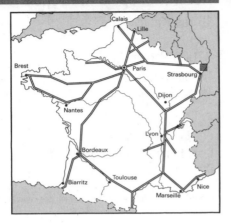

Le Valentin Sorg

6 place de l'Homme de Fer
67000 Strasbourg
Tel: 88 32 12 16 / 88 32 02 36

CC: AE, D, Eu, V
Closed Sunday evening and Tuesday,
and the last two weeks of August
and February.

Location: on the 14th floor of a building in the
center of town.

Strasbourg's oldest restaurant, founded in 1852, happens to be on the top floor of a highrise. Its original home was on the other side of the square, but was destroyed during World War II. The new location offers a great view of the city.

The menu is covered with reproductions of signatures of famous guests: Edward, Duke of Windsor; Umberto, King of Italy; Le Corbusier; Fernandel; Jean Marais... But inside the menu, the most famous name is that of an epicurean hero of Alsatian fairy tales, Fritz Kobus, bestowed by Valentin Sorg on a dish of warm goose liver and apples. Goose and duck liver are also made into truffled terrines. Then two other famous names:

Demidoff, as in *grenadins de ris de veau Demidoff*; and Rossini, of tournedos fame. Less exalted in name, if not in taste, are lamb chops with *herbes de Provence*, duckling with fruit sauce, and *fondant de volaille sauce ivoire*—breast of chicken in a creamy sauce. The menu changes with the seasons, and while the famous names remain, some unusual specialties crop up periodically. One that arouses my curiosity is a savory flan of frogs legs and green cabbage!

For dessert, try the kirsch pancakes, which have been on the menu since the Valentin Sorg was founded. Munster with caraway seeds is an Alsatian after-dinner tradition, "for the digestion."

Panoramic views in a restaurant fit for a king.

$ $

A A A

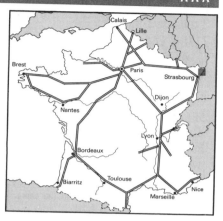

Maison Kammerzell

16 place de la Cathédrale
67000 Strasbourg
Tel: 88 32 42 14

CC: AE, D, Eu, V
Closed February.

Location: across the square from the cathedral.

There is no other place like it in all of France, a towering gingerbread house, narrow on the bottom and wide in the middle, with dormer-studded steep-pitched roof and 75 stained-glass windows. The three upper floors, added in 1589 and made of wood, project over a ground floor entirely of stone, erected in 1427 on four arches.

A winding staircase leads to dining rooms on the upper floors. The ground floor has more of a *gasthaus* atmosphere and features murals by Alsatian painter Leo Schnug, depicting scenes from the 15th century.

Recently taken over by master chef Guy-Pierre Baumann, Maison Kammerzell is just about the best restaurant in town. You can eat à la carte, or choose one of 18 fixed-price menus which start at 160F and inch their way up to 380F. Because there is such a wide range of menus, and because the same courses appear on the à la carte list, the menus seem the better choice. Consider that for 160F you get a *feuilleté* of snails in garlic butter, a *coq au vin* made with Alsace riesling, and ice milk with a thick red fruit sauce. The 170F menu features a formidable Alsatian specialty, the *baeckenofe,* a casserole of alternating layers of mutton, beef and pork marinated in Alsace wine, with slices of potatoes and onions. The 180F menu includes a *salade gourmande* which lives up to its name, and *choucroute aux poissons*, blending rascasse, salmon and smoked haddock with the tangy taste of aromatic sauerkraut.

An ancient tourist attraction specializing in great food.

119

$ $

AAA

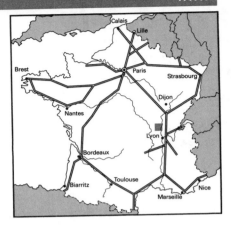

Le Rempart

2 avenue Gambetta
71700 Tournus
Tel: 85 51 10 56
Telex: 351 019

28 rooms, 10 suites
CC: AE, D, M, V
Open all year.

Location: on the A6 between Lyon and Beaune. The hotel is on the main road in the center of town.

The hotel was a coaching station in the 19th century, built around a 12th-century cloister—the medieval stone fountain can still be seen in the restaurant. The public areas have lots of atmosphere; the rooms are modern, bright, and inviting, with TV, radio, minibar, and roomy bathrooms, robes included.

Daniel Rogé's cooking is acclaimed. The 138 F menu offers a terrine of duck liver and mushrooms, broiled entrecôte with béarnaise sauce, cheese, and dessert, for the price of the steak alone at most places as good as this. The 215 F menu is even greater value, featuring a salad of langoustines with a saffron vinaigrette, an escalope of salmon in parsley cream, and a broiled lamb steak, followed by cheese, dessert, and petits fours.

A la carte treats that struck me favorably were *émincé de canard en salade, vinaigrette tiède à l'orange* (a salad of thinly sliced duck with an orange vinaigrette), steamed rock lobster tails in Burgundy sauce, a *millefeuille* of salmon with shellfish sauce, and just in case you would drive through Burgundy without tasting snails in their most classic style: *douze escargots de Bourgogne en coquille.*

The wine list has 351 vintages; the house wine is Mâcon blanc, a full-bodied classic dry white with only a hint of fruitiness and no tartness.

RATINGS: beauty 4, comfort 3, service 3, restaurant 4.

Some rooms with park view.

$ $

AAA

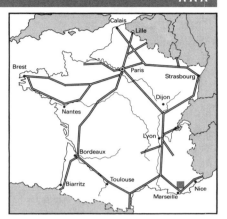

La Bastide de Tourtour

83690 Tourtour
Tel: 94 70 57 30
Telex: 970 827

25 rooms
CC: AE, D, M, V
Open March to November.
Restaurant closed Monday and lunch
Tuesday before May and during October.

Location: leave the A8 at Le Muy and drive towards
Salernes. After Flayosac, you'll see a well-marked
right turn up a small road for Tourtour.

Though it was built only two decades ago, this heavy stone bastion is evocative of ancient times. Some come here for the view, reaching as far as St-Raphaël on the coast; others for the solar-heated swimming pool, the tennis courts, the attractions of Tourtour village... The region's best restaurant under Hervé Guérin is an additional incentive for wending one's way up that fragrant, pine-scented hill.

Room comfort is largely a matter of size. Smaller rooms, at 400 F, offer pretty décor and almost minimal comfort, while the bigger rooms, at more than 500 F for two, are quite luxurious.

The cooking is stamped with lightness. *Raviolis de fromage de chèvre frais*—thin pasta dough, filled with fresh goat's cheese flavored with basil, in cream sauce; *grillade de saint-pierre*—mustard seeds sprinkled over delicate fillets of John Dory, served with a red pepper *coulis*; or roast leg of lamb previously marinated in olive oil and rosemary.

There's also roast duck breast in a wild cherry sauce laced with red wine, and regional fare like *goujonnettes de sole au pistou*—small strips of sole with the Provençal version of pesto: garlic, basil, and cheese pounded with olive oil. The *filet de bœuf poêlé, sauce à la cuvée des Abeillons de Tourtour* deserves acclaim: tender, perfectly broiled prime steak with a spicy, aromatic wine sauce.

An in-between course triumph is a sherbet made with rosemary-flavored vodka.

RATINGS: beauty 4, comfort 3, service 3, restaurant 4.

Pool, tennis, jacuzzi. 10 rooms with balcony. Panoramic views.

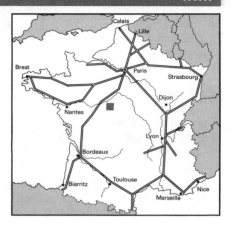

Hôtel d'Espagne

9 rue du Château
36600 Valençay
Tel: 54 00 00 02
Telex: 751 675

10 rooms, 6 suites
CC: AE, Eu, M, V
Closed January and February. Restaurant closed every Sunday evening and Monday, and all November and December.

Location: halfway between Blois and Châteauroux on D956. The hotel is almost next door to the Château de Valençay.

During the Napoleonic Wars, the Prince of Spain spent six years in exile in the Château de Valençay, while his staff had to be content with rooms at the inn. The prince left no mark on the château, but the inn never got over the panache brought by the Spanish courtiers. The Fourré family bought it in 1875 and changed its name to Hôtel d'Espagne. When you arrive by car, you follow the same route as the old stagecoaches, through an archway into a courtyard street, its old walls covered with Virginia creeper.

The rooms are neither grand nor luxurious, but offer above-average roominess and comfort, many with a sofa, all with robes in the bathroom, and a flowered balcony or terrace.

The cozy restaurant is hung with deer antlers, and decorated in maroon and gold stripes. The cooking is not devoid of inspiration: foie gras with white grapes in a red wine sauce, quail in madeira, or freshwater fish in a thick sauce made with red Chinon wine.

Local wines are the Reuilly Valençay, a dry and fragrant white made from the Sauvignon grape, and the much less full-bodied but pleasant, red Reuilly Pinot Noir.

RATINGS: beauty 4, comfort 3, service 3, restaurant 4.

In the heart of château country. All rooms with balcony.

Château Saint-Martin

Route de Coursegoules
06140 Vence
Tel: 93 58 02 02
Telex: 470 282

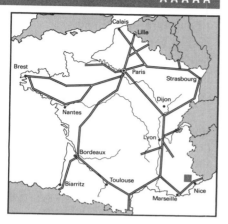

15 rooms, 10 suites
CC: AE, CG, Eu
Open mid-March to mid-November.

Location: exit A8 at Cagnes and follow signs for St-Paul and Vence. Bypass Vence "centre ville" and take D2 direction Coursegoules for 2.5 km.

The rolling hills of Vence have a rare luminescence you could never suspect youre just passing by on the *autoroute*. At an altitude of 1,650 feet, surrounded by steep hills scented by pine and myrtle, the Château St-Martin occupies a site chosen by the Knights Templar for their castle in the 12th century. Today, only one tower and a drawbridge remain of the fortress.

The main building of the present hotel was erected in 1935 in palatial style, complete with marble floors, high ceilings and tall windows to take in a view spanning 60 miles of coastline from Menton to St-Raphael. The suites, Provençal cottages scattered around the 6-acre estate, have enormous terraces.

The restaurant, in a glass-enclosed pavilion attached to the main building, has an aura of informal charm, though prices are high—300 F for a three-course menu. This is one of the last bastions of *nouvelle cuisine*. The current vogue for regional cooking doesn't seem to bother Château St-Martin's chef, Dominique Ferrière, and there's no reason why it should. Just try his *poulet de Bresse sauté au vinaigre de framboises*—sautéed Bresse chicken in a raspberry vinegar sauce. Though nothing speaks more eloquently of Ferrières' talent than *canette de Challans rôtie aux airelles*—roast duck with a surprising combination of piquant green peppers and sharp red cranberries in a triumphant harmony of color and flavor.

The small list of heady desserts is topped by plum and Armagnac ice cream.

RATINGS: beauty 5, comfort 5, service 5, restaurant 5.
Pool, tennis. Golf nearby. Most rooms with balcony.

$ $ $

A A A A

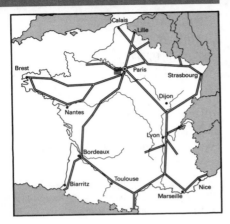

Trianon Palace

**1 boulevard de la Reine
78000 Versailles**
Tel: 39 50 34 12
Telex: 698 863
Fax: 39 49 00 77

108 rooms, 12 suites
CC: all
Open all year.

Location: 21 km from Paris via Porte de St-Cloud.
On the boulevard leading to the Trianons.

It's a special treat to stay in a palace when you're visiting one. This hotel has its own 8 acres of grounds, right next door to the vast park of Versailles. You might think this hotel-palace with its dormer windows dates back to the same century as the neighboring villas and royal châteaux, but in fact it was built in 1911. Its claim to fame is that Clemenceau, Lloyd-George and Wilson stayed here when they came to sign the Treaty of Versailles—a commemorative plaque now adorns the wall of the Salon Clemenceau.

Upstairs, the rooms could not exactly be described as palatial, but most people seem to prefer it that way. They do have a lot of character: high ceilings, French doors, huge white-tiled bathrooms. The fifth floor, which must have been intended for the guests' personal servants, is more modest, but you can save from 200 to 300 F for the small sacrifice.

In the restaurant, the service is somewhat perfunctory, but the food itself is very good. And why quibble that "pastry" becomes "patty" on the menu, when this *feuilleté* of frog legs and asparagus tastes so wonderful? Another plus is the light ravioli filled with squid, served with squash and wild mushrooms. Squab simmered with sweetbreads in Cahors wine is worthy of attention. As is moorhen in truffle sauce. The *pétale* of dark chocolate with Grand Marnier makes a happy ending. Many fine half-bottles of wine in the 50 F range.

RATINGS: beauty 5, comfort 4, service 4, restaurant 4.

22 rooms with balcony. Free use of bicycles. Park.

$ $ $ $

AAAAA

Les Trois Marches

3 rue Colbert
78002 Versailles
Tel: 39 50 13 21

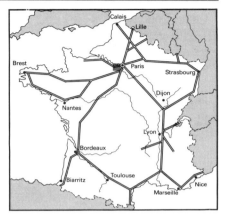

CC: AE, D, Eu, V
Closed Sunday and Monday,
and the first two weeks in February.

Location: 21 km from Paris via Porte de St-Cloud.
Or a 20-min train ride from Paris Gare St-Lazare.
On the square in front of the Château de Versailles.

A unique restaurant in an 18th-century villa overlooking the palace. Beautiful paintings bedeck the walls, and the clientele is dressy. But the setting pales in comparison to Chef Gérard Vié's cooking. Everything is unexpected. His cassolette of mushrooms and snails is served in a *fondue* of ham and sausage. His shellfish with ginger, tomatoes and olive oil. A warm *méli-mélo* of salmon in caviar butter. An astonishing turbot with boletus mushrooms and potatoes.

The baby leg of lamb baked in its own juice is about the size of a turkey drumstick and couldn't be more succulent. The duckling, braised with cider vinegar and honey, is served in two parts: the wings and breast with a purée of root vegetables; the thighs *confites en salade* with apples and pepper.

From the excellent selection of cheeses, I recommend the Pouligny-saint-pierre, and the Epoisses. The wine list is grand and more than reasonably priced. For example, grand cru Chablis for around 150 F. There is a selection of Bordeaux for 90 F, and other good wines for around 80 F. Cuvée Gérard Vié—60 F.

It would be worth coming here for the desserts alone—*mousse au chocolat et raisins parfumés au curaçao*; *soupe chaude de cassis à la poire*. Or a grande finale worthy of the Sun King, the *chariot de glaces et de sorbets*, topped with gold spun-sugar angel's hair.

As awe-inspiring as the palace it overlooks.

125

$ $

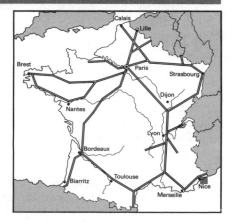

Hôtel Welcome

1 quai Colbert
06230 Villefranche-sur-Mer
Tel: 93 76 76 93
Telex: 470 281

32 rooms
CC: AE, D, Eu, M, V
Closed 20 November to 20 December.

Location: the first town on the bottom Corniche from Nice. Follow the road down to the waterfront and the municipal parking area; the hotel is just beside it.

This demure, family-owned hotel still has the charm that made Cocteau refer to it as "my dear little Hôtel Welcome." It's blessed by its romantic setting in front of Villefranche harbor. The chapel Cocteau painted, Chapelle St-Pierre, is just across the road.

The hotel he liked so much is still a modest place with functional rooms—almost all with a little balcony—and lovely views.

The **Restaurant St-Pierre** can be reached either by hotel elevator, or, more pleasantly, through its street-level doors fronting the quay. Try to get a table with a good view of the harbor. The menu, decorated with Cocteau's drawings, is an impressive affair. About half the à la carte main courses are priced over 150 F; the *menu prestige* is 295 F, featuring entrées like *la gourmande de foie gras de canard*, followed by *suprême* of John Dory in sorrel sauce, a lime and vodka sherbet, and a choice of meat courses; *filet mignon* with morels, fillet of lamb with courgettes, or fillets of duck breast with foie gras. In spite of these ambitious courses, I was told that the average price for dinner, with wine, is around 200 F per person.

A very fine selection of cheeses is only 32 F, and there's a good list of regional wines.

RATINGS: beauty 4, comfort 3, service 3, restaurant 3.

28 rooms with balcony. Private parking.

COUPONS

Note: For ease of removal, coupons should be folded vertically before being torn from the book.

Hôtel Argi-Eder
AÏNHOA
is pleased to offer

Complimentary bottle of wine
or a champagne cocktail for each guest

Valid with any room

Hôtel Argi-Eder
AÏNHOA
is pleased to offer

Complimentary bottle of wine

Valid for two guests ordering together

La Réserve
ALBI
is pleased to offer

Complimentary bottle of wine

Valid with any room

BERLITZ

This coupon is valid for the gift, complimentary offer or discount described on the reverse side. It must be presented in conjunction with the book *More France for the $*, as described in the preface on page 9. Although the author and Berlitz Guides can take no responsibility for the receipt of the benefits indicated, the publisher would greatly appreciate your communicating any difficulties encountered. Berlitz Guides intends to review and update this book regularly. No expiry date limits this coupon.

La direction de l'établissement s'engage à faire bénéficier le porteur de ce coupon des prestations mentionnées en anglais au recto, suite à l'accord pris avec l'auteur du livre *More France for the $*, M. Alan Austin. En cas de doute, veuillez vous référer au directeur de votre hôtel/restaurant.

BERLITZ

This coupon is valid for the gift, complimentary offer or discount described on the reverse side. It must be presented in conjunction with the book *More France for the $*, as described in the preface on page 9. Although the author and Berlitz Guides can take no responsibility for the receipt of the benefits indicated, the publisher would greatly appreciate your communicating any difficulties encountered. Berlitz Guides intends to review and update this book regularly. No expiry date limits this coupon.

La direction de l'établissement s'engage à faire bénéficier le porteur de ce coupon des prestations mentionnées en anglais au recto, suite à l'accord pris avec l'auteur du livre *More France for the $*, M. Alan Austin. En cas de doute, veuillez vous référer au directeur de votre hôtel/restaurant.

BERLITZ

This coupon is valid for the gift, complimentary offer or discount described on the reverse side. It must be presented in conjunction with the book *More France for the $*, as described in the preface on page 9. Although the author and Berlitz Guides can take no responsibility for the receipt of the benefits indicated, the publisher would greatly appreciate your communicating any difficulties encountered. Berlitz Guides intends to review and update this book regularly. No expiry date limits this coupon.

La direction de l'établissement s'engage à faire bénéficier le porteur de ce coupon des prestations mentionnées en anglais au recto, suite à l'accord pris avec l'auteur du livre *More France for the $*, M. Alan Austin. En cas de doute, veuillez vous référer au directeur de votre hôtel/restaurant.

La Réserve
ALBI
is pleased to offer

Complimentary bottle of wine

Valid when two meals are ordered. If a different vintage is desired, the price of the offered wine will be deducted.

Hostellerie St-Antoine
ALBI
is pleased to offer

50% reduction in room rates

Valid for two nights after two nights at the regular price

Hostellerie St-Antoine
ALBI
is pleased to offer

Complimentary bottle of wine

Valid when two meals are ordered. If a different vintage is desired, the price of the offered wine will be deducted.

BERLITZ

This coupon is valid for the gift, complimentary offer or discount described on the reverse side. It must be presented in conjunction with the book *More France for the $*, as described in the preface on page 9. Although the author and Berlitz Guides can take no responsibility for the receipt of the benefits indicated, the publisher would greatly appreciate your communicating any difficulties encountered. Berlitz Guides intends to review and update this book regularly. No expiry date limits this coupon.

La direction de l'établissement s'engage à faire bénéficier le porteur de ce coupon des prestations mentionnées en anglais au recto, suite à l'accord pris avec l'auteur du livre *More France for the $*, M. Alan Austin. En cas de doute, veuillez vous référer au directeur de votre hôtel/restaurant.

BERLITZ

This coupon is valid for the gift, complimentary offer or discount described on the reverse side. It must be presented in conjunction with the book *More France for the $*, as described in the preface on page 9. Although the author and Berlitz Guides can take no responsibility for the receipt of the benefits indicated, the publisher would greatly appreciate your communicating any difficulties encountered. Berlitz Guides intends to review and update this book regularly. No expiry date limits this coupon.

La direction de l'établissement s'engage à faire bénéficier le porteur de ce coupon des prestations mentionnées en anglais au recto, suite à l'accord pris avec l'auteur du livre *More France for the $*, M. Alan Austin. En cas de doute, veuillez vous référer au directeur de votre hôtel/restaurant.

BERLITZ

This coupon is valid for the gift, complimentary offer or discount described on the reverse side. It must be presented in conjunction with the book *More France for the $*, as described in the preface on page 9. Although the author and Berlitz Guides can take no responsibility for the receipt of the benefits indicated, the publisher would greatly appreciate your communicating any difficulties encountered. Berlitz Guides intends to review and update this book regularly. No expiry date limits this coupon.

La direction de l'établissement s'engage à faire bénéficier le porteur de ce coupon des prestations mentionnées en anglais au recto, suite à l'accord pris avec l'auteur du livre *More France for the $*, M. Alan Austin. En cas de doute, veuillez vous référer au directeur de votre hôtel/restaurant.

L'Abbaye
ANNECY-LE-VIEUX

is pleased to offer

Room upgrading at no extra cost

Valid for a superior room for the price of a standard room,
if available at time of arrival. If upgrading is not possible,
a bottle of champagne in the room.

L'Abbaye
ANNECY-LE-VIEUX

is pleased to offer

Complimentary cocktail and appetizer

Valid for all at the table

Auberge La Fenière
RAPHÈLE-LÈS-ARLES

is pleased to offer

Complimentary bottle of wine

Valid with any room

BERLITZ®

This coupon is valid for the gift, complimentary offer or discount described on the reverse side. It must be presented in conjunction with the book *More France for the $,* as described in the preface on page 9. Although the author and Berlitz Guides can take no responsibility for the receipt of the benefits indicated, the publisher would greatly appreciate your communicating any difficulties encountered. Berlitz Guides intends to review and update this book regularly. No expiry date limits this coupon.

La direction de l'établissement s'engage à faire bénéficier le porteur de ce coupon des prestations mentionnées en anglais au recto, suite à l'accord pris avec l'auteur du livre *More France for the $,* M. Alan Austin. En cas de doute, veuillez vous référer au directeur de votre hôtel/restaurant.

BERLITZ®

This coupon is valid for the gift, complimentary offer or discount described on the reverse side. It must be presented in conjunction with the book *More France for the $,* as described in the preface on page 9. Although the author and Berlitz Guides can take no responsibility for the receipt of the benefits indicated, the publisher would greatly appreciate your communicating any difficulties encountered. Berlitz Guides intends to review and update this book regularly. No expiry date limits this coupon.

La direction de l'établissement s'engage à faire bénéficier le porteur de ce coupon des prestations mentionnées en anglais au recto, suite à l'accord pris avec l'auteur du livre *More France for the $,* M. Alan Austin. En cas de doute, veuillez vous référer au directeur de votre hôtel/restaurant.

BERLITZ®

This coupon is valid for the gift, complimentary offer or discount described on the reverse side. It must be presented in conjunction with the book *More France for the $,* as described in the preface on page 9. Although the author and Berlitz Guides can take no responsibility for the receipt of the benefits indicated, the publisher would greatly appreciate your communicating any difficulties encountered. Berlitz Guides intends to review and update this book regularly. No expiry date limits this coupon.

La direction de l'établissement s'engage à faire bénéficier le porteur de ce coupon des prestations mentionnées en anglais au recto, suite à l'accord pris avec l'auteur du livre *More France for the $,* M. Alan Austin. En cas de doute, veuillez vous référer au directeur de votre hôtel/restaurant.

Auberge La Fenière
RAPHÈLE-LÈS-ARLES
is pleased to offer

10% reduction on food and drink

Valid for any meal

Hôtel Mireille
ARLES
is pleased to offer

50% reduction in room rates, plus flowers and chocolates

Valid 1 November to 15 March

Hôtel Mireille
ARLES
is pleased to offer

25% reduction in room rates, plus flowers and chocolates

Valid 16 March to 31 October

BERLITZ

This coupon is valid for the gift, complimentary offer or discount described on the reverse side. It must be presented in conjunction with the book *More France for the $,* as described in the preface on page 9. Although the author and Berlitz Guides can take no responsibility for the receipt of the benefits indicated, the publisher would greatly appreciate your communicating any difficulties encountered. Berlitz Guides intends to review and update this book regularly. No expiry date limits this coupon.

La direction de l'établissement s'engage à faire bénéficier le porteur de ce coupon des prestations mentionnées en anglais au recto, suite à l'accord pris avec l'auteur du livre *More France for the $,* M. Alan Austin. En cas de doute, veuillez vous référer au directeur de votre hôtel/restaurant.

BERLITZ

This coupon is valid for the gift, complimentary offer or discount described on the reverse side. It must be presented in conjunction with the book *More France for the $,* as described in the preface on page 9. Although the author and Berlitz Guides can take no responsibility for the receipt of the benefits indicated, the publisher would greatly appreciate your communicating any difficulties encountered. Berlitz Guides intends to review and update this book regularly. No expiry date limits this coupon.

La direction de l'établissement s'engage à faire bénéficier le porteur de ce coupon des prestations mentionnées en anglais au recto, suite à l'accord pris avec l'auteur du livre *More France for the $,* M. Alan Austin. En cas de doute, veuillez vous référer au directeur de votre hôtel/restaurant.

BERLITZ

This coupon is valid for the gift, complimentary offer or discount described on the reverse side. It must be presented in conjunction with the book *More France for the $,* as described in the preface on page 9. Although the author and Berlitz Guides can take no responsibility for the receipt of the benefits indicated, the publisher would greatly appreciate your communicating any difficulties encountered. Berlitz Guides intends to review and update this book regularly. No expiry date limits this coupon.

La direction de l'établissement s'engage à faire bénéficier le porteur de ce coupon des prestations mentionnées en anglais au recto, suite à l'accord pris avec l'auteur du livre *More France for the $,* M. Alan Austin. En cas de doute, veuillez vous référer au directeur de votre hôtel/restaurant.

La Provence
ARLES
is pleased to offer

Complimentary bottle of wine

Valid when two meals are ordered. If a different vintage is desired,
the price of the offered wine will be deducted.

Hôtel Atrium
ARLES
is pleased to offer

30% reduction in room rates

Valid 15 November to 15 March

Hôtel Atrium
ARLES
is pleased to offer

Complimentary bottle of wine

Valid with any room

BERLITZ

This coupon is valid for the gift, complimentary offer or discount described on the reverse side. It must be presented in conjunction with the book *More France for the $,* as described in the preface on page 9. Although the author and Berlitz Guides can take no responsibility for the receipt of the benefits indicated, the publisher would greatly appreciate your communicating any difficulties encountered. Berlitz Guides intends to review and update this book regularly. No expiry date limits this coupon.

La direction de l'établissement s'engage à faire bénéficier le porteur de ce coupon des prestations mentionnées en anglais au recto, suite à l'accord pris avec l'auteur du livre *More France for the $,* M. Alan Austin. En cas de doute, veuillez vous référer au directeur de votre hôtel/restaurant.

BERLITZ

This coupon is valid for the gift, complimentary offer or discount described on the reverse side. It must be presented in conjunction with the book *More France for the $,* as described in the preface on page 9. Although the author and Berlitz Guides can take no responsibility for the receipt of the benefits indicated, the publisher would greatly appreciate your communicating any difficulties encountered. Berlitz Guides intends to review and update this book regularly. No expiry date limits this coupon.

La direction de l'établissement s'engage à faire bénéficier le porteur de ce coupon des prestations mentionnées en anglais au recto, suite à l'accord pris avec l'auteur du livre *More France for the $,* M. Alan Austin. En cas de doute, veuillez vous référer au directeur de votre hôtel/restaurant.

BERLITZ

This coupon is valid for the gift, complimentary offer or discount described on the reverse side. It must be presented in conjunction with the book *More France for the $,* as described in the preface on page 9. Although the author and Berlitz Guides can take no responsibility for the receipt of the benefits indicated, the publisher would greatly appreciate your communicating any difficulties encountered. Berlitz Guides intends to review and update this book regularly. No expiry date limits this coupon.

La direction de l'établissement s'engage à faire bénéficier le porteur de ce coupon des prestations mentionnées en anglais au recto, suite à l'accord pris avec l'auteur du livre *More France for the $,* M. Alan Austin. En cas de doute, veuillez vous référer au directeur de votre hôtel/restaurant.

Restaurant Lou Marquès
ARLES
is pleased to offer

Complimentary champagne cocktail

Valid for each guest when at least two meals are ordered

Hôtel de France
AUCH
is pleased to offer

50% reduction in room rates

Valid for each night after two nights at the regular price

Restaurant Daguin
AUCH
is pleased to offer

Complimentary bottle of Colombard wine

Valid when ordering any meal

 **BERLITZ®**

This coupon is valid for the gift, complimentary offer or discount described on the reverse side. It must be presented in conjunction with the book *More France for the $*, as described in the preface on page 9. Although the author and Berlitz Guides can take no responsibility for the receipt of the benefits indicated, the publisher would greatly appreciate your communicating any difficulties encountered. Berlitz Guides intends to review and update this book regularly. No expiry date limits this coupon.

La direction de l'établissement s'engage à faire bénéficier le porteur de ce coupon des prestations mentionnées en anglais au recto, suite à l'accord pris avec l'auteur du livre *More France for the $*, M. Alan Austin. En cas de doute, veuillez vous référer au directeur de votre hôtel/restaurant.

 BERLITZ®

This coupon is valid for the gift, complimentary offer or discount described on the reverse side. It must be presented in conjunction with the book *More France for the $*, as described in the preface on page 9. Although the author and Berlitz Guides can take no responsibility for the receipt of the benefits indicated, the publisher would greatly appreciate your communicating any difficulties encountered. Berlitz Guides intends to review and update this book regularly. No expiry date limits this coupon.

La direction de l'établissement s'engage à faire bénéficier le porteur de ce coupon des prestations mentionnées en anglais au recto, suite à l'accord pris avec l'auteur du livre *More France for the $*, M. Alan Austin. En cas de doute, veuillez vous référer au directeur de votre hôtel/restaurant.

 BERLITZ®

This coupon is valid for the gift, complimentary offer or discount described on the reverse side. It must be presented in conjunction with the book *More France for the $*, as described in the preface on page 9. Although the author and Berlitz Guides can take no responsibility for the receipt of the benefits indicated, the publisher would greatly appreciate your communicating any difficulties encountered. Berlitz Guides intends to review and update this book regularly. No expiry date limits this coupon.

La direction de l'établissement s'engage à faire bénéficier le porteur de ce coupon des prestations mentionnées en anglais au recto, suite à l'accord pris avec l'auteur du livre *More France for the $*, M. Alan Austin. En cas de doute, veuillez vous référer au directeur de votre hôtel/restaurant.

La Magnaneraie
VILLENEUVE-LÈS-AVIGNON
is pleased to offer

20% reduction in room rates

Valid 15 October to 1 April

La Magnaneraie
VILLENEUVE-LÈS-AVIGNON
is pleased to offer

Complimentary bottle of wine

Valid when two meals are ordered. If a different vintage is desired, the price of the offered wine will be deducted.

Auberge de France
AVIGNON
is pleased to offer

Complimentary champagne cocktail and appetizer

Valid for all at the table

BERLITZ

This coupon is valid for the gift, complimentary offer or discount described on the reverse side. It must be presented in conjunction with the book *More France for the $*, as described in the preface on page 9. Although the author and Berlitz Guides can take no responsibility for the receipt of the benefits indicated, the publisher would greatly appreciate your communicating any difficulties encountered. Berlitz Guides intends to review and update this book regularly. No expiry date limits this coupon.

La direction de l'établissement s'engage à faire bénéficier le porteur de ce coupon des prestations mentionnées en anglais au recto, suite à l'accord pris avec l'auteur du livre *More France for the $,* M. Alan Austin. En cas de doute, veuillez vous référer au directeur de votre hôtel/restaurant.

BERLITZ

This coupon is valid for the gift, complimentary offer or discount described on the reverse side. It must be presented in conjunction with the book *More France for the $*, as described in the preface on page 9. Although the author and Berlitz Guides can take no responsibility for the receipt of the benefits indicated, the publisher would greatly appreciate your communicating any difficulties encountered. Berlitz Guides intends to review and update this book regularly. No expiry date limits this coupon.

La direction de l'établissement s'engage à faire bénéficier le porteur de ce coupon des prestations mentionnées en anglais au recto, suite à l'accord pris avec l'auteur du livre *More France for the $,* M. Alan Austin. En cas de doute, veuillez vous référer au directeur de votre hôtel/restaurant.

BERLITZ

This coupon is valid for the gift, complimentary offer or discount described on the reverse side. It must be presented in conjunction with the book *More France for the $*, as described in the preface on page 9. Although the author and Berlitz Guides can take no responsibility for the receipt of the benefits indicated, the publisher would greatly appreciate your communicating any difficulties encountered. Berlitz Guides intends to review and update this book regularly. No expiry date limits this coupon.

La direction de l'établissement s'engage à faire bénéficier le porteur de ce coupon des prestations mentionnées en anglais au recto, suite à l'accord pris avec l'auteur du livre *More France for the $,* M. Alan Austin. En cas de doute, veuillez vous référer au directeur de votre hôtel/restaurant.

Le Grand Monarque
AZAY-LE-RIDEAU
is pleased to offer

10% reduction on room and all meals

Valid with a three-night stay or longer

Le Grand Monarque
AZAY-LE-RIDEAU
is pleased to offer

Complimentary bottle of wine

Valid for two guests ordering together. If a different vintage is desired, the price of the offered wine will be deducted.

Auberge du XIIᵉ Siècle
AZAY-LE-RIDEAU
is pleased to offer

Complimentary cocktail and appetizer

Valid for all at the table

 **BERLITZ**

This coupon is valid for the gift, complimentary offer or discount described on the reverse side. It must be presented in conjunction with the book *More France for the $*, as described in the preface on page 9. Although the author and Berlitz Guides can take no responsibility for the receipt of the benefits indicated, the publisher would greatly appreciate your communicating any difficulties encountered. Berlitz Guides intends to review and update this book regularly. No expiry date limits this coupon.

La direction de l'établissement s'engage à faire bénéficier le porteur de ce coupon des prestations mentionnées en anglais au recto, suite à l'accord pris avec l'auteur du livre *More France for the $*, M. Alan Austin. En cas de doute, veuillez vous référer au directeur de votre hôtel/restaurant.

 BERLITZ

This coupon is valid for the gift, complimentary offer or discount described on the reverse side. It must be presented in conjunction with the book *More France for the $*, as described in the preface on page 9. Although the author and Berlitz Guides can take no responsibility for the receipt of the benefits indicated, the publisher would greatly appreciate your communicating any difficulties encountered. Berlitz Guides intends to review and update this book regularly. No expiry date limits this coupon.

La direction de l'établissement s'engage à faire bénéficier le porteur de ce coupon des prestations mentionnées en anglais au recto, suite à l'accord pris avec l'auteur du livre *More France for the $*, M. Alan Austin. En cas de doute, veuillez vous référer au directeur de votre hôtel/restaurant.

 BERLITZ

This coupon is valid for the gift, complimentary offer or discount described on the reverse side. It must be presented in conjunction with the book *More France for the $*, as described in the preface on page 9. Although the author and Berlitz Guides can take no responsibility for the receipt of the benefits indicated, the publisher would greatly appreciate your communicating any difficulties encountered. Berlitz Guides intends to review and update this book regularly. No expiry date limits this coupon.

La direction de l'établissement s'engage à faire bénéficier le porteur de ce coupon des prestations mentionnées en anglais au recto, suite à l'accord pris avec l'auteur du livre *More France for the $*, M. Alan Austin. En cas de doute, veuillez vous référer au directeur de votre hôtel/restaurant.

Le Lion d'Or
BAYEUX
is pleased to offer

Complimentary house cocktail

Valid for all at the table

Hostellerie de Levernois
BEAUNE
is pleased to offer

20% reduction in room rates

Valid 1 November to 31 March, except Saturdays

Hostellerie de Lavernois
BEAUNE
is pleased to offer

Complimentary bottle
of crémant de Bourgogne

Valid with any room

 **BERLITZ**

This coupon is valid for the gift, complimentary offer or discount described on the reverse side. It must be presented in conjunction with the book *More France for the $,* as described in the preface on page 9. Although the author and Berlitz Guides can take no responsibility for the receipt of the benefits indicated, the publisher would greatly appreciate your communicating any difficulties encountered. Berlitz Guides intends to review and update this book regularly. No expiry date limits this coupon.

La direction de l'établissement s'engage à faire bénéficier le porteur de ce coupon des prestations mentionnées en anglais au recto, suite à l'accord pris avec l'auteur du livre *More France for the $,* M. Alan Austin. En cas de doute, veuillez vous référer au directeur de votre hôtel/restaurant.

 BERLITZ

This coupon is valid for the gift, complimentary offer or discount described on the reverse side. It must be presented in conjunction with the book *More France for the $,* as described in the preface on page 9. Although the author and Berlitz Guides can take no responsibility for the receipt of the benefits indicated, the publisher would greatly appreciate your communicating any difficulties encountered. Berlitz Guides intends to review and update this book regularly. No expiry date limits this coupon.

La direction de l'établissement s'engage à faire bénéficier le porteur de ce coupon des prestations mentionnées en anglais au recto, suite à l'accord pris avec l'auteur du livre *More France for the $,* M. Alan Austin. En cas de doute, veuillez vous référer au directeur de votre hôtel/restaurant.

 BERLITZ

This coupon is valid for the gift, complimentary offer or discount described on the reverse side. It must be presented in conjunction with the book *More France for the $,* as described in the preface on page 9. Although the author and Berlitz Guides can take no responsibility for the receipt of the benefits indicated, the publisher would greatly appreciate your communicating any difficulties encountered. Berlitz Guides intends to review and update this book regularly. No expiry date limits this coupon.

La direction de l'établissement s'engage à faire bénéficier le porteur de ce coupon des prestations mentionnées en anglais au recto, suite à l'accord pris avec l'auteur du livre *More France for the $,* M. Alan Austin. En cas de doute, veuillez vous référer au directeur de votre hôtel/restaurant.

Hostellerie de Lavernois
BEAUNE
is pleased to offer

Complimentary house cocktail and dessert or cheese course

Valid for all at the table

L'Ermitage-Corton
CHOREY-LÈS-BEAUNE
is pleased to offer

20% reduction in room rates and a bottle of St-Romain wine

Valid any time with any room

L'Ermitage-Corton
CHOREY-LÈS-BEAUNE
is pleased to offer

Complimentary house cocktail, appetizer and dessert

Valid for all at the table

BERLITZ

This coupon is valid for the gift, complimentary offer or discount described on the reverse side. It must be presented in conjunction with the book *More France for the $,* as described in the preface on page 9. Although the author and Berlitz Guides can take no responsibility for the receipt of the benefits indicated, the publisher would greatly appreciate your communicating any difficulties encountered. Berlitz Guides intends to review and update this book regularly. No expiry date limits this coupon.

La direction de l'établissement s'engage à faire bénéficier le porteur de ce coupon des prestations mentionnées en anglais au recto, suite à l'accord pris avec l'auteur du livre *More France for the $,* M. Alan Austin. En cas de doute, veuillez vous référer au directeur de votre hôtel/restaurant.

BERLITZ

This coupon is valid for the gift, complimentary offer or discount described on the reverse side. It must be presented in conjunction with the book *More France for the $,* as described in the preface on page 9. Although the author and Berlitz Guides can take no responsibility for the receipt of the benefits indicated, the publisher would greatly appreciate your communicating any difficulties encountered. Berlitz Guides intends to review and update this book regularly. No expiry date limits this coupon.

La direction de l'établissement s'engage à faire bénéficier le porteur de ce coupon des prestations mentionnées en anglais au recto, suite à l'accord pris avec l'auteur du livre *More France for the $,* M. Alan Austin. En cas de doute, veuillez vous référer au directeur de votre hôtel/restaurant.

BERLITZ

This coupon is valid for the gift, complimentary offer or discount described on the reverse side. It must be presented in conjunction with the book *More France for the $,* as described in the preface on page 9. Although the author and Berlitz Guides can take no responsibility for the receipt of the benefits indicated, the publisher would greatly appreciate your communicating any difficulties encountered. Berlitz Guides intends to review and update this book regularly. No expiry date limits this coupon.

La direction de l'établissement s'engage à faire bénéficier le porteur de ce coupon des prestations mentionnées en anglais au recto, suite à l'accord pris avec l'auteur du livre *More France for the $,* M. Alan Austin. En cas de doute, veuillez vous référer au directeur de votre hôtel/restaurant.

Hôtel La Pommeraie
BÉNOUVILLE
is pleased to offer

20% reduction in room rates

Valid any time

Le Manoir d'Hastings
BÉNOUVILLE
is pleased to offer

Complimentary Pommereau de Normandie and calvados

Valid for all at the table

Hôtel du Palais
BIARRITZ
is pleased to offer

Room upgrading at no extra cost

Valid any time for a sea-view room for the price of a town-view room,
if available at time of arrival. If upgrading is not possible,
a bottle of champagne in the room.

BERLITZ

This coupon is valid for the gift, complimentary offer or discount described on the reverse side. It must be presented in conjunction with the book *More France for the $,* as described in the preface on page 9. Although the author and Berlitz Guides can take no responsibility for the receipt of the benefits indicated, the publisher would greatly appreciate your communicating any difficulties encountered. Berlitz Guides intends to review and update this book regularly. No expiry date limits this coupon.

La direction de l'établissement s'engage à faire bénéficier le porteur de ce coupon des prestations mentionnées en anglais au recto, suite à l'accord pris avec l'auteur du livre *More France for the $,* M. Alan Austin. En cas de doute, veuillez vous référer au directeur de votre hôtel/restaurant.

BERLITZ

This coupon is valid for the gift, complimentary offer or discount described on the reverse side. It must be presented in conjunction with the book *More France for the $,* as described in the preface on page 9. Although the author and Berlitz Guides can take no responsibility for the receipt of the benefits indicated, the publisher would greatly appreciate your communicating any difficulties encountered. Berlitz Guides intends to review and update this book regularly. No expiry date limits this coupon.

La direction de l'établissement s'engage à faire bénéficier le porteur de ce coupon des prestations mentionnées en anglais au recto, suite à l'accord pris avec l'auteur du livre *More France for the $,* M. Alan Austin. En cas de doute, veuillez vous référer au directeur de votre hôtel/restaurant.

BERLITZ

This coupon is valid for the gift, complimentary offer or discount described on the reverse side. It must be presented in conjunction with the book *More France for the $,* as described in the preface on page 9. Although the author and Berlitz Guides can take no responsibility for the receipt of the benefits indicated, the publisher would greatly appreciate your communicating any difficulties encountered. Berlitz Guides intends to review and update this book regularly. No expiry date limits this coupon.

La direction de l'établissement s'engage à faire bénéficier le porteur de ce coupon des prestations mentionnées en anglais au recto, suite à l'accord pris avec l'auteur du livre *More France for the $,* M. Alan Austin. En cas de doute, veuillez vous référer au directeur de votre hôtel/restaurant.

Hôtel du Palais
BIARRITZ
is pleased to offer

Complimentary poolside cabana

Valid May, June, September, and October

L'Hippocampe
BIARRITZ
is pleased to offer

Complimentary main course

Valid for the less expensive of two main courses
when two meals are ordered à la carte,
exclusive of tax and service

La Rotonde
BIARRITZ
is pleased to offer

Complimentary main course

Valid for the less expensive of two main courses,
when two meals are ordered à la carte,
exclusive of tax and service

BERLITZ

This coupon is valid for the gift, complimentary offer or discount described on the reverse side. It must be presented in conjunction with the book *More France for the $*, as described in the preface on page 9. Although the author and Berlitz Guides can take no responsibility for the receipt of the benefits indicated, the publisher would greatly appreciate your communicating any difficulties encountered. Berlitz Guides intends to review and update this book regularly. No expiry date limits this coupon.

La direction de l'établissement s'engage à faire bénéficier le porteur de ce coupon des prestations mentionnées en anglais au recto, suite à l'accord pris avec l'auteur du livre *More France for the $*, M. Alan Austin. En cas de doute, veuillez vous référer au directeur de votre hôtel/restaurant.

BERLITZ

This coupon is valid for the gift, complimentary offer or discount described on the reverse side. It must be presented in conjunction with the book *More France for the $*, as described in the preface on page 9. Although the author and Berlitz Guides can take no responsibility for the receipt of the benefits indicated, the publisher would greatly appreciate your communicating any difficulties encountered. Berlitz Guides intends to review and update this book regularly. No expiry date limits this coupon.

La direction de l'établissement s'engage à faire bénéficier le porteur de ce coupon des prestations mentionnées en anglais au recto, suite à l'accord pris avec l'auteur du livre *More France for the $*, M. Alan Austin. En cas de doute, veuillez vous référer au directeur de votre hôtel/restaurant.

BERLITZ

This coupon is valid for the gift, complimentary offer or discount described on the reverse side. It must be presented in conjunction with the book *More France for the $*, as described in the preface on page 9. Although the author and Berlitz Guides can take no responsibility for the receipt of the benefits indicated, the publisher would greatly appreciate your communicating any difficulties encountered. Berlitz Guides intends to review and update this book regularly. No expiry date limits this coupon.

La direction de l'établissement s'engage à faire bénéficier le porteur de ce coupon des prestations mentionnées en anglais au recto, suite à l'accord pris avec l'auteur du livre *More France for the $*, M. Alan Austin. En cas de doute, veuillez vous référer au directeur de votre hôtel/restaurant.

Le Grand Siècle
BIARRITZ
is pleased to offer

Complimentary main course

Valid for the less expensive of two main courses,
when two meals are ordered à la carte,
exclusive of tax and service

Hôtel Martinez
CANNES
is pleased to offer

Complimentary bottle of champagne, roses, chocolates, free tennis, complimentary beach mattresses

Valid with any room

L'Orangeraie
CANNES
is pleased to offer

Complimentary champagne cocktail and appetizer

Valid for all at the table

BERLITZ

This coupon is valid for the gift, complimentary offer or discount described on the reverse side. It must be presented
in conjunction with the book *More France for the $*, as
described in the preface on page 9. Although the author and
Berlitz Guides can take no responsibility for the receipt of the
benefits indicated, the publisher would greatly appreciate
your communicating any difficulties encountered. Berlitz
Guides intends to review and update this book regularly.
No expiry date limits this coupon.

La direction de l'établissement s'engage à faire bénéficier
le porteur de ce coupon des prestations mentionnées en
anglais au recto, suite à l'accord pris avec l'auteur du livre
More France for the $, M. Alan Austin. En cas de doute,
veuillez vous référer au directeur de votre hôtel/restaurant.

BERLITZ

This coupon is valid for the gift, complimentary offer or discount described on the reverse side. It must be presented
in conjunction with the book *More France for the $*, as
described in the preface on page 9. Although the author and
Berlitz Guides can take no responsibility for the receipt of the
benefits indicated, the publisher would greatly appreciate
your communicating any difficulties encountered. Berlitz
Guides intends to review and update this book regularly.
No expiry date limits this coupon.

La direction de l'établissement s'engage à faire bénéficier
le porteur de ce coupon des prestations mentionnées en
anglais au recto, suite à l'accord pris avec l'auteur du livre
More France for the $, M. Alan Austin. En cas de doute,
veuillez vous référer au directeur de votre hôtel/restaurant.

BERLITZ

This coupon is valid for the gift, complimentary offer or discount described on the reverse side. It must be presented
in conjunction with the book *More France for the $*, as
described in the preface on page 9. Although the author and
Berlitz Guides can take no responsibility for the receipt of the
benefits indicated, the publisher would greatly appreciate
your communicating any difficulties encountered. Berlitz
Guides intends to review and update this book regularly.
No expiry date limits this coupon.

La direction de l'établissement s'engage à faire bénéficier
le porteur de ce coupon des prestations mentionnées en
anglais au recto, suite à l'accord pris avec l'auteur du livre
More France for the $, M. Alan Austin. En cas de doute,
veuillez vous référer au directeur de votre hôtel/restaurant.

La Palme d'Or
CANNES
is pleased to offer

Complimentary bottle of champagne

Valid when two meals are ordered à la carte

Hôtel Carlton Inter-Continental
CANNES
is pleased to offer

Room upgrading at no extra cost

Valid any time for a deluxe room for the price of a standard room,
if available at time of arrival

Hôtel Carlton Inter-Continental
CANNES
is pleased to offer

Complimentary bottle of wine

Valid with any room

BERLITZ®

This coupon is valid for the gift, complimentary offer or discount described on the reverse side. It must be presented in conjunction with the book *More France for the $,* as described in the preface on page 9. Although the author and Berlitz Guides can take no responsibility for the receipt of the benefits indicated, the publisher would greatly appreciate your communicating any difficulties encountered. Berlitz Guides intends to review and update this book regularly. No expiry date limits this coupon.

La direction de l'établissement s'engage à faire bénéficier le porteur de ce coupon des prestations mentionnées en anglais au recto, suite à l'accord pris avec l'auteur du livre *More France for the $,* M. Alan Austin. En cas de doute, veuillez vous référer au directeur de votre hôtel/restaurant.

BERLITZ®

This coupon is valid for the gift, complimentary offer or discount described on the reverse side. It must be presented in conjunction with the book *More France for the $,* as described in the preface on page 9. Although the author and Berlitz Guides can take no responsibility for the receipt of the benefits indicated, the publisher would greatly appreciate your communicating any difficulties encountered. Berlitz Guides intends to review and update this book regularly. No expiry date limits this coupon.

La direction de l'établissement s'engage à faire bénéficier le porteur de ce coupon des prestations mentionnées en anglais au recto, suite à l'accord pris avec l'auteur du livre *More France for the $,* M. Alan Austin. En cas de doute, veuillez vous référer au directeur de votre hôtel/restaurant.

BERLITZ®

This coupon is valid for the gift, complimentary offer or discount described on the reverse side. It must be presented in conjunction with the book *More France for the $,* as described in the preface on page 9. Although the author and Berlitz Guides can take no responsibility for the receipt of the benefits indicated, the publisher would greatly appreciate your communicating any difficulties encountered. Berlitz Guides intends to review and update this book regularly. No expiry date limits this coupon.

La direction de l'établissement s'engage à faire bénéficier le porteur de ce coupon des prestations mentionnées en anglais au recto, suite à l'accord pris avec l'auteur du livre *More France for the $,* M. Alan Austin. En cas de doute, veuillez vous référer au directeur de votre hôtel/restaurant.

La Côte
CANNES
is pleased to offer

Complimentary champagne cocktail

Valid for all at the table

La Côte
CANNES
is pleased to offer

Complimentary bottle of wine

Valid when two meals are ordered. If a different vintage is desired,
the price of the offered wine will be deducted.

Hôtel Gray d'Albion
CANNES
is pleased to offer

Room upgrading at no extra cost

Valid any time for a deluxe room for the price of a standard room,
if available at time of arrival

 **BERLITZ**

This coupon is valid for the gift, complimentary offer or discount described on the reverse side. It must be presented in conjunction with the book *More France for the $,* as described in the preface on page 9. Although the author and Berlitz Guides can take no responsibility for the receipt of the benefits indicated, the publisher would greatly appreciate your communicating any difficulties encountered. Berlitz Guides intends to review and update this book regularly. No expiry date limits this coupon.

La direction de l'établissement s'engage à faire bénéficier le porteur de ce coupon des prestations mentionnées en anglais au recto, suite à l'accord pris avec l'auteur du livre *More France for the $,* M. Alan Austin. En cas de doute, veuillez vous référer au directeur de votre hôtel/restaurant.

 BERLITZ

This coupon is valid for the gift, complimentary offer or discount described on the reverse side. It must be presented in conjunction with the book *More France for the $,* as described in the preface on page 9. Although the author and Berlitz Guides can take no responsibility for the receipt of the benefits indicated, the publisher would greatly appreciate your communicating any difficulties encountered. Berlitz Guides intends to review and update this book regularly. No expiry date limits this coupon.

La direction de l'établissement s'engage à faire bénéficier le porteur de ce coupon des prestations mentionnées en anglais au recto, suite à l'accord pris avec l'auteur du livre *More France for the $,* M. Alan Austin. En cas de doute, veuillez vous référer au directeur de votre hôtel/restaurant.

 BERLITZ

This coupon is valid for the gift, complimentary offer or discount described on the reverse side. It must be presented in conjunction with the book *More France for the $,* as described in the preface on page 9. Although the author and Berlitz Guides can take no responsibility for the receipt of the benefits indicated, the publisher would greatly appreciate your communicating any difficulties encountered. Berlitz Guides intends to review and update this book regularly. No expiry date limits this coupon.

La direction de l'établissement s'engage à faire bénéficier le porteur de ce coupon des prestations mentionnées en anglais au recto, suite à l'accord pris avec l'auteur du livre *More France for the $,* M. Alan Austin. En cas de doute, veuillez vous référer au directeur de votre hôtel/restaurant.

Hôtel Gray d'Albion
CANNES
is pleased to offer

Complimentary bottle of champagne

Valid with any room

Le Royal Gray
CANNES
is pleased to offer

Complimentary champagne cocktail

Valid for all at the table

Le Royal Gray
CANNES
is pleased to offer

Complimentary bottle of wine

Valid when two meals are ordered. If a different vintage is desired, the price of the offered wine will be deducted.

BERLITZ

This coupon is valid for the gift, complimentary offer or discount described on the reverse side. It must be presented in conjunction with the book *More France for the $,* as described in the preface on page 9. Although the author and Berlitz Guides can take no responsibility for the receipt of the benefits indicated, the publisher would greatly appreciate your communicating any difficulties encountered. Berlitz Guides intends to review and update this book regularly. No expiry date limits this coupon.

La direction de l'établissement s'engage à faire bénéficier le porteur de ce coupon des prestations mentionnées en anglais au recto, suite à l'accord pris avec l'auteur du livre *More France for the $,* M. Alan Austin. En cas de doute, veuillez vous référer au directeur de votre hôtel/restaurant.

BERLITZ

This coupon is valid for the gift, complimentary offer or discount described on the reverse side. It must be presented in conjunction with the book *More France for the $,* as described in the preface on page 9. Although the author and Berlitz Guides can take no responsibility for the receipt of the benefits indicated, the publisher would greatly appreciate your communicating any difficulties encountered. Berlitz Guides intends to review and update this book regularly. No expiry date limits this coupon.

La direction de l'établissement s'engage à faire bénéficier le porteur de ce coupon des prestations mentionnées en anglais au recto, suite à l'accord pris avec l'auteur du livre *More France for the $,* M. Alan Austin. En cas de doute, veuillez vous référer au directeur de votre hôtel/restaurant.

BERLITZ

This coupon is valid for the gift, complimentary offer or discount described on the reverse side. It must be presented in conjunction with the book *More France for the $,* as described in the preface on page 9. Although the author and Berlitz Guides can take no responsibility for the receipt of the benefits indicated, the publisher would greatly appreciate your communicating any difficulties encountered. Berlitz Guides intends to review and update this book regularly. No expiry date limits this coupon.

La direction de l'établissement s'engage à faire bénéficier le porteur de ce coupon des prestations mentionnées en anglais au recto, suite à l'accord pris avec l'auteur du livre *More France for the $,* M. Alan Austin. En cas de doute, veuillez vous référer au directeur de votre hôtel/restaurant.

Hôtel Majestic
CANNES
is pleased to offer

Room upgrading at no extra cost

Valid any time for a deluxe room for the price of a standard room,
if available at time of arrival

Hôtel Majestic
CANNES
is pleased to offer

Complimentary half-bottle of champagne

Valid with any room

Le Grill
CANNES
is pleased to offer

Complimentary bottle of wine

Valid when two beach-buffet luncheons are ordered

BERLITZ®

This coupon is valid for the gift, complimentary offer or discount described on the reverse side. It must be presented
in conjunction with the book *More France for the $,* as
described in the preface on page 9. Although the author and
Berlitz Guides can take no responsibility for the receipt of the
benefits indicated, the publisher would greatly appreciate
your communicating any difficulties encountered. Berlitz
Guides intends to review and update this book regularly.
No expiry date limits this coupon.

La direction de l'établissement s'engage à faire bénéficier
le porteur de ce coupon des prestations mentionnées en
anglais au recto, suite à l'accord pris avec l'auteur du livre
More France for the $, M. Alan Austin. En cas de doute,
veuillez vous référer au directeur de votre hôtel/restaurant.

BERLITZ®

This coupon is valid for the gift, complimentary offer or discount described on the reverse side. It must be presented
in conjunction with the book *More France for the $,* as
described in the preface on page 9. Although the author and
Berlitz Guides can take no responsibility for the receipt of the
benefits indicated, the publisher would greatly appreciate
your communicating any difficulties encountered. Berlitz
Guides intends to review and update this book regularly.
No expiry date limits this coupon.

La direction de l'établissement s'engage à faire bénéficier
le porteur de ce coupon des prestations mentionnées en
anglais au recto, suite à l'accord pris avec l'auteur du livre
More France for the $, M. Alan Austin. En cas de doute,
veuillez vous référer au directeur de votre hôtel/restaurant.

BERLITZ®

This coupon is valid for the gift, complimentary offer or discount described on the reverse side. It must be presented
in conjunction with the book *More France for the $,* as
described in the preface on page 9. Although the author and
Berlitz Guides can take no responsibility for the receipt of the
benefits indicated, the publisher would greatly appreciate
your communicating any difficulties encountered. Berlitz
Guides intends to review and update this book regularly.
No expiry date limits this coupon.

La direction de l'établissement s'engage à faire bénéficier
le porteur de ce coupon des prestations mentionnées en
anglais au recto, suite à l'accord pris avec l'auteur du livre
More France for the $, M. Alan Austin. En cas de doute,
veuillez vous référer au directeur de votre hôtel/restaurant.

Lann Roz
CARNAC
is pleased to offer

25% reduction in room rates

Valid 15 May to 15 June and 1 October to 31 December,
for guests on half-board

Lann Roz
CARNAC
is pleased to offer

Complimentary bottle of wine

Valid for two guests ordering the menu "Entre amis" or better.
If a different vintage is desired,
the price of the offered wine will be deducted.

Château de la Salle
CERISY-LA-SALLE
is pleased to offer

Complimentary luncheon

Valid if booking two nights with dinner

 **BERLITZ**®

This coupon is valid for the gift, complimentary offer or discount described on the reverse side. It must be presented in conjunction with the book *More France for the $*, as described in the preface on page 9. Although the author and Berlitz Guides can take no responsibility for the receipt of the benefits indicated, the publisher would greatly appreciate your communicating any difficulties encountered. Berlitz Guides intends to review and update this book regularly. No expiry date limits this coupon.

La direction de l'établissement s'engage à faire bénéficier le porteur de ce coupon des prestations mentionnées en anglais au recto, suite à l'accord pris avec l'auteur du livre *More France for the $*, M. Alan Austin. En cas de doute, veuillez vous référer au directeur de votre hôtel/restaurant.

 BERLITZ®

This coupon is valid for the gift, complimentary offer or discount described on the reverse side. It must be presented in conjunction with the book *More France for the $*, as described in the preface on page 9. Although the author and Berlitz Guides can take no responsibility for the receipt of the benefits indicated, the publisher would greatly appreciate your communicating any difficulties encountered. Berlitz Guides intends to review and update this book regularly. No expiry date limits this coupon.

La direction de l'établissement s'engage à faire bénéficier le porteur de ce coupon des prestations mentionnées en anglais au recto, suite à l'accord pris avec l'auteur du livre *More France for the $*, M. Alan Austin. En cas de doute, veuillez vous référer au directeur de votre hôtel/restaurant.

 BERLITZ®

This coupon is valid for the gift, complimentary offer or discount described on the reverse side. It must be presented in conjunction with the book *More France for the $*, as described in the preface on page 9. Although the author and Berlitz Guides can take no responsibility for the receipt of the benefits indicated, the publisher would greatly appreciate your communicating any difficulties encountered. Berlitz Guides intends to review and update this book regularly. No expiry date limits this coupon.

La direction de l'établissement s'engage à faire bénéficier le porteur de ce coupon des prestations mentionnées en anglais au recto, suite à l'accord pris avec l'auteur du livre *More France for the $*, M. Alan Austin. En cas de doute, veuillez vous référer au directeur de votre hôtel/restaurant.

Château de la Salle
CERISY-LA-SALLE
is pleased to offer

Complimentary champagne cocktail and after-dinner drink

Valid for all at the table

Hostellerie des Clos
CHABLIS
is pleased to offer

20% reduction in room rates

Valid 1 November to 31 March

Hostellerie des Clos
CHABLIS
is pleased to offer

Escorted tour through Chablis vineyards, with wine-tasting and a gift magnum of Chablis premier cru

Valid for hotel guests on half-board

BERLITZ

This coupon is valid for the gift, complimentary offer or discount described on the reverse side. It must be presented in conjunction with the book *More France for the $,* as described in the preface on page 9. Although the author and Berlitz Guides can take no responsibility for the receipt of the benefits indicated, the publisher would greatly appreciate your communicating any difficulties encountered. Berlitz Guides intends to review and update this book regularly. No expiry date limits this coupon.

La direction de l'établissement s'engage à faire bénéficier le porteur de ce coupon des prestations mentionnées en anglais au recto, suite à l'accord pris avec l'auteur du livre *More France for the $,* M. Alan Austin. En cas de doute, veuillez vous référer au directeur de votre hôtel/restaurant.

BERLITZ

This coupon is valid for the gift, complimentary offer or discount described on the reverse side. It must be presented in conjunction with the book *More France for the $,* as described in the preface on page 9. Although the author and Berlitz Guides can take no responsibility for the receipt of the benefits indicated, the publisher would greatly appreciate your communicating any difficulties encountered. Berlitz Guides intends to review and update this book regularly. No expiry date limits this coupon.

La direction de l'établissement s'engage à faire bénéficier le porteur de ce coupon des prestations mentionnées en anglais au recto, suite à l'accord pris avec l'auteur du livre *More France for the $,* M. Alan Austin. En cas de doute, veuillez vous référer au directeur de votre hôtel/restaurant.

BERLITZ

This coupon is valid for the gift, complimentary offer or discount described on the reverse side. It must be presented in conjunction with the book *More France for the $,* as described in the preface on page 9. Although the author and Berlitz Guides can take no responsibility for the receipt of the benefits indicated, the publisher would greatly appreciate your communicating any difficulties encountered. Berlitz Guides intends to review and update this book regularly. No expiry date limits this coupon.

La direction de l'établissement s'engage à faire bénéficier le porteur de ce coupon des prestations mentionnées en anglais au recto, suite à l'accord pris avec l'auteur du livre *More France for the $,* M. Alan Austin. En cas de doute, veuillez vous référer au directeur de votre hôtel/restaurant.

Hostellerie des Clos
CHABLIS
is pleased to offer

Complimentary bottle of Chablis

Valid at lunch for two guests (half-bottle for single guest)

Hostellerie des Clos
CHABLIS
is pleased to offer

Complimentary house cocktail

Valid at dinner for all at the table

Le Royal Champagne
CHAMPILLON-BELLEVUE
is pleased to offer

Complimentary bottle of champagne

Valid with any room

BERLITZ

This coupon is valid for the gift, complimentary offer or discount described on the reverse side. It must be presented in conjunction with the book *More France for the $,* as described in the preface on page 9. Although the author and Berlitz Guides can take no responsibility for the receipt of the benefits indicated, the publisher would greatly appreciate your communicating any difficulties encountered. Berlitz Guides intends to review and update this book regularly. No expiry date limits this coupon.

La direction de l'établissement s'engage à faire bénéficier le porteur de ce coupon des prestations mentionnées en anglais au recto, suite à l'accord pris avec l'auteur du livre *More France for the $,* M. Alan Austin. En cas de doute, veuillez vous référer au directeur de votre hôtel/restaurant.

BERLITZ

This coupon is valid for the gift, complimentary offer or discount described on the reverse side. It must be presented in conjunction with the book *More France for the $,* as described in the preface on page 9. Although the author and Berlitz Guides can take no responsibility for the receipt of the benefits indicated, the publisher would greatly appreciate your communicating any difficulties encountered. Berlitz Guides intends to review and update this book regularly. No expiry date limits this coupon.

La direction de l'établissement s'engage à faire bénéficier le porteur de ce coupon des prestations mentionnées en anglais au recto, suite à l'accord pris avec l'auteur du livre *More France for the $,* M. Alan Austin. En cas de doute, veuillez vous référer au directeur de votre hôtel/restaurant.

BERLITZ

This coupon is valid for the gift, complimentary offer or discount described on the reverse side. It must be presented in conjunction with the book *More France for the $,* as described in the preface on page 9. Although the author and Berlitz Guides can take no responsibility for the receipt of the benefits indicated, the publisher would greatly appreciate your communicating any difficulties encountered. Berlitz Guides intends to review and update this book regularly. No expiry date limits this coupon.

La direction de l'établissement s'engage à faire bénéficier le porteur de ce coupon des prestations mentionnées en anglais au recto, suite à l'accord pris avec l'auteur du livre *More France for the $,* M. Alan Austin. En cas de doute, veuillez vous référer au directeur de votre hôtel/restaurant.

Le Royal Champagne
CHAMPILLON-BELLEVUE
is pleased to offer

Complimentary champagne cocktail and appetizer

Valid for all at the table

Château de Teildras
CHEFFES-SUR-SARTHE
is pleased to offer

25% reduction in room rates

Valid any time

Château de Teildras
CHEFFES-SUR-SARTHE
is pleased to offer

Complimentary bottle of wine

Valid for two guests ordering together.
If a different vintage is desired,
the price of the offered wine will be deducted.

BERLITZ®

This coupon is valid for the gift, complimentary offer or discount described on the reverse side. It must be presented in conjunction with the book *More France for the $,* as described in the preface on page 9. Although the author and Berlitz Guides can take no responsibility for the receipt of the benefits indicated, the publisher would greatly appreciate your communicating any difficulties encountered. Berlitz Guides intends to review and update this book regularly. No expiry date limits this coupon.

La direction de l'établissement s'engage à faire bénéficier le porteur de ce coupon des prestations mentionnées en anglais au recto, suite à l'accord pris avec l'auteur du livre *More France for the $,* M. Alan Austin. En cas de doute, veuillez vous référer au directeur de votre hôtel/restaurant.

BERLITZ®

This coupon is valid for the gift, complimentary offer or discount described on the reverse side. It must be presented in conjunction with the book *More France for the $,* as described in the preface on page 9. Although the author and Berlitz Guides can take no responsibility for the receipt of the benefits indicated, the publisher would greatly appreciate your communicating any difficulties encountered. Berlitz Guides intends to review and update this book regularly. No expiry date limits this coupon.

La direction de l'établissement s'engage à faire bénéficier le porteur de ce coupon des prestations mentionnées en anglais au recto, suite à l'accord pris avec l'auteur du livre *More France for the $,* M. Alan Austin. En cas de doute, veuillez vous référer au directeur de votre hôtel/restaurant.

BERLITZ®

This coupon is valid for the gift, complimentary offer or discount described on the reverse side. It must be presented in conjunction with the book *More France for the $,* as described in the preface on page 9. Although the author and Berlitz Guides can take no responsibility for the receipt of the benefits indicated, the publisher would greatly appreciate your communicating any difficulties encountered. Berlitz Guides intends to review and update this book regularly. No expiry date limits this coupon.

La direction de l'établissement s'engage à faire bénéficier le porteur de ce coupon des prestations mentionnées en anglais au recto, suite à l'accord pris avec l'auteur du livre *More France for the $,* M. Alan Austin. En cas de doute, veuillez vous référer au directeur de votre hôtel/restaurant.

Le Grand Ecuyer
CORDES
is pleased to offer

10% reduction in room rates

Valid all year except July and August

Le Grand Ecuyer
CORDES
is pleased to offer

10% reduction on food and drink

Valid for any meal

Hostellerie du Vieux Cordes
CORDES
is pleased to offer

20% reduction in room rates

Valid all year except July and August

 **BERLITZ**®

This coupon is valid for the gift, complimentary offer or discount described on the reverse side. It must be presented in conjunction with the book *More France for the $,* as described in the preface on page 9. Although the author and Berlitz Guides can take no responsibility for the receipt of the benefits indicated, the publisher would greatly appreciate your communicating any difficulties encountered. Berlitz Guides intends to review and update this book regularly. No expiry date limits this coupon.

La direction de l'établissement s'engage à faire bénéficier le porteur de ce coupon des prestations mentionnées en anglais au recto, suite à l'accord pris avec l'auteur du livre *More France for the $,* M. Alan Austin. En cas de doute, veuillez vous référer au directeur de votre hôtel/restaurant.

 BERLITZ®

This coupon is valid for the gift, complimentary offer or discount described on the reverse side. It must be presented in conjunction with the book *More France for the $,* as described in the preface on page 9. Although the author and Berlitz Guides can take no responsibility for the receipt of the benefits indicated, the publisher would greatly appreciate your communicating any difficulties encountered. Berlitz Guides intends to review and update this book regularly. No expiry date limits this coupon.

La direction de l'établissement s'engage à faire bénéficier le porteur de ce coupon des prestations mentionnées en anglais au recto, suite à l'accord pris avec l'auteur du livre *More France for the $,* M. Alan Austin. En cas de doute, veuillez vous référer au directeur de votre hôtel/restaurant.

 BERLITZ®

This coupon is valid for the gift, complimentary offer or discount described on the reverse side. It must be presented in conjunction with the book *More France for the $,* as described in the preface on page 9. Although the author and Berlitz Guides can take no responsibility for the receipt of the benefits indicated, the publisher would greatly appreciate your communicating any difficulties encountered. Berlitz Guides intends to review and update this book regularly. No expiry date limits this coupon.

La direction de l'établissement s'engage à faire bénéficier le porteur de ce coupon des prestations mentionnées en anglais au recto, suite à l'accord pris avec l'auteur du livre *More France for the $,* M. Alan Austin. En cas de doute, veuillez vous référer au directeur de votre hôtel/restaurant.

Hostellerie du Vieux Cordes
CORDES
is pleased to offer

Complimentary bottle of wine

Valid for any meal

Hostellerie du Chapeau Rouge
DIJON
is pleased to offer

Complimentary half-bottle of cassis apéritif and a boxed set of two glasses

Valid with any room

Hostellerie du Chapeau Rouge
DIJON
is pleased to offer

Complimentary apéritif, and champagne with dessert

Valid for all at the table

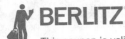

BERLITZ

This coupon is valid for the gift, complimentary offer or discount described on the reverse side. It must be presented in conjunction with the book *More France for the $*, as described in the preface on page 9. Although the author and Berlitz Guides can take no responsibility for the receipt of the benefits indicated, the publisher would greatly appreciate your communicating any difficulties encountered. Berlitz Guides intends to review and update this book regularly. No expiry date limits this coupon.

La direction de l'établissement s'engage à faire bénéficier le porteur de ce coupon des prestations mentionnées en anglais au recto, suite à l'accord pris avec l'auteur du livre *More France for the $*, M. Alan Austin. En cas de doute, veuillez vous référer au directeur de votre hôtel/restaurant.

BERLITZ

This coupon is valid for the gift, complimentary offer or discount described on the reverse side. It must be presented in conjunction with the book *More France for the $*, as described in the preface on page 9. Although the author and Berlitz Guides can take no responsibility for the receipt of the benefits indicated, the publisher would greatly appreciate your communicating any difficulties encountered. Berlitz Guides intends to review and update this book regularly. No expiry date limits this coupon.

La direction de l'établissement s'engage à faire bénéficier le porteur de ce coupon des prestations mentionnées en anglais au recto, suite à l'accord pris avec l'auteur du livre *More France for the $*, M. Alan Austin. En cas de doute, veuillez vous référer au directeur de votre hôtel/restaurant.

BERLITZ

This coupon is valid for the gift, complimentary offer or discount described on the reverse side. It must be presented in conjunction with the book *More France for the $*, as described in the preface on page 9. Although the author and Berlitz Guides can take no responsibility for the receipt of the benefits indicated, the publisher would greatly appreciate your communicating any difficulties encountered. Berlitz Guides intends to review and update this book regularly. No expiry date limits this coupon.

La direction de l'établissement s'engage à faire bénéficier le porteur de ce coupon des prestations mentionnées en anglais au recto, suite à l'accord pris avec l'auteur du livre *More France for the $*, M. Alan Austin. En cas de doute, veuillez vous référer au directeur de votre hôtel/restaurant.

Jean-Pierre Billoux
DIJON
is pleased to offer

Complimentary house cocktail, appetizer and marc de Bourgogne after-dinner drink

Valid for all at the table

Hôtel Cro-Magnon
LES EYZIES-DE-TAYAC
is pleased to offer

Complimentary luncheon

Valid with a stay of two nights with dinners

Hôtel Cro-Magnon
LES EYZIES-DE-TAYAC
is pleased to offer

Complimentary cocktail

Valid for all at the table

 **BERLITZ**

This coupon is valid for the gift, complimentary offer or discount described on the reverse side. It must be presented in conjunction with the book *More France for the $,* as described in the preface on page 9. Although the author and Berlitz Guides can take no responsibility for the receipt of the benefits indicated, the publisher would greatly appreciate your communicating any difficulties encountered. Berlitz Guides intends to review and update this book regularly. No expiry date limits this coupon.

La direction de l'établissement s'engage à faire bénéficier le porteur de ce coupon des prestations mentionnées en anglais au recto, suite à l'accord pris avec l'auteur du livre *More France for the $,* M. Alan Austin. En cas de doute, veuillez vous référer au directeur de votre hôtel/restaurant.

 BERLITZ

This coupon is valid for the gift, complimentary offer or discount described on the reverse side. It must be presented in conjunction with the book *More France for the $,* as described in the preface on page 9. Although the author and Berlitz Guides can take no responsibility for the receipt of the benefits indicated, the publisher would greatly appreciate your communicating any difficulties encountered. Berlitz Guides intends to review and update this book regularly. No expiry date limits this coupon.

La direction de l'établissement s'engage à faire bénéficier le porteur de ce coupon des prestations mentionnées en anglais au recto, suite à l'accord pris avec l'auteur du livre *More France for the $,* M. Alan Austin. En cas de doute, veuillez vous référer au directeur de votre hôtel/restaurant.

 BERLITZ

This coupon is valid for the gift, complimentary offer or discount described on the reverse side. It must be presented in conjunction with the book *More France for the $,* as described in the preface on page 9. Although the author and Berlitz Guides can take no responsibility for the receipt of the benefits indicated, the publisher would greatly appreciate your communicating any difficulties encountered. Berlitz Guides intends to review and update this book regularly. No expiry date limits this coupon.

La direction de l'établissement s'engage à faire bénéficier le porteur de ce coupon des prestations mentionnées en anglais au recto, suite à l'accord pris avec l'auteur du livre *More France for the $,* M. Alan Austin. En cas de doute, veuillez vous référer au directeur de votre hôtel/restaurant.

Château Eza
EZE-VILLAGE
is pleased to offer

Room upgrading at no extra cost

Valid any time for a deluxe room or suite
for the price of a standard room, if available at time of arrival.
If upgrading is not possible, a bottle of champagne in the room.

Château Eza
EZE-VILLAGE
is pleased to offer

Complimentary bottle of champagne

Valid when booking a suite at the regular price

Château Eza
EZE-VILLAGE
is pleased to offer

Complimentary bottle of wine

Valid when two meals are ordered. If a different vintage is desired,
the price of the offered wine will be deducted.

 **BERLITZ**

This coupon is valid for the gift, complimentary offer or discount described on the reverse side. It must be presented in conjunction with the book *More France for the $,* as described in the preface on page 9. Although the author and Berlitz Guides can take no responsibility for the receipt of the benefits indicated, the publisher would greatly appreciate your communicating any difficulties encountered. Berlitz Guides intends to review and update this book regularly. No expiry date limits this coupon.

La direction de l'établissement s'engage à faire bénéficier le porteur de ce coupon des prestations mentionnées en anglais au recto, suite à l'accord pris avec l'auteur du livre *More France for the $,* M. Alan Austin. En cas de doute, veuillez vous référer au directeur de votre hôtel/restaurant.

 BERLITZ

This coupon is valid for the gift, complimentary offer or discount described on the reverse side. It must be presented in conjunction with the book *More France for the $,* as described in the preface on page 9. Although the author and Berlitz Guides can take no responsibility for the receipt of the benefits indicated, the publisher would greatly appreciate your communicating any difficulties encountered. Berlitz Guides intends to review and update this book regularly. No expiry date limits this coupon.

La direction de l'établissement s'engage à faire bénéficier le porteur de ce coupon des prestations mentionnées en anglais au recto, suite à l'accord pris avec l'auteur du livre *More France for the $,* M. Alan Austin. En cas de doute, veuillez vous référer au directeur de votre hôtel/restaurant.

 BERLITZ

This coupon is valid for the gift, complimentary offer or discount described on the reverse side. It must be presented in conjunction with the book *More France for the $,* as described in the preface on page 9. Although the author and Berlitz Guides can take no responsibility for the receipt of the benefits indicated, the publisher would greatly appreciate your communicating any difficulties encountered. Berlitz Guides intends to review and update this book regularly. No expiry date limits this coupon.

La direction de l'établissement s'engage à faire bénéficier le porteur de ce coupon des prestations mentionnées en anglais au recto, suite à l'accord pris avec l'auteur du livre *More France for the $,* M. Alan Austin. En cas de doute, veuillez vous référer au directeur de votre hôtel/restaurant.

Château de la Chèvre d'Or
EZE-VILLAGE
is pleased to offer

Complimentary half-bottle of champagne

Valid with any room

Château de la Chèvre d'Or
EZE-VILLAGE
is pleased to offer

10% reduction on food and drink

Valid for any meal

Le Grill
EZE-VILLAGE
is pleased to offer

Complimentary kir cocktail

Valid for all at the table

 **BERLITZ**®

This coupon is valid for the gift, complimentary offer or discount described on the reverse side. It must be presented in conjunction with the book *More France for the $,* as described in the preface on page 9. Although the author and Berlitz Guides can take no responsibility for the receipt of the benefits indicated, the publisher would greatly appreciate your communicating any difficulties encountered. Berlitz Guides intends to review and update this book regularly. No expiry date limits this coupon.

La direction de l'établissement s'engage à faire bénéficier le porteur de ce coupon des prestations mentionnées en anglais au recto, suite à l'accord pris avec l'auteur du livre *More France for the $,* M. Alan Austin. En cas de doute, veuillez vous référer au directeur de votre hôtel/restaurant.

 BERLITZ®

This coupon is valid for the gift, complimentary offer or discount described on the reverse side. It must be presented in conjunction with the book *More France for the $,* as described in the preface on page 9. Although the author and Berlitz Guides can take no responsibility for the receipt of the benefits indicated, the publisher would greatly appreciate your communicating any difficulties encountered. Berlitz Guides intends to review and update this book regularly. No expiry date limits this coupon.

La direction de l'établissement s'engage à faire bénéficier le porteur de ce coupon des prestations mentionnées en anglais au recto, suite à l'accord pris avec l'auteur du livre *More France for the $,* M. Alan Austin. En cas de doute, veuillez vous référer au directeur de votre hôtel/restaurant.

 BERLITZ®

This coupon is valid for the gift, complimentary offer or discount described on the reverse side. It must be presented in conjunction with the book *More France for the $,* as described in the preface on page 9. Although the author and Berlitz Guides can take no responsibility for the receipt of the benefits indicated, the publisher would greatly appreciate your communicating any difficulties encountered. Berlitz Guides intends to review and update this book regularly. No expiry date limits this coupon.

La direction de l'établissement s'engage à faire bénéficier le porteur de ce coupon des prestations mentionnées en anglais au recto, suite à l'accord pris avec l'auteur du livre *More France for the $,* M. Alan Austin. En cas de doute, veuillez vous référer au directeur de votre hôtel/restaurant.

L'Hermitage du Col d'Eze
EZE-VILLAGE
is pleased to offer

20% reduction in room rates

Valid 1 October to 31 May

L'Hermitage du Col d'Eze
EZE-VILLAGE
is pleased to offer

Complimentary appetizer or cheese course

Valid when one meal is ordered à la carte

L'Hermitage du Col d'Eze
EZE-VILLAGE
is pleased to offer

Complimentary bottle of wine

Valid when two meals are ordered. If a different vintage is desired,
the price of the offered wine will be deducted.

BERLITZ

This coupon is valid for the gift, complimentary offer or discount described on the reverse side. It must be presented in conjunction with the book *More France for the $*, as described in the preface on page 9. Although the author and Berlitz Guides can take no responsibility for the receipt of the benefits indicated, the publisher would greatly appreciate your communicating any difficulties encountered. Berlitz Guides intends to review and update this book regularly. No expiry date limits this coupon.

La direction de l'établissement s'engage à faire bénéficier le porteur de ce coupon des prestations mentionnées en anglais au recto, suite à l'accord pris avec l'auteur du livre *More France for the $*, M. Alan Austin. En cas de doute, veuillez vous référer au directeur de votre hôtel/restaurant.

BERLITZ

This coupon is valid for the gift, complimentary offer or discount described on the reverse side. It must be presented in conjunction with the book *More France for the $*, as described in the preface on page 9. Although the author and Berlitz Guides can take no responsibility for the receipt of the benefits indicated, the publisher would greatly appreciate your communicating any difficulties encountered. Berlitz Guides intends to review and update this book regularly. No expiry date limits this coupon.

La direction de l'établissement s'engage à faire bénéficier le porteur de ce coupon des prestations mentionnées en anglais au recto, suite à l'accord pris avec l'auteur du livre *More France for the $*, M. Alan Austin. En cas de doute, veuillez vous référer au directeur de votre hôtel/restaurant.

BERLITZ

This coupon is valid for the gift, complimentary offer or discount described on the reverse side. It must be presented in conjunction with the book *More France for the $*, as described in the preface on page 9. Although the author and Berlitz Guides can take no responsibility for the receipt of the benefits indicated, the publisher would greatly appreciate your communicating any difficulties encountered. Berlitz Guides intends to review and update this book regularly. No expiry date limits this coupon.

La direction de l'établissement s'engage à faire bénéficier le porteur de ce coupon des prestations mentionnées en anglais au recto, suite à l'accord pris avec l'auteur du livre *More France for the $*, M. Alan Austin. En cas de doute, veuillez vous référer au directeur de votre hôtel/restaurant.

Hostellerie du Château
FÈRE-EN-TARDENOIS
is pleased to offer

Complimentary bottle of white wine

Valid with any room

Hostellerie du Château
FÈRE-EN-TARDENOIS
is pleased to offer

Complimentary cocktail and canapés

Valid for all at the table

Auberge La Regalido
FONTVIEILLE
is pleased to offer

30% reduction in room rates

Valid 31 October to Easter

BERLITZ®

This coupon is valid for the gift, complimentary offer or discount described on the reverse side. It must be presented in conjunction with the book *More France for the $,* as described in the preface on page 9. Although the author and Berlitz Guides can take no responsibility for the receipt of the benefits indicated, the publisher would greatly appreciate your communicating any difficulties encountered. Berlitz Guides intends to review and update this book regularly. No expiry date limits this coupon.

La direction de l'établissement s'engage à faire bénéficier le porteur de ce coupon des prestations mentionnées en anglais au recto, suite à l'accord pris avec l'auteur du livre *More France for the $,* M. Alan Austin. En cas de doute, veuillez vous référer au directeur de votre hôtel/restaurant.

BERLITZ®

This coupon is valid for the gift, complimentary offer or discount described on the reverse side. It must be presented in conjunction with the book *More France for the $,* as described in the preface on page 9. Although the author and Berlitz Guides can take no responsibility for the receipt of the benefits indicated, the publisher would greatly appreciate your communicating any difficulties encountered. Berlitz Guides intends to review and update this book regularly. No expiry date limits this coupon.

La direction de l'établissement s'engage à faire bénéficier le porteur de ce coupon des prestations mentionnées en anglais au recto, suite à l'accord pris avec l'auteur du livre *More France for the $,* M. Alan Austin. En cas de doute, veuillez vous référer au directeur de votre hôtel/restaurant.

BERLITZ®

This coupon is valid for the gift, complimentary offer or discount described on the reverse side. It must be presented in conjunction with the book *More France for the $,* as described in the preface on page 9. Although the author and Berlitz Guides can take no responsibility for the receipt of the benefits indicated, the publisher would greatly appreciate your communicating any difficulties encountered. Berlitz Guides intends to review and update this book regularly. No expiry date limits this coupon.

La direction de l'établissement s'engage à faire bénéficier le porteur de ce coupon des prestations mentionnées en anglais au recto, suite à l'accord pris avec l'auteur du livre *More France for the $,* M. Alan Austin. En cas de doute, veuillez vous référer au directeur de votre hôtel/restaurant.

Auberge la Regalido
FONTVIEILLE
is pleased to offer

Complimentary luncheon for two

Valid when two hotel guests reserve a table for dinner

Château de la Rapée
GISORS
is pleased to offer

Complimentary bottle of chilled Normandy cider

Valid with any room

Château de la Rapée
GISORS
is pleased to offer

Complimentary cheese course and aged calvados

Valid for all at the table

BERLITZ®

This coupon is valid for the gift, complimentary offer or discount described on the reverse side. It must be presented in conjunction with the book *More France for the $,* as described in the preface on page 9. Although the author and Berlitz Guides can take no responsibility for the receipt of the benefits indicated, the publisher would greatly appreciate your communicating any difficulties encountered. Berlitz Guides intends to review and update this book regularly. No expiry date limits this coupon.

La direction de l'établissement s'engage à faire bénéficier le porteur de ce coupon des prestations mentionnées en anglais au recto, suite à l'accord pris avec l'auteur du livre *More France for the $,* M. Alan Austin. En cas de doute, veuillez vous référer au directeur de votre hôtel/restaurant.

BERLITZ®

This coupon is valid for the gift, complimentary offer or discount described on the reverse side. It must be presented in conjunction with the book *More France for the $,* as described in the preface on page 9. Although the author and Berlitz Guides can take no responsibility for the receipt of the benefits indicated, the publisher would greatly appreciate your communicating any difficulties encountered. Berlitz Guides intends to review and update this book regularly. No expiry date limits this coupon.

La direction de l'établissement s'engage à faire bénéficier le porteur de ce coupon des prestations mentionnées en anglais au recto, suite à l'accord pris avec l'auteur du livre *More France for the $,* M. Alan Austin. En cas de doute, veuillez vous référer au directeur de votre hôtel/restaurant.

BERLITZ®

This coupon is valid for the gift, complimentary offer or discount described on the reverse side. It must be presented in conjunction with the book *More France for the $,* as described in the preface on page 9. Although the author and Berlitz Guides can take no responsibility for the receipt of the benefits indicated, the publisher would greatly appreciate your communicating any difficulties encountered. Berlitz Guides intends to review and update this book regularly. No expiry date limits this coupon.

La direction de l'établissement s'engage à faire bénéficier le porteur de ce coupon des prestations mentionnées en anglais au recto, suite à l'accord pris avec l'auteur du livre *More France for the $,* M. Alan Austin. En cas de doute, veuillez vous référer au directeur de votre hôtel/restaurant.

Château de Locguénolé
HENNEBONT
is pleased to offer

40% reduction in room rates

Valid 1 February to 30 April and 15 September to 31 December, except French national holiday weekends

Château de Locguénolé
HENNEBONT
is pleased to offer

Room upgrading at no extra cost

Valid any time for a superior room for the price of a standard room, if available at time of arrival. If upgrading is not possible, a bottle of champagne in the room.

Château de Locguénolé
HENNEBONT
is pleased to offer

Complimentary bottle of wine

Valid for two guests ordering together

BERLITZ®

This coupon is valid for the gift, complimentary offer or discount described on the reverse side. It must be presented in conjunction with the book *More France for the $*, as described in the preface on page 9. Although the author and Berlitz Guides can take no responsibility for the receipt of the benefits indicated, the publisher would greatly appreciate your communicating any difficulties encountered. Berlitz Guides intends to review and update this book regularly. No expiry date limits this coupon.

La direction de l'établissement s'engage à faire bénéficier le porteur de ce coupon des prestations mentionnées en anglais au recto, suite à l'accord pris avec l'auteur du livre *More France for the $*, M. Alan Austin. En cas de doute, veuillez vous référer au directeur de votre hôtel/restaurant.

BERLITZ®

This coupon is valid for the gift, complimentary offer or discount described on the reverse side. It must be presented in conjunction with the book *More France for the $*, as described in the preface on page 9. Although the author and Berlitz Guides can take no responsibility for the receipt of the benefits indicated, the publisher would greatly appreciate your communicating any difficulties encountered. Berlitz Guides intends to review and update this book regularly. No expiry date limits this coupon.

La direction de l'établissement s'engage à faire bénéficier le porteur de ce coupon des prestations mentionnées en anglais au recto, suite à l'accord pris avec l'auteur du livre *More France for the $*, M. Alan Austin. En cas de doute, veuillez vous référer au directeur de votre hôtel/restaurant.

BERLITZ®

This coupon is valid for the gift, complimentary offer or discount described on the reverse side. It must be presented in conjunction with the book *More France for the $*, as described in the preface on page 9. Although the author and Berlitz Guides can take no responsibility for the receipt of the benefits indicated, the publisher would greatly appreciate your communicating any difficulties encountered. Berlitz Guides intends to review and update this book regularly. No expiry date limits this coupon.

La direction de l'établissement s'engage à faire bénéficier le porteur de ce coupon des prestations mentionnées en anglais au recto, suite à l'accord pris avec l'auteur du livre *More France for the $*, M. Alan Austin. En cas de doute, veuillez vous référer au directeur de votre hôtel/restaurant.

Les Chaumières de Kerniaven
HENNEBONT
is pleased to offer

50% reduction in room rates

Valid all year except July and August

Ferme St-Siméon et son Manoir
HONFLEUR
is pleased to offer

Complimentary bottle of champagne

Valid with any room

Ferme St-Siméon et son Manoir
HONFLEUR
is pleased to offer

One night's accommodation at no charge

Valid after a four-night stay at the regular price

BERLITZ®

This coupon is valid for the gift, complimentary offer or discount described on the reverse side. It must be presented in conjunction with the book *More France for the $,* as described in the preface on page 9. Although the author and Berlitz Guides can take no responsibility for the receipt of the benefits indicated, the publisher would greatly appreciate your communicating any difficulties encountered. Berlitz Guides intends to review and update this book regularly. No expiry date limits this coupon.

La direction de l'établissement s'engage à faire bénéficier le porteur de ce coupon des prestations mentionnées en anglais au recto, suite à l'accord pris avec l'auteur du livre *More France for the $,* M. Alan Austin. En cas de doute, veuillez vous référer au directeur de votre hôtel/restaurant.

BERLITZ®

This coupon is valid for the gift, complimentary offer or discount described on the reverse side. It must be presented in conjunction with the book *More France for the $,* as described in the preface on page 9. Although the author and Berlitz Guides can take no responsibility for the receipt of the benefits indicated, the publisher would greatly appreciate your communicating any difficulties encountered. Berlitz Guides intends to review and update this book regularly. No expiry date limits this coupon.

La direction de l'établissement s'engage à faire bénéficier le porteur de ce coupon des prestations mentionnées en anglais au recto, suite à l'accord pris avec l'auteur du livre *More France for the $,* M. Alan Austin. En cas de doute, veuillez vous référer au directeur de votre hôtel/restaurant.

BERLITZ®

This coupon is valid for the gift, complimentary offer or discount described on the reverse side. It must be presented in conjunction with the book *More France for the $,* as described in the preface on page 9. Although the author and Berlitz Guides can take no responsibility for the receipt of the benefits indicated, the publisher would greatly appreciate your communicating any difficulties encountered. Berlitz Guides intends to review and update this book regularly. No expiry date limits this coupon.

La direction de l'établissement s'engage à faire bénéficier le porteur de ce coupon des prestations mentionnées en anglais au recto, suite à l'accord pris avec l'auteur du livre *More France for the $,* M. Alan Austin. En cas de doute, veuillez vous référer au directeur de votre hôtel/restaurant.

Ferme St-Siméon
HONFLEUR
is pleased to offer

Complimentary champagne cocktail and appetizer

Valid for all at the table

Résidence de la Côte St-Jacques
JOIGNY
is pleased to offer

Complimentary bottle of St-Jacques wine

Valid with any room

Résidence de la Côte St-Jacques
JOIGNY
is pleased to offer

Complimentary house cocktail and appetizer

Valid for all at the table

BERLITZ

This coupon is valid for the gift, complimentary offer or discount described on the reverse side. It must be presented in conjunction with the book *More France for the $*, as described in the preface on page 9. Although the author and Berlitz Guides can take no responsibility for the receipt of the benefits indicated, the publisher would greatly appreciate your communicating any difficulties encountered. Berlitz Guides intends to review and update this book regularly. No expiry date limits this coupon.

La direction de l'établissement s'engage à faire bénéficier le porteur de ce coupon des prestations mentionnées en anglais au recto, suite à l'accord pris avec l'auteur du livre *More France for the $*, M. Alan Austin. En cas de doute, veuillez vous référer au directeur de votre hôtel/restaurant.

BERLITZ

This coupon is valid for the gift, complimentary offer or discount described on the reverse side. It must be presented in conjunction with the book *More France for the $*, as described in the preface on page 9. Although the author and Berlitz Guides can take no responsibility for the receipt of the benefits indicated, the publisher would greatly appreciate your communicating any difficulties encountered. Berlitz Guides intends to review and update this book regularly. No expiry date limits this coupon.

La direction de l'établissement s'engage à faire bénéficier le porteur de ce coupon des prestations mentionnées en anglais au recto, suite à l'accord pris avec l'auteur du livre *More France for the $*, M. Alan Austin. En cas de doute, veuillez vous référer au directeur de votre hôtel/restaurant.

BERLITZ

This coupon is valid for the gift, complimentary offer or discount described on the reverse side. It must be presented in conjunction with the book *More France for the $*, as described in the preface on page 9. Although the author and Berlitz Guides can take no responsibility for the receipt of the benefits indicated, the publisher would greatly appreciate your communicating any difficulties encountered. Berlitz Guides intends to review and update this book regularly. No expiry date limits this coupon.

La direction de l'établissement s'engage à faire bénéficier le porteur de ce coupon des prestations mentionnées en anglais au recto, suite à l'accord pris avec l'auteur du livre *More France for the $*, M. Alan Austin. En cas de doute, veuillez vous référer au directeur de votre hôtel/restaurant.

La Bannière de France
LAON
is pleased to offer

Complimentary bottle of wine

Valid with any room

La Bannière de France
LAON
is pleased to offer

Complimentary kir royal champagne cocktail

Valid for all at the table

Les Vannes
LIVERDUN
is pleased to offer

Complimentary bottle of Perlé, white or red

Valid with any room

BERLITZ®

This coupon is valid for the gift, complimentary offer or discount described on the reverse side. It must be presented in conjunction with the book *More France for the $*, as described in the preface on page 9. Although the author and Berlitz Guides can take no responsibility for the receipt of the benefits indicated, the publisher would greatly appreciate your communicating any difficulties encountered. Berlitz Guides intends to review and update this book regularly. No expiry date limits this coupon.

La direction de l'établissement s'engage à faire bénéficier le porteur de ce coupon des prestations mentionnées en anglais au recto, suite à l'accord pris avec l'auteur du livre *More France for the $*, M. Alan Austin. En cas de doute, veuillez vous référer au directeur de votre hôtel/restaurant.

BERLITZ®

This coupon is valid for the gift, complimentary offer or discount described on the reverse side. It must be presented in conjunction with the book *More France for the $*, as described in the preface on page 9. Although the author and Berlitz Guides can take no responsibility for the receipt of the benefits indicated, the publisher would greatly appreciate your communicating any difficulties encountered. Berlitz Guides intends to review and update this book regularly. No expiry date limits this coupon.

La direction de l'établissement s'engage à faire bénéficier le porteur de ce coupon des prestations mentionnées en anglais au recto, suite à l'accord pris avec l'auteur du livre *More France for the $*, M. Alan Austin. En cas de doute, veuillez vous référer au directeur de votre hôtel/restaurant.

BERLITZ®

This coupon is valid for the gift, complimentary offer or discount described on the reverse side. It must be presented in conjunction with the book *More France for the $*, as described in the preface on page 9. Although the author and Berlitz Guides can take no responsibility for the receipt of the benefits indicated, the publisher would greatly appreciate your communicating any difficulties encountered. Berlitz Guides intends to review and update this book regularly. No expiry date limits this coupon.

La direction de l'établissement s'engage à faire bénéficier le porteur de ce coupon des prestations mentionnées en anglais au recto, suite à l'accord pris avec l'auteur du livre *More France for the $*, M. Alan Austin. En cas de doute, veuillez vous référer au directeur de votre hôtel/restaurant.

Les Vannes
LIVERDUN
is pleased to offer

Complimentary main course

Valid for the less expensive of two main courses, when two meals are ordered together à la carte, exclusive of tax and service

Grand Hôtel Concorde
LYON
is pleased to offer

25% reduction in room rates

Valid any time

Le Fiorelle
LYON
is pleased to offer

Complimentary champagne cocktail

Valid for each guest at the table

BERLITZ

This coupon is valid for the gift, complimentary offer or discount described on the reverse side. It must be presented in conjunction with the book *More France for the $,* as described in the preface on page 9. Although the author and Berlitz Guides can take no responsibility for the receipt of the benefits indicated, the publisher would greatly appreciate your communicating any difficulties encountered. Berlitz Guides intends to review and update this book regularly. No expiry date limits this coupon.

La direction de l'établissement s'engage à faire bénéficier le porteur de ce coupon des prestations mentionnées en anglais au recto, suite à l'accord pris avec l'auteur du livre *More France for the $,* M. Alan Austin. En cas de doute, veuillez vous référer au directeur de votre hôtel/restaurant.

BERLITZ

This coupon is valid for the gift, complimentary offer or discount described on the reverse side. It must be presented in conjunction with the book *More France for the $,* as described in the preface on page 9. Although the author and Berlitz Guides can take no responsibility for the receipt of the benefits indicated, the publisher would greatly appreciate your communicating any difficulties encountered. Berlitz Guides intends to review and update this book regularly. No expiry date limits this coupon.

La direction de l'établissement s'engage à faire bénéficier le porteur de ce coupon des prestations mentionnées en anglais au recto, suite à l'accord pris avec l'auteur du livre *More France for the $,* M. Alan Austin. En cas de doute, veuillez vous référer au directeur de votre hôtel/restaurant.

BERLITZ

This coupon is valid for the gift, complimentary offer or discount described on the reverse side. It must be presented in conjunction with the book *More France for the $,* as described in the preface on page 9. Although the author and Berlitz Guides can take no responsibility for the receipt of the benefits indicated, the publisher would greatly appreciate your communicating any difficulties encountered. Berlitz Guides intends to review and update this book regularly. No expiry date limits this coupon.

La direction de l'établissement s'engage à faire bénéficier le porteur de ce coupon des prestations mentionnées en anglais au recto, suite à l'accord pris avec l'auteur du livre *More France for the $,* M. Alan Austin. En cas de doute, veuillez vous référer au directeur de votre hôtel/restaurant.

Restaurant Orsi
LYON
is pleased to offer

Complimentary kir royal champagne cocktail and appetizer

Valid for each guest at the table

Restaurant Henry
LYON
is pleased to offer

Complimentary main course

Valid for the less expensive of two main courses,
when two meals are ordered à la carte,
exclusive of tax and service

La Musardière
MILLAU
is pleased to offer

Complimentary bottle of wine

Valid with any room

BERLITZ

This coupon is valid for the gift, complimentary offer or discount described on the reverse side. It must be presented in conjunction with the book *More France for the $,* as described in the preface on page 9. Although the author and Berlitz Guides can take no responsibility for the receipt of the benefits indicated, the publisher would greatly appreciate your communicating any difficulties encountered. Berlitz Guides intends to review and update this book regularly. No expiry date limits this coupon.

La direction de l'établissement s'engage à faire bénéficier le porteur de ce coupon des prestations mentionnées en anglais au recto, suite à l'accord pris avec l'auteur du livre *More France for the $,* M. Alan Austin. En cas de doute, veuillez vous référer au directeur de votre hôtel/restaurant.

BERLITZ

This coupon is valid for the gift, complimentary offer or discount described on the reverse side. It must be presented in conjunction with the book *More France for the $,* as described in the preface on page 9. Although the author and Berlitz Guides can take no responsibility for the receipt of the benefits indicated, the publisher would greatly appreciate your communicating any difficulties encountered. Berlitz Guides intends to review and update this book regularly. No expiry date limits this coupon.

La direction de l'établissement s'engage à faire bénéficier le porteur de ce coupon des prestations mentionnées en anglais au recto, suite à l'accord pris avec l'auteur du livre *More France for the $,* M. Alan Austin. En cas de doute, veuillez vous référer au directeur de votre hôtel/restaurant.

BERLITZ

This coupon is valid for the gift, complimentary offer or discount described on the reverse side. It must be presented in conjunction with the book *More France for the $,* as described in the preface on page 9. Although the author and Berlitz Guides can take no responsibility for the receipt of the benefits indicated, the publisher would greatly appreciate your communicating any difficulties encountered. Berlitz Guides intends to review and update this book regularly. No expiry date limits this coupon.

La direction de l'établissement s'engage à faire bénéficier le porteur de ce coupon des prestations mentionnées en anglais au recto, suite à l'accord pris avec l'auteur du livre *More France for the $,* M. Alan Austin. En cas de doute, veuillez vous référer au directeur de votre hôtel/restaurant.

La Musardière
MILLAU
is pleased to offer

Complimentary champagne cocktail and appetizer

Valid for all at the table

International Hotel
MILLAU
is pleased to offer

20% reduction in room rates

Valid any time

International Hotel
MILLAU
is pleased to offer

Complimentary bottle of champagne

Valid when a suite is ordered

BERLITZ

This coupon is valid for the gift, complimentary offer or discount described on the reverse side. It must be presented in conjunction with the book *More France for the $,* as described in the preface on page 9. Although the author and Berlitz Guides can take no responsibility for the receipt of the benefits indicated, the publisher would greatly appreciate your communicating any difficulties encountered. Berlitz Guides intends to review and update this book regularly. No expiry date limits this coupon.

La direction de l'établissement s'engage à faire bénéficier le porteur de ce coupon des prestations mentionnées en anglais au recto, suite à l'accord pris avec l'auteur du livre *More France for the $,* M. Alan Austin. En cas de doute, veuillez vous référer au directeur de votre hôtel/restaurant.

BERLITZ

This coupon is valid for the gift, complimentary offer or discount described on the reverse side. It must be presented in conjunction with the book *More France for the $,* as described in the preface on page 9. Although the author and Berlitz Guides can take no responsibility for the receipt of the benefits indicated, the publisher would greatly appreciate your communicating any difficulties encountered. Berlitz Guides intends to review and update this book regularly. No expiry date limits this coupon.

La direction de l'établissement s'engage à faire bénéficier le porteur de ce coupon des prestations mentionnées en anglais au recto, suite à l'accord pris avec l'auteur du livre *More France for the $,* M. Alan Austin. En cas de doute, veuillez vous référer au directeur de votre hôtel/restaurant.

BERLITZ

This coupon is valid for the gift, complimentary offer or discount described on the reverse side. It must be presented in conjunction with the book *More France for the $,* as described in the preface on page 9. Although the author and Berlitz Guides can take no responsibility for the receipt of the benefits indicated, the publisher would greatly appreciate your communicating any difficulties encountered. Berlitz Guides intends to review and update this book regularly. No expiry date limits this coupon.

La direction de l'établissement s'engage à faire bénéficier le porteur de ce coupon des prestations mentionnées en anglais au recto, suite à l'accord pris avec l'auteur du livre *More France for the $,* M. Alan Austin. En cas de doute, veuillez vous référer au directeur de votre hôtel/restaurant.

International Hotel
MILLAU
is pleased to offer

Complimentary bottle of wine, house digestif and coffee

Valid when two meals are ordered. If a different vintage is desired, the price of the offered wine will be deducted.

La Braconne
MILLAU
is pleased to offer

Complimentary bottle of wine, house digestif and coffee

Valid when two meals are ordered. If a different vintage is desired, the price of the offered wine will be deducted.

Hôtel St-Christophe
MIRAMAR
is pleased to offer

50% reduction in room rates

Valid for two nights after a stay of five nights at the regular price

BERLITZ®

This coupon is valid for the gift, complimentary offer or discount described on the reverse side. It must be presented in conjunction with the book *More France for the $,* as described in the preface on page 9. Although the author and Berlitz Guides can take no responsibility for the receipt of the benefits indicated, the publisher would greatly appreciate your communicating any difficulties encountered. Berlitz Guides intends to review and update this book regularly. No expiry date limits this coupon.

La direction de l'établissement s'engage à faire bénéficier le porteur de ce coupon des prestations mentionnées en anglais au recto, suite à l'accord pris avec l'auteur du livre *More France for the $,* M. Alan Austin. En cas de doute, veuillez vous référer au directeur de votre hôtel/restaurant.

BERLITZ®

This coupon is valid for the gift, complimentary offer or discount described on the reverse side. It must be presented in conjunction with the book *More France for the $,* as described in the preface on page 9. Although the author and Berlitz Guides can take no responsibility for the receipt of the benefits indicated, the publisher would greatly appreciate your communicating any difficulties encountered. Berlitz Guides intends to review and update this book regularly. No expiry date limits this coupon.

La direction de l'établissement s'engage à faire bénéficier le porteur de ce coupon des prestations mentionnées en anglais au recto, suite à l'accord pris avec l'auteur du livre *More France for the $,* M. Alan Austin. En cas de doute, veuillez vous référer au directeur de votre hôtel/restaurant.

BERLITZ®

This coupon is valid for the gift, complimentary offer or discount described on the reverse side. It must be presented in conjunction with the book *More France for the $,* as described in the preface on page 9. Although the author and Berlitz Guides can take no responsibility for the receipt of the benefits indicated, the publisher would greatly appreciate your communicating any difficulties encountered. Berlitz Guides intends to review and update this book regularly. No expiry date limits this coupon.

La direction de l'établissement s'engage à faire bénéficier le porteur de ce coupon des prestations mentionnées en anglais au recto, suite à l'accord pris avec l'auteur du livre *More France for the $,* M. Alan Austin. En cas de doute, veuillez vous référer au directeur de votre hôtel/restaurant.

Hôtel St-Christophe
MIRAMAR
is pleased to offer

15% reduction in room rates

Valid from opening to 15 June and
from 16 September to closing

Hôtel St-Christophe
MIRAMAR
is pleased to offer

Complimentary cocktail or after-dinner drink

Valid for all at the table

Château d'Artigny
MONTBAZON
is pleased to offer

20% reduction in room rates

Valid January, February, March, and November

BERLITZ®

This coupon is valid for the gift, complimentary offer or discount described on the reverse side. It must be presented in conjunction with the book *More France for the $,* as described in the preface on page 9. Although the author and Berlitz Guides can take no responsibility for the receipt of the benefits indicated, the publisher would greatly appreciate your communicating any difficulties encountered. Berlitz Guides intends to review and update this book regularly. No expiry date limits this coupon.

La direction de l'établissement s'engage à faire bénéficier le porteur de ce coupon des prestations mentionnées en anglais au recto, suite à l'accord pris avec l'auteur du livre *More France for the $,* M. Alan Austin. En cas de doute, veuillez vous référer au directeur de votre hôtel/restaurant.

BERLITZ®

This coupon is valid for the gift, complimentary offer or discount described on the reverse side. It must be presented in conjunction with the book *More France for the $,* as described in the preface on page 9. Although the author and Berlitz Guides can take no responsibility for the receipt of the benefits indicated, the publisher would greatly appreciate your communicating any difficulties encountered. Berlitz Guides intends to review and update this book regularly. No expiry date limits this coupon.

La direction de l'établissement s'engage à faire bénéficier le porteur de ce coupon des prestations mentionnées en anglais au recto, suite à l'accord pris avec l'auteur du livre *More France for the $,* M. Alan Austin. En cas de doute, veuillez vous référer au directeur de votre hôtel/restaurant.

BERLITZ®

This coupon is valid for the gift, complimentary offer or discount described on the reverse side. It must be presented in conjunction with the book *More France for the $,* as described in the preface on page 9. Although the author and Berlitz Guides can take no responsibility for the receipt of the benefits indicated, the publisher would greatly appreciate your communicating any difficulties encountered. Berlitz Guides intends to review and update this book regularly. No expiry date limits this coupon.

La direction de l'établissement s'engage à faire bénéficier le porteur de ce coupon des prestations mentionnées en anglais au recto, suite à l'accord pris avec l'auteur du livre *More France for the $,* M. Alan Austin. En cas de doute, veuillez vous référer au directeur de votre hôtel/restaurant.

Château d'Artigny
MONTBAZON
is pleased to offer

Complimentary champagne cocktail and appetizer

Valid for all at the table

Hôtel Hermitage
MONTE CARLO
is pleased to offer

Complimentary entry to the Casino and Terrace swimming pool club; transportation and entry to Monte Carlo beach club; and 50% reduction at Golf and Tennis clubs

Valid with any room

Restaurant Belle Epoque
MONTE CARLO
is pleased to offer

Complimentary Grand Prix cocktail and appetizers

Valid for all at the table

BERLITZ

This coupon is valid for the gift, complimentary offer or discount described on the reverse side. It must be presented in conjunction with the book *More France for the $,* as described in the preface on page 9. Although the author and Berlitz Guides can take no responsibility for the receipt of the benefits indicated, the publisher would greatly appreciate your communicating any difficulties encountered. Berlitz Guides intends to review and update this book regularly. No expiry date limits this coupon.

La direction de l'établissement s'engage à faire bénéficier le porteur de ce coupon des prestations mentionnées en anglais au recto, suite à l'accord pris avec l'auteur du livre *More France for the $,* M. Alan Austin. En cas de doute, veuillez vous référer au directeur de votre hôtel/restaurant.

BERLITZ

This coupon is valid for the gift, complimentary offer or discount described on the reverse side. It must be presented in conjunction with the book *More France for the $,* as described in the preface on page 9. Although the author and Berlitz Guides can take no responsibility for the receipt of the benefits indicated, the publisher would greatly appreciate your communicating any difficulties encountered. Berlitz Guides intends to review and update this book regularly. No expiry date limits this coupon.

La direction de l'établissement s'engage à faire bénéficier le porteur de ce coupon des prestations mentionnées en anglais au recto, suite à l'accord pris avec l'auteur du livre *More France for the $,* M. Alan Austin. En cas de doute, veuillez vous référer au directeur de votre hôtel/restaurant.

BERLITZ

This coupon is valid for the gift, complimentary offer or discount described on the reverse side. It must be presented in conjunction with the book *More France for the $,* as described in the preface on page 9. Although the author and Berlitz Guides can take no responsibility for the receipt of the benefits indicated, the publisher would greatly appreciate your communicating any difficulties encountered. Berlitz Guides intends to review and update this book regularly. No expiry date limits this coupon.

La direction de l'établissement s'engage à faire bénéficier le porteur de ce coupon des prestations mentionnées en anglais au recto, suite à l'accord pris avec l'auteur du livre *More France for the $,* M. Alan Austin. En cas de doute, veuillez vous référer au directeur de votre hôtel/restaurant.

Hôtel Beach Plaza
MONTE CARLO
is pleased to offer

Room upgrading at no extra cost

Valid 1 November to 31 March (or up to Easter weekend, if earlier)
for a sea-view room with balcony for the price of an inside
room, if available at time of arrival. If upgrading is not possible,
a bottle of champagne in the room.

Le Gratin
MONTE CARLO
is pleased to offer

Complimentary bottle of wine

Valid when two dinners are ordered. If a different vintage is desired,
the price of the offered wine will be deducted.

Restaurant Louis XV
MONTE CARLO
is pleased to offer

Complimentary champagne cocktails and appetizer

Valid for two guests

BERLITZ

This coupon is valid for the gift, complimentary offer or discount described on the reverse side. It must be presented in conjunction with the book *More France for the $*, as described in the preface on page 9. Although the author and Berlitz Guides can take no responsibility for the receipt of the benefits indicated, the publisher would greatly appreciate your communicating any difficulties encountered. Berlitz Guides intends to review and update this book regularly. No expiry date limits this coupon.

La direction de l'établissement s'engage à faire bénéficier le porteur de ce coupon des prestations mentionnées en anglais au recto, suite à l'accord pris avec l'auteur du livre *More France for the $*, M. Alan Austin. En cas de doute, veuillez vous référer au directeur de votre hôtel/restaurant.

BERLITZ

This coupon is valid for the gift, complimentary offer or discount described on the reverse side. It must be presented in conjunction with the book *More France for the $*, as described in the preface on page 9. Although the author and Berlitz Guides can take no responsibility for the receipt of the benefits indicated, the publisher would greatly appreciate your communicating any difficulties encountered. Berlitz Guides intends to review and update this book regularly. No expiry date limits this coupon.

La direction de l'établissement s'engage à faire bénéficier le porteur de ce coupon des prestations mentionnées en anglais au recto, suite à l'accord pris avec l'auteur du livre *More France for the $*, M. Alan Austin. En cas de doute, veuillez vous référer au directeur de votre hôtel/restaurant.

BERLITZ

This coupon is valid for the gift, complimentary offer or discount described on the reverse side. It must be presented in conjunction with the book *More France for the $*, as described in the preface on page 9. Although the author and Berlitz Guides can take no responsibility for the receipt of the benefits indicated, the publisher would greatly appreciate your communicating any difficulties encountered. Berlitz Guides intends to review and update this book regularly. No expiry date limits this coupon.

La direction de l'établissement s'engage à faire bénéficier le porteur de ce coupon des prestations mentionnées en anglais au recto, suite à l'accord pris avec l'auteur du livre *More France for the $*, M. Alan Austin. En cas de doute, veuillez vous référer au directeur de votre hôtel/restaurant.

Restaurant Polpetta
MONTE CARLO
is pleased to offer

Complimentary kir royal champagne cocktail and Polpetta after-dinner liqueur

Valid for all at the table

La Ferme de Mougins
MOUGINS
is pleased to offer

Complimentary house champagne cocktail and appetizer, or choice of after-dinner drink

Valid for all at the table

Hôtel Belle Rive
NAJAC
is pleased to offer

20% reduction in room rates

Valid all year except July and August

BERLITZ®

This coupon is valid for the gift, complimentary offer or discount described on the reverse side. It must be presented in conjunction with the book *More France for the $*, as described in the preface on page 9. Although the author and Berlitz Guides can take no responsibility for the receipt of the benefits indicated, the publisher would greatly appreciate your communicating any difficulties encountered. Berlitz Guides intends to review and update this book regularly. No expiry date limits this coupon.

La direction de l'établissement s'engage à faire bénéficier le porteur de ce coupon des prestations mentionnées en anglais au recto, suite à l'accord pris avec l'auteur du livre *More France for the $*, M. Alan Austin. En cas de doute, veuillez vous référer au directeur de votre hôtel/restaurant.

BERLITZ®

This coupon is valid for the gift, complimentary offer or discount described on the reverse side. It must be presented in conjunction with the book *More France for the $*, as described in the preface on page 9. Although the author and Berlitz Guides can take no responsibility for the receipt of the benefits indicated, the publisher would greatly appreciate your communicating any difficulties encountered. Berlitz Guides intends to review and update this book regularly. No expiry date limits this coupon.

La direction de l'établissement s'engage à faire bénéficier le porteur de ce coupon des prestations mentionnées en anglais au recto, suite à l'accord pris avec l'auteur du livre *More France for the $*, M. Alan Austin. En cas de doute, veuillez vous référer au directeur de votre hôtel/restaurant.

BERLITZ®

This coupon is valid for the gift, complimentary offer or discount described on the reverse side. It must be presented in conjunction with the book *More France for the $*, as described in the preface on page 9. Although the author and Berlitz Guides can take no responsibility for the receipt of the benefits indicated, the publisher would greatly appreciate your communicating any difficulties encountered. Berlitz Guides intends to review and update this book regularly. No expiry date limits this coupon.

La direction de l'établissement s'engage à faire bénéficier le porteur de ce coupon des prestations mentionnées en anglais au recto, suite à l'accord pris avec l'auteur du livre *More France for the $*, M. Alan Austin. En cas de doute, veuillez vous référer au directeur de votre hôtel/restaurant.

Hôtel Belle Rive
NAJAC
is pleased to offer

Complimentary picnic lunch, including wine

Valid any time if room and dinner are booked

Grand Hôtel de la Reine
NANCY
is pleased to offer

25% reduction in room rates

Valid at all times

Le Stanislas
NANCY
is pleased to offer

Complimentary bottle of champagne

Valid for two guests ordering together

BERLITZ

This coupon is valid for the gift, complimentary offer or discount described on the reverse side. It must be presented in conjunction with the book *More France for the $,* as described in the preface on page 9. Although the author and Berlitz Guides can take no responsibility for the receipt of the benefits indicated, the publisher would greatly appreciate your communicating any difficulties encountered. Berlitz Guides intends to review and update this book regularly. No expiry date limits this coupon.

La direction de l'établissement s'engage à faire bénéficier le porteur de ce coupon des prestations mentionnées en anglais au recto, suite à l'accord pris avec l'auteur du livre *More France for the $,* M. Alan Austin. En cas de doute, veuillez vous référer au directeur de votre hôtel/restaurant.

BERLITZ

This coupon is valid for the gift, complimentary offer or discount described on the reverse side. It must be presented in conjunction with the book *More France for the $,* as described in the preface on page 9. Although the author and Berlitz Guides can take no responsibility for the receipt of the benefits indicated, the publisher would greatly appreciate your communicating any difficulties encountered. Berlitz Guides intends to review and update this book regularly. No expiry date limits this coupon.

La direction de l'établissement s'engage à faire bénéficier le porteur de ce coupon des prestations mentionnées en anglais au recto, suite à l'accord pris avec l'auteur du livre *More France for the $,* M. Alan Austin. En cas de doute, veuillez vous référer au directeur de votre hôtel/restaurant.

BERLITZ

This coupon is valid for the gift, complimentary offer or discount described on the reverse side. It must be presented in conjunction with the book *More France for the $,* as described in the preface on page 9. Although the author and Berlitz Guides can take no responsibility for the receipt of the benefits indicated, the publisher would greatly appreciate your communicating any difficulties encountered. Berlitz Guides intends to review and update this book regularly. No expiry date limits this coupon.

La direction de l'établissement s'engage à faire bénéficier le porteur de ce coupon des prestations mentionnées en anglais au recto, suite à l'accord pris avec l'auteur du livre *More France for the $,* M. Alan Austin. En cas de doute, veuillez vous référer au directeur de votre hôtel/restaurant.

Le Goéland
NANCY
is pleased to offer

Complimentary cocktail and appetizer

Valid for all at the table

Hôtel Négresco
NICE
is pleased to offer

Room upgrading at no extra cost, plus flowers and basket of fruit

Valid any time for a sea-view or deluxe room for the price
of an inside or standard room, if available at time of arrival

Le Chantecler
NICE
is pleased to offer

Complimentary champagne cocktail Négresco and appetizer

Valid for all at the table

BERLITZ

This coupon is valid for the gift, complimentary offer or discount described on the reverse side. It must be presented in conjunction with the book *More France for the $*, as described in the preface on page 9. Although the author and Berlitz Guides can take no responsibility for the receipt of the benefits indicated, the publisher would greatly appreciate your communicating any difficulties encountered. Berlitz Guides intends to review and update this book regularly. No expiry date limits this coupon.

La direction de l'établissement s'engage à faire bénéficier le porteur de ce coupon des prestations mentionnées en anglais au recto, suite à l'accord pris avec l'auteur du livre *More France for the $*, M. Alan Austin. En cas de doute, veuillez vous référer au directeur de votre hôtel/restaurant.

BERLITZ

This coupon is valid for the gift, complimentary offer or discount described on the reverse side. It must be presented in conjunction with the book *More France for the $*, as described in the preface on page 9. Although the author and Berlitz Guides can take no responsibility for the receipt of the benefits indicated, the publisher would greatly appreciate your communicating any difficulties encountered. Berlitz Guides intends to review and update this book regularly. No expiry date limits this coupon.

La direction de l'établissement s'engage à faire bénéficier le porteur de ce coupon des prestations mentionnées en anglais au recto, suite à l'accord pris avec l'auteur du livre *More France for the $*, M. Alan Austin. En cas de doute, veuillez vous référer au directeur de votre hôtel/restaurant.

BERLITZ

This coupon is valid for the gift, complimentary offer or discount described on the reverse side. It must be presented in conjunction with the book *More France for the $*, as described in the preface on page 9. Although the author and Berlitz Guides can take no responsibility for the receipt of the benefits indicated, the publisher would greatly appreciate your communicating any difficulties encountered. Berlitz Guides intends to review and update this book regularly. No expiry date limits this coupon.

La direction de l'établissement s'engage à faire bénéficier le porteur de ce coupon des prestations mentionnées en anglais au recto, suite à l'accord pris avec l'auteur du livre *More France for the $*, M. Alan Austin. En cas de doute, veuillez vous référer au directeur de votre hôtel/restaurant.

La Rotonde
NICE
is pleased to offer

Complimentary half-liter carafe of wine

Valid for two guests ordering a meal

Hôtel Beach Regency
NICE
is pleased to offer

Room upgrading at no extra cost

Valid any time for a sea-view room with balcony for the price of
a standard room, if available at time of arrival.
If upgrading is not possible, a bottle of champagne in the room.

Le Regency
NICE
is pleased to offer

Complimentary bottle of wine

Valid when two meals are ordered. If a different vintage is desired,
the price of the wine offered will be deducted.

BERLITZ

This coupon is valid for the gift, complimentary offer or discount described on the reverse side. It must be presented in conjunction with the book *More France for the $,* as described in the preface on page 9. Although the author and Berlitz Guides can take no responsibility for the receipt of the benefits indicated, the publisher would greatly appreciate your communicating any difficulties encountered. Berlitz Guides intends to review and update this book regularly. No expiry date limits this coupon.

La direction de l'établissement s'engage à faire bénéficier le porteur de ce coupon des prestations mentionnées en anglais au recto, suite à l'accord pris avec l'auteur du livre *More France for the $,* M. Alan Austin. En cas de doute, veuillez vous référer au directeur de votre hôtel/restaurant.

BERLITZ

This coupon is valid for the gift, complimentary offer or discount described on the reverse side. It must be presented in conjunction with the book *More France for the $,* as described in the preface on page 9. Although the author and Berlitz Guides can take no responsibility for the receipt of the benefits indicated, the publisher would greatly appreciate your communicating any difficulties encountered. Berlitz Guides intends to review and update this book regularly. No expiry date limits this coupon.

La direction de l'établissement s'engage à faire bénéficier le porteur de ce coupon des prestations mentionnées en anglais au recto, suite à l'accord pris avec l'auteur du livre *More France for the $,* M. Alan Austin. En cas de doute, veuillez vous référer au directeur de votre hôtel/restaurant.

BERLITZ

This coupon is valid for the gift, complimentary offer or discount described on the reverse side. It must be presented in conjunction with the book *More France for the $,* as described in the preface on page 9. Although the author and Berlitz Guides can take no responsibility for the receipt of the benefits indicated, the publisher would greatly appreciate your communicating any difficulties encountered. Berlitz Guides intends to review and update this book regularly. No expiry date limits this coupon.

La direction de l'établissement s'engage à faire bénéficier le porteur de ce coupon des prestations mentionnées en anglais au recto, suite à l'accord pris avec l'auteur du livre *More France for the $,* M. Alan Austin. En cas de doute, veuillez vous référer au directeur de votre hôtel/restaurant.

Le Regency
NICE
is pleased to offer

Complimentary kir royal champagne cocktail and appetizer

Valid when a single meal is ordered

Le Gourmet Lorrain
NICE
is pleased to offer

Complimentary bottle of champagne

Valid with any room

Le Gourmet Lorrain
NICE
is pleased to offer

Complimentary 100-year-old armagnac

Valid for all at the table

BERLITZ

This coupon is valid for the gift, complimentary offer or discount described on the reverse side. It must be presented in conjunction with the book *More France for the $,* as described in the preface on page 9. Although the author and Berlitz Guides can take no responsibility for the receipt of the benefits indicated, the publisher would greatly appreciate your communicating any difficulties encountered. Berlitz Guides intends to review and update this book regularly. No expiry date limits this coupon.

La direction de l'établissement s'engage à faire bénéficier le porteur de ce coupon des prestations mentionnées en anglais au recto, suite à l'accord pris avec l'auteur du livre *More France for the $,* M. Alan Austin. En cas de doute, veuillez vous référer au directeur de votre hôtel/restaurant.

BERLITZ

This coupon is valid for the gift, complimentary offer or discount described on the reverse side. It must be presented in conjunction with the book *More France for the $,* as described in the preface on page 9. Although the author and Berlitz Guides can take no responsibility for the receipt of the benefits indicated, the publisher would greatly appreciate your communicating any difficulties encountered. Berlitz Guides intends to review and update this book regularly. No expiry date limits this coupon.

La direction de l'établissement s'engage à faire bénéficier le porteur de ce coupon des prestations mentionnées en anglais au recto, suite à l'accord pris avec l'auteur du livre *More France for the $,* M. Alan Austin. En cas de doute, veuillez vous référer au directeur de votre hôtel/restaurant.

BERLITZ

This coupon is valid for the gift, complimentary offer or discount described on the reverse side. It must be presented in conjunction with the book *More France for the $,* as described in the preface on page 9. Although the author and Berlitz Guides can take no responsibility for the receipt of the benefits indicated, the publisher would greatly appreciate your communicating any difficulties encountered. Berlitz Guides intends to review and update this book regularly. No expiry date limits this coupon.

La direction de l'établissement s'engage à faire bénéficier le porteur de ce coupon des prestations mentionnées en anglais au recto, suite à l'accord pris avec l'auteur du livre *More France for the $,* M. Alan Austin. En cas de doute, veuillez vous référer au directeur de votre hôtel/restaurant.

Hôtel de Lausanne
NICE
is pleased to offer

50% reduction in room rates

Valid for one night after a stay of three nights at the regular price,
1 April to 31 October

Hôtel de Lausanne
NICE
is pleased to offer

30% reduction in room rates

Valid 1 November to 20 December and 3 January to 31 March

Hôtel Pullman
NICE
is pleased to offer

30% reduction in room rates

Valid 1 November to 31 March

BERLITZ

This coupon is valid for the gift, complimentary offer or discount described on the reverse side. It must be presented in conjunction with the book *More France for the $,* as described in the preface on page 9. Although the author and Berlitz Guides can take no responsibility for the receipt of the benefits indicated, the publisher would greatly appreciate your communicating any difficulties encountered. Berlitz Guides intends to review and update this book regularly. No expiry date limits this coupon.

La direction de l'établissement s'engage à faire bénéficier le porteur de ce coupon des prestations mentionnées en anglais au recto, suite à l'accord pris avec l'auteur du livre *More France for the $,* M. Alan Austin. En cas de doute, veuillez vous référer au directeur de votre hôtel/restaurant.

BERLITZ

This coupon is valid for the gift, complimentary offer or discount described on the reverse side. It must be presented in conjunction with the book *More France for the $,* as described in the preface on page 9. Although the author and Berlitz Guides can take no responsibility for the receipt of the benefits indicated, the publisher would greatly appreciate your communicating any difficulties encountered. Berlitz Guides intends to review and update this book regularly. No expiry date limits this coupon.

La direction de l'établissement s'engage à faire bénéficier le porteur de ce coupon des prestations mentionnées en anglais au recto, suite à l'accord pris avec l'auteur du livre *More France for the $,* M. Alan Austin. En cas de doute, veuillez vous référer au directeur de votre hôtel/restaurant.

BERLITZ

This coupon is valid for the gift, complimentary offer or discount described on the reverse side. It must be presented in conjunction with the book *More France for the $,* as described in the preface on page 9. Although the author and Berlitz Guides can take no responsibility for the receipt of the benefits indicated, the publisher would greatly appreciate your communicating any difficulties encountered. Berlitz Guides intends to review and update this book regularly. No expiry date limits this coupon.

La direction de l'établissement s'engage à faire bénéficier le porteur de ce coupon des prestations mentionnées en anglais au recto, suite à l'accord pris avec l'auteur du livre *More France for the $,* M. Alan Austin. En cas de doute, veuillez vous référer au directeur de votre hôtel/restaurant.

Neptune Plage
NICE
is pleased to offer

Complimentary entry to the beach club and mattresses

Valid for each guest ordering lunch

La Côte d'Or
NUITS-ST-GEORGES
is pleased to offer

20% reduction in room rates

Valid 1 November to 31 March, except Saturdays

La Côte d'Or
NUITS-ST-GEORGES
is pleased to offer

Complimentary bottle of crémant de Bourgogne

Valid with any room

This coupon is valid for the gift, complimentary offer or discount described on the reverse side. It must be presented in conjunction with the book *More France for the $*, as described in the preface on page 9. Although the author and Berlitz Guides can take no responsibility for the receipt of the benefits indicated, the publisher would greatly appreciate your communicating any difficulties encountered. Berlitz Guides intends to review and update this book regularly. No expiry date limits this coupon.

La direction de l'établissement s'engage à faire bénéficier le porteur de ce coupon des prestations mentionnées en anglais au recto, suite à l'accord pris avec l'auteur du livre *More France for the $*, M. Alan Austin. En cas de doute, veuillez vous référer au directeur de votre hôtel/restaurant.

This coupon is valid for the gift, complimentary offer or discount described on the reverse side. It must be presented in conjunction with the book *More France for the $*, as described in the preface on page 9. Although the author and Berlitz Guides can take no responsibility for the receipt of the benefits indicated, the publisher would greatly appreciate your communicating any difficulties encountered. Berlitz Guides intends to review and update this book regularly. No expiry date limits this coupon.

La direction de l'établissement s'engage à faire bénéficier le porteur de ce coupon des prestations mentionnées en anglais au recto, suite à l'accord pris avec l'auteur du livre *More France for the $*, M. Alan Austin. En cas de doute, veuillez vous référer au directeur de votre hôtel/restaurant.

This coupon is valid for the gift, complimentary offer or discount described on the reverse side. It must be presented in conjunction with the book *More France for the $*, as described in the preface on page 9. Although the author and Berlitz Guides can take no responsibility for the receipt of the benefits indicated, the publisher would greatly appreciate your communicating any difficulties encountered. Berlitz Guides intends to review and update this book regularly. No expiry date limits this coupon.

La direction de l'établissement s'engage à faire bénéficier le porteur de ce coupon des prestations mentionnées en anglais au recto, suite à l'accord pris avec l'auteur du livre *More France for the $*, M. Alan Austin. En cas de doute, veuillez vous référer au directeur de votre hôtel/restaurant.

La Côte d'Or
NUITS-ST-GEORGES
is pleased to offer

Complimentary house cocktail and dessert

Valid for all at the table

Domaine des Hauts-de-Loire
ONZAIN
is pleased to offer

50% reduction in room rates

Valid 1 February to 15 April (except Easter) and November

Domaine des Hauts-de-Loire
ONZAIN
is pleased to offer
Complimentary bottle of wine
plus dessert of the day

Valid at lunch (except Sunday) for two guests ordering together.
If a different vintage is desired, the price of the offered wine
will be deducted.

BERLITZ

This coupon is valid for the gift, complimentary offer or discount described on the reverse side. It must be presented in conjunction with the book *More France for the $*, as described in the preface on page 9. Although the author and Berlitz Guides can take no responsibility for the receipt of the benefits indicated, the publisher would greatly appreciate your communicating any difficulties encountered. Berlitz Guides intends to review and update this book regularly. No expiry date limits this coupon.

La direction de l'établissement s'engage à faire bénéficier le porteur de ce coupon des prestations mentionnées en anglais au recto, suite à l'accord pris avec l'auteur du livre *More France for the $*, M. Alan Austin. En cas de doute, veuillez vous référer au directeur de votre hôtel/restaurant.

BERLITZ

This coupon is valid for the gift, complimentary offer or discount described on the reverse side. It must be presented in conjunction with the book *More France for the $*, as described in the preface on page 9. Although the author and Berlitz Guides can take no responsibility for the receipt of the benefits indicated, the publisher would greatly appreciate your communicating any difficulties encountered. Berlitz Guides intends to review and update this book regularly. No expiry date limits this coupon.

La direction de l'établissement s'engage à faire bénéficier le porteur de ce coupon des prestations mentionnées en anglais au recto, suite à l'accord pris avec l'auteur du livre *More France for the $*, M. Alan Austin. En cas de doute, veuillez vous référer au directeur de votre hôtel/restaurant.

BERLITZ

This coupon is valid for the gift, complimentary offer or discount described on the reverse side. It must be presented in conjunction with the book *More France for the $*, as described in the preface on page 9. Although the author and Berlitz Guides can take no responsibility for the receipt of the benefits indicated, the publisher would greatly appreciate your communicating any difficulties encountered. Berlitz Guides intends to review and update this book regularly. No expiry date limits this coupon.

La direction de l'établissement s'engage à faire bénéficier le porteur de ce coupon des prestations mentionnées en anglais au recto, suite à l'accord pris avec l'auteur du livre *More France for the $*, M. Alan Austin. En cas de doute, veuillez vous référer au directeur de votre hôtel/restaurant.

Domaine des Hauts-de-Loire
ONZAIN
is pleased to offer

Complimentary bottle of wine

Valid at dinner (except Sunday) for two guests ordering together.
If a different vintage is desired, the price of the offered wine
will be deducted.

Hôtel Lotti
PARIS
is pleased to offer

Room upgrading at no extra cost

Valid any time for a deluxe room for the price
of a mid-category room, if available at time of arrival

Hôtel Lotti
PARIS
is pleased to offer

A gift box of red, white and rosé wines

Valid with any room

This coupon is valid for the gift, complimentary offer or discount described on the reverse side. It must be presented in conjunction with the book *More France for the $*, as described in the preface on page 9. Although the author and Berlitz Guides can take no responsibility for the receipt of the benefits indicated, the publisher would greatly appreciate your communicating any difficulties encountered. Berlitz Guides intends to review and update this book regularly. No expiry date limits this coupon.

La direction de l'établissement s'engage à faire bénéficier le porteur de ce coupon des prestations mentionnées en anglais au recto, suite à l'accord pris avec l'auteur du livre *More France for the $*, M. Alan Austin. En cas de doute, veuillez vous référer au directeur de votre hôtel/restaurant.

This coupon is valid for the gift, complimentary offer or discount described on the reverse side. It must be presented in conjunction with the book *More France for the $*, as described in the preface on page 9. Although the author and Berlitz Guides can take no responsibility for the receipt of the benefits indicated, the publisher would greatly appreciate your communicating any difficulties encountered. Berlitz Guides intends to review and update this book regularly. No expiry date limits this coupon.

La direction de l'établissement s'engage à faire bénéficier le porteur de ce coupon des prestations mentionnées en anglais au recto, suite à l'accord pris avec l'auteur du livre *More France for the $*, M. Alan Austin. En cas de doute, veuillez vous référer au directeur de votre hôtel/restaurant.

This coupon is valid for the gift, complimentary offer or discount described on the reverse side. It must be presented in conjunction with the book *More France for the $*, as described in the preface on page 9. Although the author and Berlitz Guides can take no responsibility for the receipt of the benefits indicated, the publisher would greatly appreciate your communicating any difficulties encountered. Berlitz Guides intends to review and update this book regularly. No expiry date limits this coupon.

La direction de l'établissement s'engage à faire bénéficier le porteur de ce coupon des prestations mentionnées en anglais au recto, suite à l'accord pris avec l'auteur du livre *More France for the $*, M. Alan Austin. En cas de doute, veuillez vous référer au directeur de votre hôtel/restaurant.

Le Lotti
PARIS
is pleased to offer

Complimentary hors-d'œuvre or cheese course

Valid for each guest ordering a meal à la carte

Hôtel Westminster
PARIS
is pleased to offer

Room upgrading at no extra cost

Valid any time for a deluxe double or suite for the price
of a standard double, if available at time of arrival.
If upgrading is not possible, a bottle of champagne in the room.

Le Céladon
PARIS
is pleased to offer

10% reduction on food and drink

Valid with any meal

BERLITZ

This coupon is valid for the gift, complimentary offer or discount described on the reverse side. It must be presented in conjunction with the book *More France for the $*, as described in the preface on page 9. Although the author and Berlitz Guides can take no responsibility for the receipt of the benefits indicated, the publisher would greatly appreciate your communicating any difficulties encountered. Berlitz Guides intends to review and update this book regularly. No expiry date limits this coupon.

La direction de l'établissement s'engage à faire bénéficier le porteur de ce coupon des prestations mentionnées en anglais au recto, suite à l'accord pris avec l'auteur du livre *More France for the $*, M. Alan Austin. En cas de doute, veuillez vous référer au directeur de votre hôtel/restaurant.

BERLITZ

This coupon is valid for the gift, complimentary offer or discount described on the reverse side. It must be presented in conjunction with the book *More France for the $*, as described in the preface on page 9. Although the author and Berlitz Guides can take no responsibility for the receipt of the benefits indicated, the publisher would greatly appreciate your communicating any difficulties encountered. Berlitz Guides intends to review and update this book regularly. No expiry date limits this coupon.

La direction de l'établissement s'engage à faire bénéficier le porteur de ce coupon des prestations mentionnées en anglais au recto, suite à l'accord pris avec l'auteur du livre *More France for the $*, M. Alan Austin. En cas de doute, veuillez vous référer au directeur de votre hôtel/restaurant.

BERLITZ

This coupon is valid for the gift, complimentary offer or discount described on the reverse side. It must be presented in conjunction with the book *More France for the $*, as described in the preface on page 9. Although the author and Berlitz Guides can take no responsibility for the receipt of the benefits indicated, the publisher would greatly appreciate your communicating any difficulties encountered. Berlitz Guides intends to review and update this book regularly. No expiry date limits this coupon.

La direction de l'établissement s'engage à faire bénéficier le porteur de ce coupon des prestations mentionnées en anglais au recto, suite à l'accord pris avec l'auteur du livre *More France for the $*, M. Alan Austin. En cas de doute, veuillez vous référer au directeur de votre hôtel/restaurant.

Le Miravile
PARIS
is pleased to offer

Complimentary champagne cocktail and appetizer

Valid for each guest at the table

Hôtel Lutétia
PARIS
is pleased to offer

25% reduction in room rates

Valid July, August, and from 1 November to 30 April

Hôtel Lutétia
PARIS
is pleased to offer

Room upgrading at no extra cost

Valid any time for a deluxe double or suite for the price
of a standard double, if available at time of arrival. If upgrading
is not possible, a half-bottle of champagne in the room.

BERLITZ

This coupon is valid for the gift, complimentary offer or discount described on the reverse side. It must be presented in conjunction with the book *More France for the $*, as described in the preface on page 9. Although the author and Berlitz Guides can take no responsibility for the receipt of the benefits indicated, the publisher would greatly appreciate your communicating any difficulties encountered. Berlitz Guides intends to review and update this book regularly. No expiry date limits this coupon.

La direction de l'établissement s'engage à faire bénéficier le porteur de ce coupon des prestations mentionnées en anglais au recto, suite à l'accord pris avec l'auteur du livre *More France for the $*, M. Alan Austin. En cas de doute, veuillez vous référer au directeur de votre hôtel/restaurant.

BERLITZ

This coupon is valid for the gift, complimentary offer or discount described on the reverse side. It must be presented in conjunction with the book *More France for the $*, as described in the preface on page 9. Although the author and Berlitz Guides can take no responsibility for the receipt of the benefits indicated, the publisher would greatly appreciate your communicating any difficulties encountered. Berlitz Guides intends to review and update this book regularly. No expiry date limits this coupon.

La direction de l'établissement s'engage à faire bénéficier le porteur de ce coupon des prestations mentionnées en anglais au recto, suite à l'accord pris avec l'auteur du livre *More France for the $*, M. Alan Austin. En cas de doute, veuillez vous référer au directeur de votre hôtel/restaurant.

BERLITZ

This coupon is valid for the gift, complimentary offer or discount described on the reverse side. It must be presented in conjunction with the book *More France for the $*, as described in the preface on page 9. Although the author and Berlitz Guides can take no responsibility for the receipt of the benefits indicated, the publisher would greatly appreciate your communicating any difficulties encountered. Berlitz Guides intends to review and update this book regularly. No expiry date limits this coupon.

La direction de l'établissement s'engage à faire bénéficier le porteur de ce coupon des prestations mentionnées en anglais au recto, suite à l'accord pris avec l'auteur du livre *More France for the $*, M. Alan Austin. En cas de doute, veuillez vous référer au directeur de votre hôtel/restaurant.

Brasserie Lutétia
PARIS
is pleased to offer

Complimentary kir aligoté cocktail

Valid for each guest at the table

Le Paris
PARIS
is pleased to offer

Complimentary bottle of champagne

Valid when two meals are ordered

Hôtel Pont-Royal
PARIS
is pleased to offer

20% reduction in room rates

Valid 1 November to 30 April

BERLITZ®

This coupon is valid for the gift, complimentary offer or discount described on the reverse side. It must be presented in conjunction with the book *More France for the $,* as described in the preface on page 9. Although the author and Berlitz Guides can take no responsibility for the receipt of the benefits indicated, the publisher would greatly appreciate your communicating any difficulties encountered. Berlitz Guides intends to review and update this book regularly. No expiry date limits this coupon.

La direction de l'établissement s'engage à faire bénéficier le porteur de ce coupon des prestations mentionnées en anglais au recto, suite à l'accord pris avec l'auteur du livre *More France for the $,* M. Alan Austin. En cas de doute, veuillez vous référer au directeur de votre hôtel/restaurant.

BERLITZ®

This coupon is valid for the gift, complimentary offer or discount described on the reverse side. It must be presented in conjunction with the book *More France for the $,* as described in the preface on page 9. Although the author and Berlitz Guides can take no responsibility for the receipt of the benefits indicated, the publisher would greatly appreciate your communicating any difficulties encountered. Berlitz Guides intends to review and update this book regularly. No expiry date limits this coupon.

La direction de l'établissement s'engage à faire bénéficier le porteur de ce coupon des prestations mentionnées en anglais au recto, suite à l'accord pris avec l'auteur du livre *More France for the $,* M. Alan Austin. En cas de doute, veuillez vous référer au directeur de votre hôtel/restaurant.

BERLITZ®

This coupon is valid for the gift, complimentary offer or discount described on the reverse side. It must be presented in conjunction with the book *More France for the $,* as described in the preface on page 9. Although the author and Berlitz Guides can take no responsibility for the receipt of the benefits indicated, the publisher would greatly appreciate your communicating any difficulties encountered. Berlitz Guides intends to review and update this book regularly. No expiry date limits this coupon.

La direction de l'établissement s'engage à faire bénéficier le porteur de ce coupon des prestations mentionnées en anglais au recto, suite à l'accord pris avec l'auteur du livre *More France for the $,* M. Alan Austin. En cas de doute, veuillez vous référer au directeur de votre hôtel/restaurant.

Hôtel Pont-Royal
PARIS
is pleased to offer

Room upgrading at no extra cost

Valid any time for a superior or deluxe category room for the price
of a standard room, if available at time of arrival

Hôtel Pont-Royal
PARIS
is pleased to offer

Complimentary bottle of champagne

Valid with any room

Les Antiquaires
PARIS
is pleased to offer

Complimentary house cocktail

Valid for all at the table

BERLITZ

This coupon is valid for the gift, complimentary offer or discount described on the reverse side. It must be presented in conjunction with the book *More France for the $,* as described in the preface on page 9. Although the author and Berlitz Guides can take no responsibility for the receipt of the benefits indicated, the publisher would greatly appreciate your communicating any difficulties encountered. Berlitz Guides intends to review and update this book regularly. No expiry date limits this coupon.

La direction de l'établissement s'engage à faire bénéficier le porteur de ce coupon des prestations mentionnées en anglais au recto, suite à l'accord pris avec l'auteur du livre *More France for the $,* M. Alan Austin. En cas de doute, veuillez vous référer au directeur de votre hôtel/restaurant.

BERLITZ

This coupon is valid for the gift, complimentary offer or discount described on the reverse side. It must be presented in conjunction with the book *More France for the $,* as described in the preface on page 9. Although the author and Berlitz Guides can take no responsibility for the receipt of the benefits indicated, the publisher would greatly appreciate your communicating any difficulties encountered. Berlitz Guides intends to review and update this book regularly. No expiry date limits this coupon.

La direction de l'établissement s'engage à faire bénéficier le porteur de ce coupon des prestations mentionnées en anglais au recto, suite à l'accord pris avec l'auteur du livre *More France for the $,* M. Alan Austin. En cas de doute, veuillez vous référer au directeur de votre hôtel/restaurant.

BERLITZ

This coupon is valid for the gift, complimentary offer or discount described on the reverse side. It must be presented in conjunction with the book *More France for the $,* as described in the preface on page 9. Although the author and Berlitz Guides can take no responsibility for the receipt of the benefits indicated, the publisher would greatly appreciate your communicating any difficulties encountered. Berlitz Guides intends to review and update this book regularly. No expiry date limits this coupon.

La direction de l'établissement s'engage à faire bénéficier le porteur de ce coupon des prestations mentionnées en anglais au recto, suite à l'accord pris avec l'auteur du livre *More France for the $,* M. Alan Austin. En cas de doute, veuillez vous référer au directeur de votre hôtel/restaurant.

Hôtel St-Dominique
PARIS
is pleased to offer

Complimentary bottle of champagne

Valid with any room

La Ferme St-Simon
PARIS
is pleased to offer

Complimentary champagne cocktail

Valid for all at the table

Hôtel Concorde St-Lazare
PARIS
is pleased to offer

50% reduction in room rates

Valid for three nights after a stay of four nights
at the regular price

BERLITZ®

This coupon is valid for the gift, complimentary offer or discount described on the reverse side. It must be presented in conjunction with the book *More France for the $,* as described in the preface on page 9. Although the author and Berlitz Guides can take no responsibility for the receipt of the benefits indicated, the publisher would greatly appreciate your communicating any difficulties encountered. Berlitz Guides intends to review and update this book regularly. No expiry date limits this coupon.

La direction de l'établissement s'engage à faire bénéficier le porteur de ce coupon des prestations mentionnées en anglais au recto, suite à l'accord pris avec l'auteur du livre *More France for the $,* M. Alan Austin. En cas de doute, veuillez vous référer au directeur de votre hôtel/restaurant.

BERLITZ®

This coupon is valid for the gift, complimentary offer or discount described on the reverse side. It must be presented in conjunction with the book *More France for the $,* as described in the preface on page 9. Although the author and Berlitz Guides can take no responsibility for the receipt of the benefits indicated, the publisher would greatly appreciate your communicating any difficulties encountered. Berlitz Guides intends to review and update this book regularly. No expiry date limits this coupon.

La direction de l'établissement s'engage à faire bénéficier le porteur de ce coupon des prestations mentionnées en anglais au recto, suite à l'accord pris avec l'auteur du livre *More France for the $,* M. Alan Austin. En cas de doute, veuillez vous référer au directeur de votre hôtel/restaurant.

BERLITZ®

This coupon is valid for the gift, complimentary offer or discount described on the reverse side. It must be presented in conjunction with the book *More France for the $,* as described in the preface on page 9. Although the author and Berlitz Guides can take no responsibility for the receipt of the benefits indicated, the publisher would greatly appreciate your communicating any difficulties encountered. Berlitz Guides intends to review and update this book regularly. No expiry date limits this coupon.

La direction de l'établissement s'engage à faire bénéficier le porteur de ce coupon des prestations mentionnées en anglais au recto, suite à l'accord pris avec l'auteur du livre *More France for the $,* M. Alan Austin. En cas de doute, veuillez vous référer au directeur de votre hôtel/restaurant.

Hôtel Concorde St-Lazare
PARIS
is pleased to offer

Room upgrading at no extra cost

Valid any time for a superior room for the price of a standard room,
if available at time of arrival

Café Terminus
PARIS
is pleased to offer

Complimentary cocktail and coffee

Valid for all at the table

Hôtel Royal Monceau
PARIS
is pleased to offer

Room upgrading at no extra cost

Valid any time for a deluxe room for the price of a standard room,
if available at time of arrival

BERLITZ®

This coupon is valid for the gift, complimentary offer or discount described on the reverse side. It must be presented
in conjunction with the book *More France for the $*, as
described in the preface on page 9. Although the author and
Berlitz Guides can take no responsibility for the receipt of the
benefits indicated, the publisher would greatly appreciate
your communicating any difficulties encountered. Berlitz
Guides intends to review and update this book regularly.
No expiry date limits this coupon.

La direction de l'établissement s'engage à faire bénéficier
le porteur de ce coupon des prestations mentionnées en
anglais au recto, suite à l'accord pris avec l'auteur du livre
More France for the $, M. Alan Austin. En cas de doute,
veuillez vous référer au directeur de votre hôtel/restaurant.

BERLITZ®

This coupon is valid for the gift, complimentary offer or discount described on the reverse side. It must be presented
in conjunction with the book *More France for the $*, as
described in the preface on page 9. Although the author and
Berlitz Guides can take no responsibility for the receipt of the
benefits indicated, the publisher would greatly appreciate
your communicating any difficulties encountered. Berlitz
Guides intends to review and update this book regularly.
No expiry date limits this coupon.

La direction de l'établissement s'engage à faire bénéficier
le porteur de ce coupon des prestations mentionnées en
anglais au recto, suite à l'accord pris avec l'auteur du livre
More France for the $, M. Alan Austin. En cas de doute,
veuillez vous référer au directeur de votre hôtel/restaurant.

BERLITZ®

This coupon is valid for the gift, complimentary offer or discount described on the reverse side. It must be presented
in conjunction with the book *More France for the $*, as
described in the preface on page 9. Although the author and
Berlitz Guides can take no responsibility for the receipt of the
benefits indicated, the publisher would greatly appreciate
your communicating any difficulties encountered. Berlitz
Guides intends to review and update this book regularly.
No expiry date limits this coupon.

La direction de l'établissement s'engage à faire bénéficier
le porteur de ce coupon des prestations mentionnées en
anglais au recto, suite à l'accord pris avec l'auteur du livre
More France for the $, M. Alan Austin. En cas de doute,
veuillez vous référer au directeur de votre hôtel/restaurant.

Hôtel Royal Monceau
PARIS
is pleased to offer

Complimentary bottle of champagne

Valid with any room

Baumann Marbeuf
PARIS
is pleased to offer

Complimentary crémant d'Alsace cocktail and appetizer

Valid for all at the table

Restaurant Napoléon
PARIS
is pleased to offer

Complimentary kir royal champagne cocktail and appetizer

Valid for all at the table

BERLITZ

This coupon is valid for the gift, complimentary offer or discount described on the reverse side. It must be presented in conjunction with the book *More France for the $*, as described in the preface on page 9. Although the author and Berlitz Guides can take no responsibility for the receipt of the benefits indicated, the publisher would greatly appreciate your communicating any difficulties encountered. Berlitz Guides intends to review and update this book regularly. No expiry date limits this coupon.

La direction de l'établissement s'engage à faire bénéficier le porteur de ce coupon des prestations mentionnées en anglais au recto, suite à l'accord pris avec l'auteur du livre *More France for the $*, M. Alan Austin. En cas de doute, veuillez vous référer au directeur de votre hôtel/restaurant.

BERLITZ

This coupon is valid for the gift, complimentary offer or discount described on the reverse side. It must be presented in conjunction with the book *More France for the $*, as described in the preface on page 9. Although the author and Berlitz Guides can take no responsibility for the receipt of the benefits indicated, the publisher would greatly appreciate your communicating any difficulties encountered. Berlitz Guides intends to review and update this book regularly. No expiry date limits this coupon.

La direction de l'établissement s'engage à faire bénéficier le porteur de ce coupon des prestations mentionnées en anglais au recto, suite à l'accord pris avec l'auteur du livre *More France for the $*, M. Alan Austin. En cas de doute, veuillez vous référer au directeur de votre hôtel/restaurant.

BERLITZ

This coupon is valid for the gift, complimentary offer or discount described on the reverse side. It must be presented in conjunction with the book *More France for the $*, as described in the preface on page 9. Although the author and Berlitz Guides can take no responsibility for the receipt of the benefits indicated, the publisher would greatly appreciate your communicating any difficulties encountered. Berlitz Guides intends to review and update this book regularly. No expiry date limits this coupon.

La direction de l'établissement s'engage à faire bénéficier le porteur de ce coupon des prestations mentionnées en anglais au recto, suite à l'accord pris avec l'auteur du livre *More France for the $*, M. Alan Austin. En cas de doute, veuillez vous référer au directeur de votre hôtel/restaurant.

Hôtel Scribe
PARIS
is pleased to offer

Room upgrading at no extra cost

Valid any time for a deluxe double or suite for the price
of a standard double, if available at time of arrival. If upgrading
is not possible, a bottle of champagne in the room.

Les Muses
PARIS
is pleased to offer

Complimentary champagne cocktail

Valid for all at the table

Hôtel Ambassador Concorde
PARIS
is pleased to offer

Room upgrading at no extra cost

Valid any time for a superior room for the price of a standard room.
If upgrading is not possible, a half-bottle of champagne per guest,
in the room.

 **BERLITZ**

This coupon is valid for the gift, complimentary offer or discount described on the reverse side. It must be presented
in conjunction with the book *More France for the $,* as
described in the preface on page 9. Although the author and
Berlitz Guides can take no responsibility for the receipt of the
benefits indicated, the publisher would greatly appreciate
your communicating any difficulties encountered. Berlitz
Guides intends to review and update this book regularly.
No expiry date limits this coupon.

La direction de l'établissement s'engage à faire bénéficier
le porteur de ce coupon des prestations mentionnées en
anglais au recto, suite à l'accord pris avec l'auteur du livre
More France for the $, M. Alan Austin. En cas de doute,
veuillez vous référer au directeur de votre hôtel/restaurant.

 BERLITZ

This coupon is valid for the gift, complimentary offer or discount described on the reverse side. It must be presented
in conjunction with the book *More France for the $,* as
described in the preface on page 9. Although the author and
Berlitz Guides can take no responsibility for the receipt of the
benefits indicated, the publisher would greatly appreciate
your communicating any difficulties encountered. Berlitz
Guides intends to review and update this book regularly.
No expiry date limits this coupon.

La direction de l'établissement s'engage à faire bénéficier
le porteur de ce coupon des prestations mentionnées en
anglais au recto, suite à l'accord pris avec l'auteur du livre
More France for the $, M. Alan Austin. En cas de doute,
veuillez vous référer au directeur de votre hôtel/restaurant.

 BERLITZ

This coupon is valid for the gift, complimentary offer or discount described on the reverse side. It must be presented
in conjunction with the book *More France for the $,* as
described in the preface on page 9. Although the author and
Berlitz Guides can take no responsibility for the receipt of the
benefits indicated, the publisher would greatly appreciate
your communicating any difficulties encountered. Berlitz
Guides intends to review and update this book regularly.
No expiry date limits this coupon.

La direction de l'établissement s'engage à faire bénéficier
le porteur de ce coupon des prestations mentionnées en
anglais au recto, suite à l'accord pris avec l'auteur du livre
More France for the $, M. Alan Austin. En cas de doute,
veuillez vous référer au directeur de votre hôtel/restaurant.

Le Lindbergh
PARIS
is pleased to offer

Complimentary cocktail and coffee

Valid for each guest at the table

Hôtel Raphaël
PARIS
is pleased to offer

Room upgrading at no extra cost

Valid any time for a deluxe double or suite for the price
of a standard double, if available at time of arrival.
If upgrading is not possible, a bottle of wine in the room.

Restaurant Raphaël
PARIS
is pleased to offer

Complimentary main course

Valid for the less expensive of two main courses,
when two meals are ordered à la carte, exclusive of
tax and service

This coupon is valid for the gift, complimentary offer or discount described on the reverse side. It must be presented in conjunction with the book *More France for the $*, as described in the preface on page 9. Although the author and Berlitz Guides can take no responsibility for the receipt of the benefits indicated, the publisher would greatly appreciate your communicating any difficulties encountered. Berlitz Guides intends to review and update this book regularly. No expiry date limits this coupon.

La direction de l'établissement s'engage à faire bénéficier le porteur de ce coupon des prestations mentionnées en anglais au recto, suite à l'accord pris avec l'auteur du livre *More France for the $*, M. Alan Austin. En cas de doute, veuillez vous référer au directeur de votre hôtel/restaurant.

This coupon is valid for the gift, complimentary offer or discount described on the reverse side. It must be presented in conjunction with the book *More France for the $*, as described in the preface on page 9. Although the author and Berlitz Guides can take no responsibility for the receipt of the benefits indicated, the publisher would greatly appreciate your communicating any difficulties encountered. Berlitz Guides intends to review and update this book regularly. No expiry date limits this coupon.

La direction de l'établissement s'engage à faire bénéficier le porteur de ce coupon des prestations mentionnées en anglais au recto, suite à l'accord pris avec l'auteur du livre *More France for the $*, M. Alan Austin. En cas de doute, veuillez vous référer au directeur de votre hôtel/restaurant.

This coupon is valid for the gift, complimentary offer or discount described on the reverse side. It must be presented in conjunction with the book *More France for the $*, as described in the preface on page 9. Although the author and Berlitz Guides can take no responsibility for the receipt of the benefits indicated, the publisher would greatly appreciate your communicating any difficulties encountered. Berlitz Guides intends to review and update this book regularly. No expiry date limits this coupon.

La direction de l'établissement s'engage à faire bénéficier le porteur de ce coupon des prestations mentionnées en anglais au recto, suite à l'accord pris avec l'auteur du livre *More France for the $*, M. Alan Austin. En cas de doute, veuillez vous référer au directeur de votre hôtel/restaurant.

Hôtel Centre-Ville Etoile
PARIS
is pleased to offer

50% reduction in room rates

Valid August, November, December, and all Saturdays
and Sundays when no commercial fair is scheduled

Le Cougar
PARIS
is pleased to offer

Complimentary main course and cocktails

Valid at dinner for the less expensive of two main
courses, when two meals are ordered à la carte,
exclusive of tax and service

Le Manoir de Paris
PARIS
is pleased to offer

Complimentary champagne cocktail

Valid for all at the table

BERLITZ

This coupon is valid for the gift, complimentary offer or discount described on the reverse side. It must be presented in conjunction with the book *More France for the $*, as described in the preface on page 9. Although the author and Berlitz Guides can take no responsibility for the receipt of the benefits indicated, the publisher would greatly appreciate your communicating any difficulties encountered. Berlitz Guides intends to review and update this book regularly. No expiry date limits this coupon.

La direction de l'établissement s'engage à faire bénéficier le porteur de ce coupon des prestations mentionnées en anglais au recto, suite à l'accord pris avec l'auteur du livre *More France for the $*, M. Alan Austin. En cas de doute, veuillez vous référer au directeur de votre hôtel/restaurant.

BERLITZ

This coupon is valid for the gift, complimentary offer or discount described on the reverse side. It must be presented in conjunction with the book *More France for the $*, as described in the preface on page 9. Although the author and Berlitz Guides can take no responsibility for the receipt of the benefits indicated, the publisher would greatly appreciate your communicating any difficulties encountered. Berlitz Guides intends to review and update this book regularly. No expiry date limits this coupon.

La direction de l'établissement s'engage à faire bénéficier le porteur de ce coupon des prestations mentionnées en anglais au recto, suite à l'accord pris avec l'auteur du livre *More France for the $*, M. Alan Austin. En cas de doute, veuillez vous référer au directeur de votre hôtel/restaurant.

BERLITZ

This coupon is valid for the gift, complimentary offer or discount described on the reverse side. It must be presented in conjunction with the book *More France for the $*, as described in the preface on page 9. Although the author and Berlitz Guides can take no responsibility for the receipt of the benefits indicated, the publisher would greatly appreciate your communicating any difficulties encountered. Berlitz Guides intends to review and update this book regularly. No expiry date limits this coupon.

La direction de l'établissement s'engage à faire bénéficier le porteur de ce coupon des prestations mentionnées en anglais au recto, suite à l'accord pris avec l'auteur du livre *More France for the $*, M. Alan Austin. En cas de doute, veuillez vous référer au directeur de votre hôtel/restaurant.

Terass'Hôtel
PARIS
is pleased to offer

Room upgrading at no extra cost

Valid any time for a superior double or suite for the price
of a standard double, if available at time of arrival. If upgrading
is not possible, a bottle of champagne in the room.

Le Guerlande
PARIS
is pleased to offer

Complimentary bottle of wine

Valid when two meals are ordered. If a different vintage
is desired, the price of the offered wine will be deducted. Choice
of apéritif, cognac or liqueur when only one meal is ordered.

Les Hospitaliers
LE POËT-LAVAL
is pleased to offer

Room upgrading at no extra cost

Valid for a superior room for the price of a standard room,
if available at arrival

 **BERLITZ**®

This coupon is valid for the gift, complimentary offer or discount described on the reverse side. It must be presented in conjunction with the book *More France for the $*, as described in the preface on page 9. Although the author and Berlitz Guides can take no responsibility for the receipt of the benefits indicated, the publisher would greatly appreciate your communicating any difficulties encountered. Berlitz Guides intends to review and update this book regularly. No expiry date limits this coupon.

La direction de l'établissement s'engage à faire bénéficier le porteur de ce coupon des prestations mentionnées en anglais au recto, suite à l'accord pris avec l'auteur du livre *More France for the $*, M. Alan Austin. En cas de doute, veuillez vous référer au directeur de votre hôtel/restaurant.

 BERLITZ®

This coupon is valid for the gift, complimentary offer or discount described on the reverse side. It must be presented in conjunction with the book *More France for the $*, as described in the preface on page 9. Although the author and Berlitz Guides can take no responsibility for the receipt of the benefits indicated, the publisher would greatly appreciate your communicating any difficulties encountered. Berlitz Guides intends to review and update this book regularly. No expiry date limits this coupon.

La direction de l'établissement s'engage à faire bénéficier le porteur de ce coupon des prestations mentionnées en anglais au recto, suite à l'accord pris avec l'auteur du livre *More France for the $*, M. Alan Austin. En cas de doute, veuillez vous référer au directeur de votre hôtel/restaurant.

 BERLITZ®

This coupon is valid for the gift, complimentary offer or discount described on the reverse side. It must be presented in conjunction with the book *More France for the $*, as described in the preface on page 9. Although the author and Berlitz Guides can take no responsibility for the receipt of the benefits indicated, the publisher would greatly appreciate your communicating any difficulties encountered. Berlitz Guides intends to review and update this book regularly. No expiry date limits this coupon.

La direction de l'établissement s'engage à faire bénéficier le porteur de ce coupon des prestations mentionnées en anglais au recto, suite à l'accord pris avec l'auteur du livre *More France for the $*, M. Alan Austin. En cas de doute, veuillez vous référer au directeur de votre hôtel/restaurant.

Les Hospitaliers
LE POËT-LAVAL
is pleased to offer

House cocktail and complimentary appetizer or cheese course

Valid for all at the table ordering à la carte

Michel Chabran
PONT-DE-L'ISÈRE
is pleased to offer

20% reduction in room rates

Valid 1 November to 30 April

Michel Chabran
PONT-DE-L'ISÈRE
is pleased to offer

Complimentary champagne cocktail and appetizer

Valid for all at the table

BERLITZ®

This coupon is valid for the gift, complimentary offer or discount described on the reverse side. It must be presented in conjunction with the book *More France for the $,* as described in the preface on page 9. Although the author and Berlitz Guides can take no responsibility for the receipt of the benefits indicated, the publisher would greatly appreciate your communicating any difficulties encountered. Berlitz Guides intends to review and update this book regularly. No expiry date limits this coupon.

La direction de l'établissement s'engage à faire bénéficier le porteur de ce coupon des prestations mentionnées en anglais au recto, suite à l'accord pris avec l'auteur du livre *More France for the $,* M. Alan Austin. En cas de doute, veuillez vous référer au directeur de votre hôtel/restaurant.

BERLITZ®

This coupon is valid for the gift, complimentary offer or discount described on the reverse side. It must be presented in conjunction with the book *More France for the $,* as described in the preface on page 9. Although the author and Berlitz Guides can take no responsibility for the receipt of the benefits indicated, the publisher would greatly appreciate your communicating any difficulties encountered. Berlitz Guides intends to review and update this book regularly. No expiry date limits this coupon.

La direction de l'établissement s'engage à faire bénéficier le porteur de ce coupon des prestations mentionnées en anglais au recto, suite à l'accord pris avec l'auteur du livre *More France for the $,* M. Alan Austin. En cas de doute, veuillez vous référer au directeur de votre hôtel/restaurant.

BERLITZ®

This coupon is valid for the gift, complimentary offer or discount described on the reverse side. It must be presented in conjunction with the book *More France for the $,* as described in the preface on page 9. Although the author and Berlitz Guides can take no responsibility for the receipt of the benefits indicated, the publisher would greatly appreciate your communicating any difficulties encountered. Berlitz Guides intends to review and update this book regularly. No expiry date limits this coupon.

La direction de l'établissement s'engage à faire bénéficier le porteur de ce coupon des prestations mentionnées en anglais au recto, suite à l'accord pris avec l'auteur du livre *More France for the $,* M. Alan Austin. En cas de doute, veuillez vous référer au directeur de votre hôtel/restaurant.

Le Chardonnay
REIMS
is pleased to offer

Complimentary half-bottle of champagne rosé

Valid for two guests ordering together

Le Florence
REIMS
is pleased to offer

Complimentary house cocktail, appetizer and after-dinner drink

Valid for all at the table

Le Florence
REIMS
is pleased to offer

Complimentary bottle of vin blanc de champagne

Valid for two guests ordering the *dégustation* menu

BERLITZ

This coupon is valid for the gift, complimentary offer or discount described on the reverse side. It must be presented in conjunction with the book *More France for the $*, as described in the preface on page 9. Although the author and Berlitz Guides can take no responsibility for the receipt of the benefits indicated, the publisher would greatly appreciate your communicating any difficulties encountered. Berlitz Guides intends to review and update this book regularly. No expiry date limits this coupon.

La direction de l'établissement s'engage à faire bénéficier le porteur de ce coupon des prestations mentionnées en anglais au recto, suite à l'accord pris avec l'auteur du livre *More France for the $*, M. Alan Austin. En cas de doute, veuillez vous référer au directeur de votre hôtel/restaurant.

BERLITZ

This coupon is valid for the gift, complimentary offer or discount described on the reverse side. It must be presented in conjunction with the book *More France for the $*, as described in the preface on page 9. Although the author and Berlitz Guides can take no responsibility for the receipt of the benefits indicated, the publisher would greatly appreciate your communicating any difficulties encountered. Berlitz Guides intends to review and update this book regularly. No expiry date limits this coupon.

La direction de l'établissement s'engage à faire bénéficier le porteur de ce coupon des prestations mentionnées en anglais au recto, suite à l'accord pris avec l'auteur du livre *More France for the $*, M. Alan Austin. En cas de doute, veuillez vous référer au directeur de votre hôtel/restaurant.

BERLITZ

This coupon is valid for the gift, complimentary offer or discount described on the reverse side. It must be presented in conjunction with the book *More France for the $*, as described in the preface on page 9. Although the author and Berlitz Guides can take no responsibility for the receipt of the benefits indicated, the publisher would greatly appreciate your communicating any difficulties encountered. Berlitz Guides intends to review and update this book regularly. No expiry date limits this coupon.

La direction de l'établissement s'engage à faire bénéficier le porteur de ce coupon des prestations mentionnées en anglais au recto, suite à l'accord pris avec l'auteur du livre *More France for the $*, M. Alan Austin. En cas de doute, veuillez vous référer au directeur de votre hôtel/restaurant.

Hôtel Beau-Site
ROCAMADOUR
is pleased to offer

50% reduction in room rates

Valid April, July, October, if at least one meal is taken

Le Jehan de Valon
ROCAMADOUR
is pleased to offer

Complimentary champagne cocktail

Valid for all at the table

Château d'Isenbourg
ROUFFACH
is pleased to offer

50% reduction in room rates

Valid March, April, November, December;
at all other times, after each three-night stay
at the regular price

BERLITZ

This coupon is valid for the gift, complimentary offer or discount described on the reverse side. It must be presented in conjunction with the book *More France for the $*, as described in the preface on page 9. Although the author and Berlitz Guides can take no responsibility for the receipt of the benefits indicated, the publisher would greatly appreciate your communicating any difficulties encountered. Berlitz Guides intends to review and update this book regularly. No expiry date limits this coupon.

La direction de l'établissement s'engage à faire bénéficier le porteur de ce coupon des prestations mentionnées en anglais au recto, suite à l'accord pris avec l'auteur du livre *More France for the $*, M. Alan Austin. En cas de doute, veuillez vous référer au directeur de votre hôtel/restaurant.

BERLITZ

This coupon is valid for the gift, complimentary offer or discount described on the reverse side. It must be presented in conjunction with the book *More France for the $*, as described in the preface on page 9. Although the author and Berlitz Guides can take no responsibility for the receipt of the benefits indicated, the publisher would greatly appreciate your communicating any difficulties encountered. Berlitz Guides intends to review and update this book regularly. No expiry date limits this coupon.

La direction de l'établissement s'engage à faire bénéficier le porteur de ce coupon des prestations mentionnées en anglais au recto, suite à l'accord pris avec l'auteur du livre *More France for the $*, M. Alan Austin. En cas de doute, veuillez vous référer au directeur de votre hôtel/restaurant.

BERLITZ

This coupon is valid for the gift, complimentary offer or discount described on the reverse side. It must be presented in conjunction with the book *More France for the $*, as described in the preface on page 9. Although the author and Berlitz Guides can take no responsibility for the receipt of the benefits indicated, the publisher would greatly appreciate your communicating any difficulties encountered. Berlitz Guides intends to review and update this book regularly. No expiry date limits this coupon.

La direction de l'établissement s'engage à faire bénéficier le porteur de ce coupon des prestations mentionnées en anglais au recto, suite à l'accord pris avec l'auteur du livre *More France for the $*, M. Alan Austin. En cas de doute, veuillez vous référer au directeur de votre hôtel/restaurant.

Les Tommeries
ROUFFACH
is pleased to offer

Complimentary bottle of wine

Valid when two meals are ordered.
If a different vintage is desired,
the price of the offered wine will be deducted.

Hôtel Radio
ROYAT-CHAMALIÈRES
is pleased to offer

20% reduction in room rates

Valid any time

Hôtel Radio
ROYAT-CHAMALIÈRES
is pleased to offer

Complimentary champagne cocktail and appetizer

Valid for all at the table

BERLITZ

This coupon is valid for the gift, complimentary offer or discount described on the reverse side. It must be presented in conjunction with the book *More France for the $*, as described in the preface on page 9. Although the author and Berlitz Guides can take no responsibility for the receipt of the benefits indicated, the publisher would greatly appreciate your communicating any difficulties encountered. Berlitz Guides intends to review and update this book regularly. No expiry date limits this coupon.

La direction de l'établissement s'engage à faire bénéficier le porteur de ce coupon des prestations mentionnées en anglais au recto, suite à l'accord pris avec l'auteur du livre *More France for the $*, M. Alan Austin. En cas de doute, veuillez vous référer au directeur de votre hôtel/restaurant.

BERLITZ

This coupon is valid for the gift, complimentary offer or discount described on the reverse side. It must be presented in conjunction with the book *More France for the $*, as described in the preface on page 9. Although the author and Berlitz Guides can take no responsibility for the receipt of the benefits indicated, the publisher would greatly appreciate your communicating any difficulties encountered. Berlitz Guides intends to review and update this book regularly. No expiry date limits this coupon.

La direction de l'établissement s'engage à faire bénéficier le porteur de ce coupon des prestations mentionnées en anglais au recto, suite à l'accord pris avec l'auteur du livre *More France for the $*, M. Alan Austin. En cas de doute, veuillez vous référer au directeur de votre hôtel/restaurant.

BERLITZ

This coupon is valid for the gift, complimentary offer or discount described on the reverse side. It must be presented in conjunction with the book *More France for the $*, as described in the preface on page 9. Although the author and Berlitz Guides can take no responsibility for the receipt of the benefits indicated, the publisher would greatly appreciate your communicating any difficulties encountered. Berlitz Guides intends to review and update this book regularly. No expiry date limits this coupon.

La direction de l'établissement s'engage à faire bénéficier le porteur de ce coupon des prestations mentionnées en anglais au recto, suite à l'accord pris avec l'auteur du livre *More France for the $*, M. Alan Austin. En cas de doute, veuillez vous référer au directeur de votre hôtel/restaurant.

La Belle Meunière
ROYAT
is pleased to offer

20% reduction on food and drink

Valid when two meals are ordered

Hostellerie de Plaisance
ST-EMILION
is pleased to offer

50% reduction in room rates

Valid February, March, April, November, December

Hostellerie de Plaisance
ST-EMILION
is pleased to offer

Room upgrading at no extra cost

Valid any time for a superior room for the price of a standard room,
if available at time of arrival. If upgrading is not possible,
a bottle of St-Emilion in the room.

BERLITZ

This coupon is valid for the gift, complimentary offer or discount described on the reverse side. It must be presented in conjunction with the book *More France for the $,* as described in the preface on page 9. Although the author and Berlitz Guides can take no responsibility for the receipt of the benefits indicated, the publisher would greatly appreciate your communicating any difficulties encountered. Berlitz Guides intends to review and update this book regularly. No expiry date limits this coupon.

La direction de l'établissement s'engage à faire bénéficier le porteur de ce coupon des prestations mentionnées en anglais au recto, suite à l'accord pris avec l'auteur du livre *More France for the $,* M. Alan Austin. En cas de doute, veuillez vous référer au directeur de votre hôtel/restaurant.

BERLITZ

This coupon is valid for the gift, complimentary offer or discount described on the reverse side. It must be presented in conjunction with the book *More France for the $,* as described in the preface on page 9. Although the author and Berlitz Guides can take no responsibility for the receipt of the benefits indicated, the publisher would greatly appreciate your communicating any difficulties encountered. Berlitz Guides intends to review and update this book regularly. No expiry date limits this coupon.

La direction de l'établissement s'engage à faire bénéficier le porteur de ce coupon des prestations mentionnées en anglais au recto, suite à l'accord pris avec l'auteur du livre *More France for the $,* M. Alan Austin. En cas de doute, veuillez vous référer au directeur de votre hôtel/restaurant.

BERLITZ

This coupon is valid for the gift, complimentary offer or discount described on the reverse side. It must be presented in conjunction with the book *More France for the $,* as described in the preface on page 9. Although the author and Berlitz Guides can take no responsibility for the receipt of the benefits indicated, the publisher would greatly appreciate your communicating any difficulties encountered. Berlitz Guides intends to review and update this book regularly. No expiry date limits this coupon.

La direction de l'établissement s'engage à faire bénéficier le porteur de ce coupon des prestations mentionnées en anglais au recto, suite à l'accord pris avec l'auteur du livre *More France for the $,* M. Alan Austin. En cas de doute, veuillez vous référer au directeur de votre hôtel/restaurant.

Hostellerie de Plaisance
ST-EMILION
is pleased to offer

Complimentary bottle of wine

Valid when two meals are ordered.
If a different vintage is desired, the price of the offered wine
will be deducted.

Grand Hôtel du Cap-Ferrat
ST-JEAN-CAP-FERRAT
is pleased to offer

Complimentary bottle of champagne

Valid with any room

Grand Hôtel du Cap-Ferrat
ST-JEAN-CAP-FERRAT
is pleased to offer

Complimentary champagne cocktail and appetizer

Valid for all at the table

BERLITZ

This coupon is valid for the gift, complimentary offer or discount described on the reverse side. It must be presented in conjunction with the book *More France for the $*, as described in the preface on page 9. Although the author and Berlitz Guides can take no responsibility for the receipt of the benefits indicated, the publisher would greatly appreciate your communicating any difficulties encountered. Berlitz Guides intends to review and update this book regularly. No expiry date limits this coupon.

La direction de l'établissement s'engage à faire bénéficier le porteur de ce coupon des prestations mentionnées en anglais au recto, suite à l'accord pris avec l'auteur du livre *More France for the $*, M. Alan Austin. En cas de doute, veuillez vous référer au directeur de votre hôtel/restaurant.

BERLITZ

This coupon is valid for the gift, complimentary offer or discount described on the reverse side. It must be presented in conjunction with the book *More France for the $*, as described in the preface on page 9. Although the author and Berlitz Guides can take no responsibility for the receipt of the benefits indicated, the publisher would greatly appreciate your communicating any difficulties encountered. Berlitz Guides intends to review and update this book regularly. No expiry date limits this coupon.

La direction de l'établissement s'engage à faire bénéficier le porteur de ce coupon des prestations mentionnées en anglais au recto, suite à l'accord pris avec l'auteur du livre *More France for the $*, M. Alan Austin. En cas de doute, veuillez vous référer au directeur de votre hôtel/restaurant.

BERLITZ

This coupon is valid for the gift, complimentary offer or discount described on the reverse side. It must be presented in conjunction with the book *More France for the $*, as described in the preface on page 9. Although the author and Berlitz Guides can take no responsibility for the receipt of the benefits indicated, the publisher would greatly appreciate your communicating any difficulties encountered. Berlitz Guides intends to review and update this book regularly. No expiry date limits this coupon.

La direction de l'établissement s'engage à faire bénéficier le porteur de ce coupon des prestations mentionnées en anglais au recto, suite à l'accord pris avec l'auteur du livre *More France for the $*, M. Alan Austin. En cas de doute, veuillez vous référer au directeur de votre hôtel/restaurant.

Club Dauphin
ST-JEAN-CAP-FERRAT
is pleased to offer

Complimentary entry and use of facilities

Valid if lunch is taken at the seaside terrace restaurant

Club Dauphin
ST-JEAN-CAP-FERRAT
is pleased to offer

50% reduction on entry fee, and use of facilities

Valid for non-hotel guests not taking lunch

Grand Hôtel
ST-JEAN-DE-LUZ
is pleased to offer

20% reduction in room rates

Valid 16 September to 14 June

BERLITZ®

This coupon is valid for the gift, complimentary offer or discount described on the reverse side. It must be presented in conjunction with the book *More France for the $*, as described in the preface on page 9. Although the author and Berlitz Guides can take no responsibility for the receipt of the benefits indicated, the publisher would greatly appreciate your communicating any difficulties encountered. Berlitz Guides intends to review and update this book regularly. No expiry date limits this coupon.

La direction de l'établissement s'engage à faire bénéficier le porteur de ce coupon des prestations mentionnées en anglais au recto, suite à l'accord pris avec l'auteur du livre *More France for the $*, M. Alan Austin. En cas de doute, veuillez vous référer au directeur de votre hôtel/restaurant.

BERLITZ®

This coupon is valid for the gift, complimentary offer or discount described on the reverse side. It must be presented in conjunction with the book *More France for the $*, as described in the preface on page 9. Although the author and Berlitz Guides can take no responsibility for the receipt of the benefits indicated, the publisher would greatly appreciate your communicating any difficulties encountered. Berlitz Guides intends to review and update this book regularly. No expiry date limits this coupon.

La direction de l'établissement s'engage à faire bénéficier le porteur de ce coupon des prestations mentionnées en anglais au recto, suite à l'accord pris avec l'auteur du livre *More France for the $*, M. Alan Austin. En cas de doute, veuillez vous référer au directeur de votre hôtel/restaurant.

BERLITZ®

This coupon is valid for the gift, complimentary offer or discount described on the reverse side. It must be presented in conjunction with the book *More France for the $*, as described in the preface on page 9. Although the author and Berlitz Guides can take no responsibility for the receipt of the benefits indicated, the publisher would greatly appreciate your communicating any difficulties encountered. Berlitz Guides intends to review and update this book regularly. No expiry date limits this coupon.

La direction de l'établissement s'engage à faire bénéficier le porteur de ce coupon des prestations mentionnées en anglais au recto, suite à l'accord pris avec l'auteur du livre *More France for the $*, M. Alan Austin. En cas de doute, veuillez vous référer au directeur de votre hôtel/restaurant.

Grand Hôtel
ST-JEAN-DE-LUZ
is pleased to offer

**Complimentary champagne cocktail
and appetizer, plus a glass of Sauternes
or Banyuls with petits fours**

Valid for all at the table

Relais du Bois St-Georges
SAINTES
is pleased to offer

50% reduction in room rates

Valid after a three-night stay at the regular price,
or unconditionally in November and February

Relais du Bois St-Georges
SAINTES
is pleased to offer

**Complimentary cheese course
and Merlin cognac**

Valid for two guests ordering à la carte

 **BERLITZ**®

This coupon is valid for the gift, complimentary offer or discount described on the reverse side. It must be presented in conjunction with the book *More France for the $,* as described in the preface on page 9. Although the author and Berlitz Guides can take no responsibility for the receipt of the benefits indicated, the publisher would greatly appreciate your communicating any difficulties encountered. Berlitz Guides intends to review and update this book regularly. No expiry date limits this coupon.

La direction de l'établissement s'engage à faire bénéficier le porteur de ce coupon des prestations mentionnées en anglais au recto, suite à l'accord pris avec l'auteur du livre *More France for the $,* M. Alan Austin. En cas de doute, veuillez vous référer au directeur de votre hôtel/restaurant.

 BERLITZ®

This coupon is valid for the gift, complimentary offer or discount described on the reverse side. It must be presented in conjunction with the book *More France for the $,* as described in the preface on page 9. Although the author and Berlitz Guides can take no responsibility for the receipt of the benefits indicated, the publisher would greatly appreciate your communicating any difficulties encountered. Berlitz Guides intends to review and update this book regularly. No expiry date limits this coupon.

La direction de l'établissement s'engage à faire bénéficier le porteur de ce coupon des prestations mentionnées en anglais au recto, suite à l'accord pris avec l'auteur du livre *More France for the $,* M. Alan Austin. En cas de doute, veuillez vous référer au directeur de votre hôtel/restaurant.

 BERLITZ®

This coupon is valid for the gift, complimentary offer or discount described on the reverse side. It must be presented in conjunction with the book *More France for the $,* as described in the preface on page 9. Although the author and Berlitz Guides can take no responsibility for the receipt of the benefits indicated, the publisher would greatly appreciate your communicating any difficulties encountered. Berlitz Guides intends to review and update this book regularly. No expiry date limits this coupon.

La direction de l'établissement s'engage à faire bénéficier le porteur de ce coupon des prestations mentionnées en anglais au recto, suite à l'accord pris avec l'auteur du livre *More France for the $,* M. Alan Austin. En cas de doute, veuillez vous référer au directeur de votre hôtel/restaurant.

Mas de la Fouque
SAINTES-MARIES-DE-LA-MER
is pleased to offer

Complimentary bottle of vin du Mas

Valid with any room

Mas de la Fouque
SAINTES-MARIES-DE-LA-MER
is pleased to offer

Complimentary house cocktail

Valid for all at the table

Abbaye de Sainte-Croix
SALON-DE-PROVENCE
is pleased to offer

20% reduction in room rates

Valid from 30 September to 15 June

BERLITZ

This coupon is valid for the gift, complimentary offer or discount described on the reverse side. It must be presented in conjunction with the book *More France for the $*, as described in the preface on page 9. Although the author and Berlitz Guides can take no responsibility for the receipt of the benefits indicated, the publisher would greatly appreciate your communicating any difficulties encountered. Berlitz Guides intends to review and update this book regularly. No expiry date limits this coupon.

La direction de l'établissement s'engage à faire bénéficier le porteur de ce coupon des prestations mentionnées en anglais au recto, suite à l'accord pris avec l'auteur du livre *More France for the $*, M. Alan Austin. En cas de doute, veuillez vous référer au directeur de votre hôtel/restaurant.

BERLITZ

This coupon is valid for the gift, complimentary offer or discount described on the reverse side. It must be presented in conjunction with the book *More France for the $*, as described in the preface on page 9. Although the author and Berlitz Guides can take no responsibility for the receipt of the benefits indicated, the publisher would greatly appreciate your communicating any difficulties encountered. Berlitz Guides intends to review and update this book regularly. No expiry date limits this coupon.

La direction de l'établissement s'engage à faire bénéficier le porteur de ce coupon des prestations mentionnées en anglais au recto, suite à l'accord pris avec l'auteur du livre *More France for the $*, M. Alan Austin. En cas de doute, veuillez vous référer au directeur de votre hôtel/restaurant.

BERLITZ

This coupon is valid for the gift, complimentary offer or discount described on the reverse side. It must be presented in conjunction with the book *More France for the $*, as described in the preface on page 9. Although the author and Berlitz Guides can take no responsibility for the receipt of the benefits indicated, the publisher would greatly appreciate your communicating any difficulties encountered. Berlitz Guides intends to review and update this book regularly. No expiry date limits this coupon.

La direction de l'établissement s'engage à faire bénéficier le porteur de ce coupon des prestations mentionnées en anglais au recto, suite à l'accord pris avec l'auteur du livre *More France for the $*, M. Alan Austin. En cas de doute, veuillez vous référer au directeur de votre hôtel/restaurant.

Abbaye de Sainte-Croix
SALON-DE-PROVENCE
is pleased to offer

20% reduction on food and drink

Valid any time, except dinner in July and August

Château de la Treyne
SOUILLAC
is pleased to offer

30% reduction in room rates

Valid April through November,
if less than 80% booked at time of reservation

Château de la Treyne
SOUILLAC
is pleased to offer

Complimentary lunch

Valid with a three-night stay

BERLITZ®

This coupon is valid for the gift, complimentary offer or discount described on the reverse side. It must be presented in conjunction with the book *More France for the $,* as described in the preface on page 9. Although the author and Berlitz Guides can take no responsibility for the receipt of the benefits indicated, the publisher would greatly appreciate your communicating any difficulties encountered. Berlitz Guides intends to review and update this book regularly. No expiry date limits this coupon.

La direction de l'établissement s'engage à faire bénéficier le porteur de ce coupon des prestations mentionnées en anglais au recto, suite à l'accord pris avec l'auteur du livre *More France for the $,* M. Alan Austin. En cas de doute, veuillez vous référer au directeur de votre hôtel/restaurant.

BERLITZ®

This coupon is valid for the gift, complimentary offer or discount described on the reverse side. It must be presented in conjunction with the book *More France for the $,* as described in the preface on page 9. Although the author and Berlitz Guides can take no responsibility for the receipt of the benefits indicated, the publisher would greatly appreciate your communicating any difficulties encountered. Berlitz Guides intends to review and update this book regularly. No expiry date limits this coupon.

La direction de l'établissement s'engage à faire bénéficier le porteur de ce coupon des prestations mentionnées en anglais au recto, suite à l'accord pris avec l'auteur du livre *More France for the $,* M. Alan Austin. En cas de doute, veuillez vous référer au directeur de votre hôtel/restaurant.

BERLITZ®

This coupon is valid for the gift, complimentary offer or discount described on the reverse side. It must be presented in conjunction with the book *More France for the $,* as described in the preface on page 9. Although the author and Berlitz Guides can take no responsibility for the receipt of the benefits indicated, the publisher would greatly appreciate your communicating any difficulties encountered. Berlitz Guides intends to review and update this book regularly. No expiry date limits this coupon.

La direction de l'établissement s'engage à faire bénéficier le porteur de ce coupon des prestations mentionnées en anglais au recto, suite à l'accord pris avec l'auteur du livre *More France for the $,* M. Alan Austin. En cas de doute, veuillez vous référer au directeur de votre hôtel/restaurant.

Château de la Treyne
SOUILLAC
is pleased to offer

20% reduction on food and drink

Valid at lunch for all at the table

Château de la Treyne
SOUILLAC
is pleased to offer

Complimentary digestif and coffee

Valid at dinner for all at the table

Hôtel Monopole-Métropole
STRASBOURG
is pleased to offer

25% reduction in room rates

Valid weekends all year, and every day July and August

BERLITZ®

This coupon is valid for the gift, complimentary offer or discount described on the reverse side. It must be presented in conjunction with the book *More France for the $,* as described in the preface on page 9. Although the author and Berlitz Guides can take no responsibility for the receipt of the benefits indicated, the publisher would greatly appreciate your communicating any difficulties encountered. Berlitz Guides intends to review and update this book regularly. No expiry date limits this coupon.

La direction de l'établissement s'engage à faire bénéficier le porteur de ce coupon des prestations mentionnées en anglais au recto, suite à l'accord pris avec l'auteur du livre *More France for the $,* M. Alan Austin. En cas de doute, veuillez vous référer au directeur de votre hôtel/restaurant.

BERLITZ®

This coupon is valid for the gift, complimentary offer or discount described on the reverse side. It must be presented in conjunction with the book *More France for the $,* as described in the preface on page 9. Although the author and Berlitz Guides can take no responsibility for the receipt of the benefits indicated, the publisher would greatly appreciate your communicating any difficulties encountered. Berlitz Guides intends to review and update this book regularly. No expiry date limits this coupon.

La direction de l'établissement s'engage à faire bénéficier le porteur de ce coupon des prestations mentionnées en anglais au recto, suite à l'accord pris avec l'auteur du livre *More France for the $,* M. Alan Austin. En cas de doute, veuillez vous référer au directeur de votre hôtel/restaurant.

BERLITZ®

This coupon is valid for the gift, complimentary offer or discount described on the reverse side. It must be presented in conjunction with the book *More France for the $,* as described in the preface on page 9. Although the author and Berlitz Guides can take no responsibility for the receipt of the benefits indicated, the publisher would greatly appreciate your communicating any difficulties encountered. Berlitz Guides intends to review and update this book regularly. No expiry date limits this coupon.

La direction de l'établissement s'engage à faire bénéficier le porteur de ce coupon des prestations mentionnées en anglais au recto, suite à l'accord pris avec l'auteur du livre *More France for the $,* M. Alan Austin. En cas de doute, veuillez vous référer au directeur de votre hôtel/restaurant.

Le Valentin-Sorg
STRASBOURG
is pleased to offer

Complimentary bottle of wine

Valid when two meals are ordered.
If a different vintage is desired, the price of the offered wine
will be deducted.

Maison KAMMERZELL
STRASBOURG
is pleased to offer

Complimentary glass of Gewurztraminer and appetizer

Valid for all at the table

Le Rempart
TOURNUS
is pleased to offer

Room upgrading at no extra cost

Valid any time for a deluxe room or suite for the price
of a standard room. If upgrading is not possible,
a bottle of crémant de Bourgogne in the room.

BERLITZ®

This coupon is valid for the gift, complimentary offer or discount described on the reverse side. It must be presented in conjunction with the book *More France for the $,* as described in the preface on page 9. Although the author and Berlitz Guides can take no responsibility for the receipt of the benefits indicated, the publisher would greatly appreciate your communicating any difficulties encountered. Berlitz Guides intends to review and update this book regularly. No expiry date limits this coupon.

La direction de l'établissement s'engage à faire bénéficier le porteur de ce coupon des prestations mentionnées en anglais au recto, suite à l'accord pris avec l'auteur du livre *More France for the $,* M. Alan Austin. En cas de doute, veuillez vous référer au directeur de votre hôtel/restaurant.

BERLITZ®

This coupon is valid for the gift, complimentary offer or discount described on the reverse side. It must be presented in conjunction with the book *More France for the $,* as described in the preface on page 9. Although the author and Berlitz Guides can take no responsibility for the receipt of the benefits indicated, the publisher would greatly appreciate your communicating any difficulties encountered. Berlitz Guides intends to review and update this book regularly. No expiry date limits this coupon.

La direction de l'établissement s'engage à faire bénéficier le porteur de ce coupon des prestations mentionnées en anglais au recto, suite à l'accord pris avec l'auteur du livre *More France for the $,* M. Alan Austin. En cas de doute, veuillez vous référer au directeur de votre hôtel/restaurant.

BERLITZ®

This coupon is valid for the gift, complimentary offer or discount described on the reverse side. It must be presented in conjunction with the book *More France for the $,* as described in the preface on page 9. Although the author and Berlitz Guides can take no responsibility for the receipt of the benefits indicated, the publisher would greatly appreciate your communicating any difficulties encountered. Berlitz Guides intends to review and update this book regularly. No expiry date limits this coupon.

La direction de l'établissement s'engage à faire bénéficier le porteur de ce coupon des prestations mentionnées en anglais au recto, suite à l'accord pris avec l'auteur du livre *More France for the $,* M. Alan Austin. En cas de doute, veuillez vous référer au directeur de votre hôtel/restaurant.

Le Rempart
TOURNUS
is pleased to offer

Complimentary cocktail and appetizer, plus after-dinner drink

Valid for all at the table

La Bastide de Tourtour
TOURTOUR
is pleased to offer

Room upgrading at no extra cost

Valid for a superior room for the price of a standard room, if available at time of arrival. If upgrading is not possible, a bottle of champagne in the room.

La Bastide de Tourtour
TOURTOUR
is pleased to offer

Complimentary bottle of wine

Valid for two guests ordering together.
If a different vintage is desired, the price of the offered wine will be deducted.

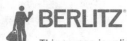

BERLITZ

This coupon is valid for the gift, complimentary offer or discount described on the reverse side. It must be presented in conjunction with the book *More France for the $*, as described in the preface on page 9. Although the author and Berlitz Guides can take no responsibility for the receipt of the benefits indicated, the publisher would greatly appreciate your communicating any difficulties encountered. Berlitz Guides intends to review and update this book regularly. No expiry date limits this coupon.

La direction de l'établissement s'engage à faire bénéficier le porteur de ce coupon des prestations mentionnées en anglais au recto, suite à l'accord pris avec l'auteur du livre *More France for the $*, M. Alan Austin. En cas de doute, veuillez vous référer au directeur de votre hôtel/restaurant.

BERLITZ

This coupon is valid for the gift, complimentary offer or discount described on the reverse side. It must be presented in conjunction with the book *More France for the $*, as described in the preface on page 9. Although the author and Berlitz Guides can take no responsibility for the receipt of the benefits indicated, the publisher would greatly appreciate your communicating any difficulties encountered. Berlitz Guides intends to review and update this book regularly. No expiry date limits this coupon.

La direction de l'établissement s'engage à faire bénéficier le porteur de ce coupon des prestations mentionnées en anglais au recto, suite à l'accord pris avec l'auteur du livre *More France for the $*, M. Alan Austin. En cas de doute, veuillez vous référer au directeur de votre hôtel/restaurant.

BERLITZ

This coupon is valid for the gift, complimentary offer or discount described on the reverse side. It must be presented in conjunction with the book *More France for the $*, as described in the preface on page 9. Although the author and Berlitz Guides can take no responsibility for the receipt of the benefits indicated, the publisher would greatly appreciate your communicating any difficulties encountered. Berlitz Guides intends to review and update this book regularly. No expiry date limits this coupon.

La direction de l'établissement s'engage à faire bénéficier le porteur de ce coupon des prestations mentionnées en anglais au recto, suite à l'accord pris avec l'auteur du livre *More France for the $*, M. Alan Austin. En cas de doute, veuillez vous référer au directeur de votre hôtel/restaurant.

Hôtel d'Espagne
VALENÇAY
is pleased to offer

10% reduction on room and all meals

Valid for a stay of three nights or longer

Hôtel d'Espagne
VALENÇAY
is pleased to offer

Complimentary bottle of crémant de Loire

Valid with any room

Hôtel d'Espagne
VALENÇAY
is pleased to offer

Complimentary bottle of wine

Valid for two guests ordering together.
If a different vintage is desired, the price of the offered wine
will be deducted.

BERLITZ

This coupon is valid for the gift, complimentary offer or discount described on the reverse side. It must be presented in conjunction with the book *More France for the $,* as described in the preface on page 9. Although the author and Berlitz Guides can take no responsibility for the receipt of the benefits indicated, the publisher would greatly appreciate your communicating any difficulties encountered. Berlitz Guides intends to review and update this book regularly. No expiry date limits this coupon.

La direction de l'établissement s'engage à faire bénéficier le porteur de ce coupon des prestations mentionnées en anglais au recto, suite à l'accord pris avec l'auteur du livre *More France for the $,* M. Alan Austin. En cas de doute, veuillez vous référer au directeur de votre hôtel/restaurant.

BERLITZ

This coupon is valid for the gift, complimentary offer or discount described on the reverse side. It must be presented in conjunction with the book *More France for the $,* as described in the preface on page 9. Although the author and Berlitz Guides can take no responsibility for the receipt of the benefits indicated, the publisher would greatly appreciate your communicating any difficulties encountered. Berlitz Guides intends to review and update this book regularly. No expiry date limits this coupon.

La direction de l'établissement s'engage à faire bénéficier le porteur de ce coupon des prestations mentionnées en anglais au recto, suite à l'accord pris avec l'auteur du livre *More France for the $,* M. Alan Austin. En cas de doute, veuillez vous référer au directeur de votre hôtel/restaurant.

BERLITZ

This coupon is valid for the gift, complimentary offer or discount described on the reverse side. It must be presented in conjunction with the book *More France for the $,* as described in the preface on page 9. Although the author and Berlitz Guides can take no responsibility for the receipt of the benefits indicated, the publisher would greatly appreciate your communicating any difficulties encountered. Berlitz Guides intends to review and update this book regularly. No expiry date limits this coupon.

La direction de l'établissement s'engage à faire bénéficier le porteur de ce coupon des prestations mentionnées en anglais au recto, suite à l'accord pris avec l'auteur du livre *More France for the $,* M. Alan Austin. En cas de doute, veuillez vous référer au directeur de votre hôtel/restaurant.

Château St-Martin
VENCE
is pleased to offer

Complimentary bottle of champagne

Valid with any room

Château St-Martin
VENCE
is pleased to offer

Complimentary champagne cocktail and appetizer

Valid for all at the table

Trianon Palace
VERSAILLES
is pleased to offer

20% reduction in room rates

Valid 1 November to 31 March

BERLITZ

This coupon is valid for the gift, complimentary offer or discount described on the reverse side. It must be presented in conjunction with the book *More France for the $,* as described in the preface on page 9. Although the author and Berlitz Guides can take no responsibility for the receipt of the benefits indicated, the publisher would greatly appreciate your communicating any difficulties encountered. Berlitz Guides intends to review and update this book regularly. No expiry date limits this coupon.

La direction de l'établissement s'engage à faire bénéficier le porteur de ce coupon des prestations mentionnées en anglais au recto, suite à l'accord pris avec l'auteur du livre *More France for the $,* M. Alan Austin. En cas de doute, veuillez vous référer au directeur de votre hôtel/restaurant.

BERLITZ

This coupon is valid for the gift, complimentary offer or discount described on the reverse side. It must be presented in conjunction with the book *More France for the $,* as described in the preface on page 9. Although the author and Berlitz Guides can take no responsibility for the receipt of the benefits indicated, the publisher would greatly appreciate your communicating any difficulties encountered. Berlitz Guides intends to review and update this book regularly. No expiry date limits this coupon.

La direction de l'établissement s'engage à faire bénéficier le porteur de ce coupon des prestations mentionnées en anglais au recto, suite à l'accord pris avec l'auteur du livre *More France for the $,* M. Alan Austin. En cas de doute, veuillez vous référer au directeur de votre hôtel/restaurant.

BERLITZ

This coupon is valid for the gift, complimentary offer or discount described on the reverse side. It must be presented in conjunction with the book *More France for the $,* as described in the preface on page 9. Although the author and Berlitz Guides can take no responsibility for the receipt of the benefits indicated, the publisher would greatly appreciate your communicating any difficulties encountered. Berlitz Guides intends to review and update this book regularly. No expiry date limits this coupon.

La direction de l'établissement s'engage à faire bénéficier le porteur de ce coupon des prestations mentionnées en anglais au recto, suite à l'accord pris avec l'auteur du livre *More France for the $,* M. Alan Austin. En cas de doute, veuillez vous référer au directeur de votre hôtel/restaurant.

Trianon Palace
VERSAILLES
is pleased to offer

Complimentary champagne cocktail, appetizer and coffee

Valid for all at the table

Les Trois Marches
VERSAILLES
is pleased to offer

Complimentary champagne cocktail, petits fours, cheese course and dessert

Valid for all at the table ordering à la carte

Hôtel Welcome
VILLEFRANCHE
is pleased to offer

30% reduction in room rates

Valid January, February, March, November,
except Fridays and Saturdays

BERLITZ®

This coupon is valid for the gift, complimentary offer or discount described on the reverse side. It must be presented in conjunction with the book *More France for the $*, as described in the preface on page 9. Although the author and Berlitz Guides can take no responsibility for the receipt of the benefits indicated, the publisher would greatly appreciate your communicating any difficulties encountered. Berlitz Guides intends to review and update this book regularly. No expiry date limits this coupon.

La direction de l'établissement s'engage à faire bénéficier le porteur de ce coupon des prestations mentionnées en anglais au recto, suite à l'accord pris avec l'auteur du livre *More France for the $*, M. Alan Austin. En cas de doute, veuillez vous référer au directeur de votre hôtel/restaurant.

BERLITZ®

This coupon is valid for the gift, complimentary offer or discount described on the reverse side. It must be presented in conjunction with the book *More France for the $*, as described in the preface on page 9. Although the author and Berlitz Guides can take no responsibility for the receipt of the benefits indicated, the publisher would greatly appreciate your communicating any difficulties encountered. Berlitz Guides intends to review and update this book regularly. No expiry date limits this coupon.

La direction de l'établissement s'engage à faire bénéficier le porteur de ce coupon des prestations mentionnées en anglais au recto, suite à l'accord pris avec l'auteur du livre *More France for the $*, M. Alan Austin. En cas de doute, veuillez vous référer au directeur de votre hôtel/restaurant.

BERLITZ®

This coupon is valid for the gift, complimentary offer or discount described on the reverse side. It must be presented in conjunction with the book *More France for the $*, as described in the preface on page 9. Although the author and Berlitz Guides can take no responsibility for the receipt of the benefits indicated, the publisher would greatly appreciate your communicating any difficulties encountered. Berlitz Guides intends to review and update this book regularly. No expiry date limits this coupon.

La direction de l'établissement s'engage à faire bénéficier le porteur de ce coupon des prestations mentionnées en anglais au recto, suite à l'accord pris avec l'auteur du livre *More France for the $*, M. Alan Austin. En cas de doute, veuillez vous référer au directeur de votre hôtel/restaurant.

Hôtel Welcome
VILLEFRANCHE
is pleased to offer

Room upgrading at no extra cost

Valid for a sea-view room with balcony for the price
of a standard room, if available at time of arrival

Restaurant St-Pierre
VILLEFRANCHE
is pleased to offer

Complimentary apéritif and appetizer

Valid for one guest ordering a meal

BERLITZ®

This coupon is valid for the gift, complimentary offer or discount described on the reverse side. It must be presented in conjunction with the book *More France for the $,* as described in the preface on page 9. Although the author and Berlitz Guides can take no responsibility for the receipt of the benefits indicated, the publisher would greatly appreciate your communicating any difficulties encountered. Berlitz Guides intends to review and update this book regularly. No expiry date limits this coupon.

La direction de l'établissement s'engage à faire bénéficier le porteur de ce coupon des prestations mentionnées en anglais au recto, suite à l'accord pris avec l'auteur du livre *More France for the $,* M. Alan Austin. En cas de doute, veuillez vous référer au directeur de votre hôtel/restaurant.

BERLITZ®

This coupon is valid for the gift, complimentary offer or discount described on the reverse side. It must be presented in conjunction with the book *More France for the $,* as described in the preface on page 9. Although the author and Berlitz Guides can take no responsibility for the receipt of the benefits indicated, the publisher would greatly appreciate your communicating any difficulties encountered. Berlitz Guides intends to review and update this book regularly. No expiry date limits this coupon.

La direction de l'établissement s'engage à faire bénéficier le porteur de ce coupon des prestations mentionnées en anglais au recto, suite à l'accord pris avec l'auteur du livre *More France for the $,* M. Alan Austin. En cas de doute, veuillez vous référer au directeur de votre hôtel/restaurant.

Hertz Chauffeur Service
FRANCE
is pleased to offer

Complimentary Chauffeured Limousine

Valid for transfer to or from the airport,
any time after purchase of a one-day excursion

Europcar ≋ National
FRANCE
is pleased to offer

20% on time and mileage rate

on any *Europcar ≋ National* rental of the car of your choice

Car Rental in France

To rent a car you must produce a valid driving licence (held for at least one year) and your passport. Minimum age is 21 (23 for certain makes of car). A substantial, refundable deposit is required (minimum 1,500 F), except for holders of major credit cards. Unlimited third-party insurance is automatically included.

BERLITZ

This coupon is valid for the gift, complimentary offer or discount described on the reverse side. It must be presented in conjunction with the book *More France for the $*, as described in the preface on page 9. Although the author and Berlitz Guides can take no responsibility for the receipt of the benefits indicated, the publisher would greatly appreciate your communicating any difficulties encountered. Berlitz Guides intends to review and update this book regularly. No expiry date limits this coupon.

La direction de l'établissement s'engage à faire bénéficier le porteur de ce coupon des prestations mentionnées en anglais au recto, suite à l'accord pris avec l'auteur du livre *More France for the $*, M. Alan Austin. En cas de doute, veuillez vous référer au directeur de votre entreprise.

BERLITZ

This coupon is valid for the gift, complimentary offer or discount described on the reverse side. It must be presented in conjunction with the book *More France for the $*, as described in the preface on page 9. Although the author and Berlitz Guides can take no responsibility for the receipt of the benefits indicated, the publisher would greatly appreciate your communicating any difficulties encountered. Berlitz Guides intends to review and update this book regularly. No expiry date limits this coupon.

La direction de l'établissement s'engage à faire bénéficier le porteur de ce coupon des prestations mentionnées en anglais au recto, suite à l'accord pris avec l'auteur du livre *More France for the $*, M. Alan Austin. En cas de doute, veuillez vous référer au directeur de votre entreprise.

Driving in France

Drivers and front-seat passengers are required by law to wear seat belts. Children under 10 are not allowed to travel in the front. Drive on the right, overtake on the left. In built-up areas, give automatic priority to vehicles coming from the right. Outside built-up areas, at junctions marked by signs with a cross or a yellow diamond on a white background, the more important of the two roads has right of way. Cars already engaged on traffic circles have priority over those entering.

BERLITZ Ready-Reference Coupon

BERLITZ Ready-Reference Coupon

BERLITZ Ready-Reference Coupon

Speed limits

On dry roads:
Autoroute (expressways): 130 kph (81 mph);
Divided highways: 110 kph (63 mph);
Other main roads: 90 kph (56 mph);
Boulevard périphérique (Paris ring-road): 80 kph (50 mph);
Towns and built-up areas: 45 or 60 kph (28 or 37 mph).
When roads are wet, limits are reduced by 10 kph (6 mph)
except for expressways, where maximum speed in fog, rain
or snow is reduced by 20 kph (12 mph). For cars fitted with
studded tires, the maximum speed is 90 kph.

Fuel and Oil

Fuel is available in super (98 octane), normal (90 octane),
lead-free (95 octane, *sans plomb*) and diesel *(gas-oil).*

Fluid measures

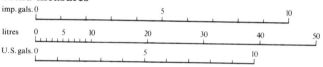

Distance

Tipping

A 15% service charge is generally included automatically in
hotel and restaurant bills (indicated by the mention *service
compris*). But rounding off the overall bill by a few francs
does help cement an entente cordiale with waiters. It is
considered normal to hand bell-boys, doormen, cinema and
theatre ushers, service-station attendants, etc., a coin or two
for their services. The chart overleaf will give you some
guidelines.

Parking

You'll encounter two systems of parking: *zone bleue* (blue zone) and meters. If you want to leave your car in a blue zone you will need a *disque de stationnement,* a parking disc obtainable from a petrol station, newsagent or stationer. Display it in the car, visible through the windscreen.

   Stationnement interdit means "No parking". Don't leave your vehicle in a *zone piétonne* (pedestrian precinct) or near a sign saying *Stationnement gênant* (parking obstructive)— it will be clamped or towed away.

Conversion Charts

France uses the metric system.

Length

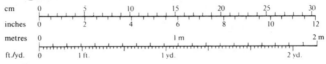

Weight

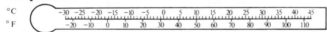

Temperature

°C °F

Tipping Chart

Hotel porter, per bag	5 F
Hotel maid, per week	50–100 F
Restroom attendant	2 F
Waiter	5–10% (optional)
Taxi driver	10–15%
Hairdresser	10%

The French Telephone

Long distance and international calls can be made from any phone box, but if you need assistance in placing the call, go to the post office or ask your hotel concierge (though there's usually a surcharge on hotel calls). Pay phones are operated by coins or cards *(télécarte)* sold at post offices, railway ticket counters and shops displaying the Télécarte sign.

Calling home. To call the U.S.A. or Canada, dial 19, wait for the continuous burring tone, dial 1 + the area code + the subscriber's number. To call the U.K., dial 19 + 44 + area code + subscriber's number.

Average Temperatures

° Fahrenheit		Jan	Feb	Mar	Apr	May	Jun	Jul	Aug	Sep	Oct	Nov	Dec
Lyon	max.	41	45	55	61	68	75	81	79	73	61	50	43
	min.	30	32	37	43	48	55	59	57	54	45	39	32
Marseille	max.	50	54	59	64	72	79	84	82	77	68	59	52
	min.	36	36	41	46	52	59	63	63	59	50	43	37
Paris	max.	43	45	54	61	68	73	77	75	70	61	50	45
	min.	34	34	39	43	50	55	59	57	54	46	41	36

*Minimum temperatures are measured just before sunrise, maximum temperatures in the afternoon.

Public Holidays

See chart overleaf.

If a national holiday falls on a Tuesday or Thursday, many French people take the Monday or Friday off as well to make a long weekend. This rarely affects shops or businesses but does mean the roads are busier.

School holidays vary from region to region, but resorts fill up in the summer, while Paris is much calmer than usual.

BERLITZ Ready-Reference Coupon

BERLITZ Ready-Reference Coupon

BERLITZ Ready-Reference Coupon

Phoning in France

There are no area codes—just dial the 8-digit number of the person you want to call. But if you are in Paris or the Ile-de-France and want to phone to the provinces, dial 16 and wait for the burring tone before dialling the 8-digit number. From the provinces to Paris or the Ile-de-France, dial 16, wait for the burr, then dial 1 and the 8-digit number. If all else fails, call the operator for help (12).

Minitel

The Minitel is the French teletext, offering about 7,000 services, several of which are in English. To call up the directory, switch on the Minitel, lift the telephone receiver and dial 36 15. As soon as you hear a loud beep, press the "Connexion/Fin" key and put the phone receiver back. Type in the letters MGS, and press the green "Envoi" key. Proceed forwards through the directory using the "Suite" key, and backwards with "Retour". For the British news, type 36 15 BBC. The code 36 15 LIBE will give you the news in English from USA Today, and 36 15 UPI the international news from the United Press International agency. 36 14 ED calls up the electronic phone directory in English.

Public Holidays

January 1	*Jour de l'An*	New Year's Day
May 1	*Fête du Travail*	Labour Day
May 8	*Armistice 1945*	Victory Day
July 14	*Fête Nationale*	Bastille Day
August 15	*Assomption*	Assumption
November 1	*Toussaint*	All Saints' Day
November 11	*Armistice 1918*	Armistice Day
December 25	*Noël*	Christmas Day
Movable dates:	*Lundi de Pâques*	Easter Monday
	Ascension	Ascension
	Lundi de Pentecôte	Whit Monday